Urban Life and Urban Landscape Series

THE MYSTERIES OF THE GREAT CITY

The Politics of Urban Design, 1877–1937

JOHN D. FAIRFIELD

OHIO STATE UNIVERSITY PRESS
Columbus

HT
167
F35
1993

Library of Congress Cataloging-in-Publication Data

Fairfield, John D., 1955–
    The mysteries of the great city : the politics of urban design,
1877–1937 / John D. Fairfield.
        p.   cm.—(Urban life and urban landscape series)
    Includes bibliographical references and index.
    ISBN 0–8142–0604–2
    1. City planning—United States—History. 2. Cities and towns—
United States—Growth—History. 3. Urbanization—United States.
I. Title.   II. Series.
HT167.F35   1993
307.1'216'0973—dc20   93–18133
                                                                CIP

Text and jacket design by Donna Hartwick.
Type set in Bembo by G&S Typesetters, Austin, TX.
Printed by McNaughton & Gunn, Inc., Saline, MI.

9   8   7   6   5   4   3   2   1

To my brother and sister

Contents

Acknowledgments

This work began during my years as an undergraduate and graduate student in the Department of History at the University of Rochester from 1974 to 1984. The department was an exciting place to study, and I owe a great debt to its faculty. From my first wonderful course on the Old South with Eugene D. Genovese to my final graduate seminars my teachers encouraged intellectual rigor, independence, and ambition. I was also fortunate to study with a talented, diverse, and often unconventional group of graduate students; they reinforced my commitment and opened my eyes to aspects of history of which I had been unaware. My greatest intellectual debt is to Christopher Lasch, my model of what a teacher and scholar should be. He took a critical interest in my work long before there was good reason to do so. I hope this book will in some measure justify his patience and his friendship.

I wrote this book while teaching at Xavier University for the past seven years. Both the administration and my colleagues in the history department have supported my work. I especially benefited from two faculty development grants without which I could not have completed this project. The teaching and scholarship of my colleague Roger Fortin has set a graceful example that has helped me adjust to the challenges and frustrations of faculty life and to focus on its joys.

I also owe a great debt to my editors. Henry Shapiro has forced me again and again to rethink and to clarify my arguments. The anonymous reader for OSU Press gave me important early encouragement and made a series of practical suggestions that helped turn a manuscript into a book. Alex Holzman has guided me through what has not always been an easy process of publication. One of the greatest joys of the whole endeavor has been my relationship with Zane L. Miller. While I suspect he remains unconvinced by elements of my argument, he has spent many hours helping me strengthen it. I could not have asked for a better colleague.

Parts of this book have appeared elsewhere in different form. Part of chapter 3 appeared in *The Old Northwest* 14 (Fall 1988) as "Cincinnati's Hole in the Ground: Rapid Transit, City Planning, and the New Urban Discipline." Part of chapter 6 appeared in *Planning Perspectives* 7 (1992) as "Alienation of Social Control: The Chicago Sociologists and the Origins of Urban Planning." Part of chapter 4 appeared in the *Journal of Urban History* (1993) as "The Scientific Management of Urban Space: The Professionalization of Planning and the Legacy of Progressive Reform." I wish to thank the editors of those journals for their permission to reprint the material. I also wish to thank Alan Trachtenberg for allowing me to borrow a chapter title from *The Incorporation of America* for the title of this book. Trachtenberg is first among the scores of scholars, acknowledged in the endnotes, to whom I am deeply indebted.

In many ways I have seen this work as an investigation of my own family's past. My paternal grandparents, Leslie and Frances Fairfield, came to Chicago from middle Tennessee in 1927. My maternal grandfather, Walter Denis, was a lifelong resident of the city. My parents, John L. and Adelaide M. Fairfield, who grew up in Chicago, have always stood behind me even when they must have had doubts about the choices I was making. I am grateful for that. Jeff and Patti will understand what the dedication is for. Their early and continued academic success fired my ambition and forced me to find my own intellectual passions. They were, in many ways, my first and best teachers.

My greatest debt of all is to my wife, Mary McPartland. I could not have accomplished what I have without her. Still my favorite historian, she has helped me build both a house and a family. She has cheerfully borne more than her fair share of family responsibilities while I have completed this book. I also owe a great debt to Sally, Thomas, Mary Frances, and Polly, who have helped remind their father that, after all, at least a few things are more important than the history of American cities.

Introduction

URBAN DESIGN AND THE NEW METROPOLITAN FORM

American society and particularly its urban component underwent dramatic economic change in the sixty years after 1877. By the turn of the century, the completion of the railroad network had helped to create ever-larger regional, national, and international markets and to promote the emergence of a system of metropolitan centers that served as the financial and managerial headquarters of that expanding commerce. The subsequent concentration of capital, the rise of national corporations, and the development of the urban market meant that the expansion of industrial production would also occur within a metropolitan context during this period. By 1937, as the newly published federal study *Our Cities: Their Role in the National Economy* made clear, the national system of metropolitan centers had become the dominant element within American society.[1] Not only had American cities grown in population and in number, but the larger cities experienced both physi-

1

cal expansion and internal reorganization. By the end of the century, a new metropolitan form had supplanted the physically constricted walking city of the mid-nineteenth century (named for its easiest, cheapest, and most common mode of transportation) and its heterogeneous jumble of commercial, industrial, and residential districts.[2]

The economic and physical changes associated with the new metropolitan form were only one part of a more profound transformation of American society during that sixty-year period. Although the new metropolitan form incorporated the political, social, and intellectual as well as the economic aspects of the transformation, contemporary observers tended to focus only on the outward physical aspects of metropolitan development. Early in the period the expansion of manufacturing crowded the urban core; by the turn of the century, giant new industrial enterprises increasingly located on the urban periphery along the metropolitan corridors of rail and water transportation. Combined with the exodus of the middle class to residential suburbs, the suburbanization of industry generated more rapid growth at the urban periphery than at the core, a characteristic that was the most salient aspect of the new metropolitan form. At the same time the central business district, relieved of both manufacturing and residential functions, became the commercial showcase and financial command center of the corporate economy. In a ring of speculative real estate surrounding the central business district, the urban poor squeezed into tenement neighborhoods that were more segregated and in some cases more densely populated than those of a generation before.[3]

The most visible symbol of the transformation of American society, the metropolis also served to disguise that transformation and to give it an apparent physical implacability and inevitability, which placed it beyond criticism and control. A major purpose of this study is to unravel the mystery of the new metropolitan form.[4] A variety of factors, from the availability and location of natural resources and the ups and downs of regional, national, and world markets to technological innovation and the development

2

of scientific knowledge and professional expertise, shaped metropolitan development. Although some of those factors were beyond human control, this study argues that the new metropolitan form and the social order it embodied were primarily the result of conscious, political decisions. Reflecting the conviction that human design plays a decisive role in urban development, the central thesis of this work is that the American city was in important ways "planned" before the rise of professional city planning.

In describing the great cities of the Gilded Age, Alan Trachtenberg has made a similar point.

> Cities did not expand and change mindlessly, by mere entropy. If they lacked democratic planning, they submitted to corporate planning—which is to say, to the overlapping, planned evolution of many private competitive enterprises. The visible forms make this clear: the power of organized wealth, answerable only to the limits of the possible.

That sort of corporate planning remained a major factor in urban development even after the rise of professional planning. Addressing a group of professional planners in 1926, Charles Beard quoted President Coolidge's remarks to the leaders of the automobile industry. Among "the problems with which you gentlemen are dealing," Coolidge had told the assembled capitalists, are the "physical configuration of our cities" and "the elementals of social organization." Beard reminded the professional planners that the actions of transportation corporations and "speculation in traction stocks and bonds" had long been among "the prime factors in the dynamics of planning" and that such powerful agencies must still be taken into account.[5]

But corporate planning has always been answerable to more than simply the limits of the possible. The private market decisions of millions of individuals have provided at least a limited check upon corporate power. More importantly, a variety of individuals and social groups (less powerful or less conscious of their power than the great corporations but still influential) shaped metropolitan development through various forms of mass action, the articulation of new ideas, and the creation of new institutions. Many of those individuals and groups developed public visions of the urban future in an effort to challenge and to transform the private city of corporate and individual decision-making. Thus a public debate about what the city could and ought to be, as well as the private pursuit of wealth, shaped the new metropolitan form.[6]

REPUBLICANS AND REALISTS

In writing an intellectual and political history of the new metropolitan form that attempts to make sense of the complex motivations and often chaotic activities of both individuals and social groups, I have isolated two distinct traditions in urban thought and urban reform. In the Gilded Age a republican and idealistic vision of the urban future imagined an urban commonwealth free of class conflict, populated by virtuous republicans, and shaped by Christian ethics. That vision, which began to emerge in the 1840s and 1850s based upon traditional republican and free labor values, is represented in this study chiefly by Frederick Law Olmsted and Henry George.[7] In calling for a balance between the city and the country, a balance that would mediate urban artifice, structure, and organization with rural nature, spontaneity, and community, the republicans hoped to inject the urban order with the civic and political equality, economic opportunity, and, perhaps most importantly, the social harmony they associated with the free labor republic.[8]

Only one of several approaches to the city in the Gilded Age, and one that was by no means completely successful, the republican tradition was the most dynamic in calling for active reform measures. Challenging the dominant laissez-faire and social Darwinist view, which accepted the urban status quo as a filtering mechanism in which the competent and energetic rose and the lazy and improvident sank, the republicans generated a popular demand

4

for a more just and humane urban order. While the republicans achieved only limited success, their attack upon complacency and their invigoration of public debate helped to open the way for a variety of reform initiatives in the Progressive Era, including some based upon assumptions very different from their own.[9]

Although the republican vision was to receive its most powerful expression in the intellectual and political career of Henry George and would bequeath an important legacy to the twentieth century, the economic depression and social upheavals of the 1870s had already begun to erode the confidence and the influence of the republicans. The economic and social consequences of the depression tended to undermine the belief that urban development could be accommodated to republican and free labor values. In the wake of the depression, the mechanized factory and corporate capitalism crowded out the small workshop and the artisan mode of production; and an increasingly bitter conflict between capital and labor reshaped social and political allegiances. In that new economic and social context, the republicans, whose economic and social ideals celebrated the small independent craftsman and the harmony of the producing classes (which included both capital and labor), were unable to develop an effective political strategy to implement their ideas.[10]

The economic and social transformation that began during the depression of the 1870s sparked the development of the new metropolitan form and generated new initiatives in urban thought and urban reform. Beginning in the wake of the depression, reaching maturity in the 1920s, and paralleling metropolitan development, a new realistic and pragmatic tradition emerged.[11] The realists, a group that included corporate leaders, good-government reformers, city and social planners, and urban academics, and whose most important theorist was the sociologist Robert E. Park, were less interested in imagining alternatives to the increasingly hierarchical, corporate, and artificial character of metropolitan America. Embracing the new developments in the name of progress, the realists accepted the metropolis on its own terms, viewing its unrepublican political order and class conflicts as problems to be

5

managed rather than resolved. Notwithstanding their desire to make the metropolis more efficient, rational, and just, an overriding concern with stabilizing and legitimating the metropolitan order weakened the realists' ability to challenge powerful interests and to tackle politically controversial problems. While the republicans failed to build a viable political coalition for change, the realists generally saw no need for one. Thus, neither republicans nor realists succeeded in reconciling the private city of individual and corporate decision-making with their public vision of the urban future.

CITY BUILDING AND URBAN PLANNING

Treating urban thought and urban reform in terms of competing republican and realistic traditions fosters a certain artificiality. Few if any of the theorists and reformers examined in this book fit perfectly into either category. The most complex figures, Frederic Howe and Robert Park for example, at times drew on both traditions. Neither do the categories of republican and realistic fully comprehend the variety of urban thought and urban reform in the period; there were undoubtedly other ways of looking at the city. An analysis of urban thought and urban reform in light of those categories does, however, illuminate certain aspects of the intellectual, social, political, and economic transformation of American society between 1877 and 1937.

While certain elements of the republican tradition survived into the twentieth century, what I describe as the city building debate was unique to the Gilded Age.[12] In the Gilded Age the industrial city was still seen as alien to the American experience and threatening to the cultural values of republican and free labor America; consequently, the republicans were eager, indeed anxious, to imagine alternatives and to transform the city. But they were relatively unprepared to do so, not only because of their limited understanding of the political implications of the changing economic and so-

6

cial structure of metropolitan America, but also because they had only a limited faith and interest in public planning.

The city building debate reflected the belief that human choice shaped urban development and that city building should remain an essentially individual process in which the average citizen had a crucial and largely private role to play. Its most innovative element was the suggestion that a small but profoundly important public role in urban development could have a dramatic and beneficent effect on urban life (as with George's single tax and the public ownership of urban utilities or Olmsted's parks, boulevards, and more flexible street layouts). And yet for all their innovation the republicans only slowly and partially dismantled the individualistic and laissez-faire assumptions that precluded a passionate embrace of public planning.

While taking a significantly broader view of the role of public planning in urban development, the realists, whose influence grew during and after the Progressive Era, doubted whether republican and free labor values could be preserved in metropolitan America. That doubt was linked to their belief that the city was a natural phenomenon that was beyond human control to a significant degree; realistic planners insisted on working with rather than against inevitable urban trends. Realists thus tended to see planning as more of a managerial and less of a political undertaking, a conviction further reinforced by their embrace of the expert and their view of the limited role the average citizen could play in planning. Thus, urban planning became an expert activity carried on through public agencies with a minimum of popular participation and reflected a tendency to minimize the role of human design in urban development. Ironically, the more the realists embraced public planning, the less they believed in its capacity to reshape significantly the urban future.

To be sure, the tendency to minimize the potential for change reflected in part a recognition of enormous investments in the built environment that had been made between 1877 and 1937. Increasingly, the built environment became a serious obstacle to change.[13] Moreover, certain elements of that environment, especially the complex corridors of rail transportation, heralded the rise of the expert builder and systems engineer whose scientific knowledge presumably placed them above the capricious world of human choice.[14] But the growing influence of the realistic perspective also had its origins in a changing intellectual environment.

Henry George had only a limited faith in public planning, but he still believed that the city could be changed in fundamental ways because he recognized the political choices that shaped it. About George's great work, *Progress and Poverty*, labor editor John Swinton wrote:

> [It] came to the weary and heavy laden as the talisman of a lost hope. All their lives long they had been taught that poverty was a 'dispensation of Providence' needful to keep them humble and teach them patience, but if cheerfully borne, it would somehow contribute to their happiness in the dim beyond. 'Progress and Poverty' reversed all this, teaching that poverty is an artificial condition of man's invention, the result of unjust social conditions which compel one to toil that another may eat. . . . Workingmen and women, learning all this, conceived the thought 'if this be truth, then existence even here in this world may be something more than continued striving to supply the most urgent physical demands,' and immediately they commenced to wrestle with their chains.

In the same way George insisted that, if the public made a different set of political choices, both the shape and the character of the metropolis could be dramatically changed for the better.[15]

As befit someone who came to intellectual maturity in the Progressive Era, Robert Park had a greater faith in public planning than did George. But Park doubted the capacity of planning to alter existing urban trends precisely because he minimized the role of political choice in urban development. He believed that a set of natural factors beyond conscious human control outweighed those of human design. Defining the city as "a state of mind, a body of customs and traditions, and of the organized attitudes and sentiments that inhere in these customs and are transmitted with this tradition," Park surely recognized the city as the product of human nature. But the main thrust of his thinking went in a different direction. Rooted in the habits and customs of its inhabitants, the city possessed a moral organization; it was, however, "the structure of the city which first impresses us by its visible vastness and complexity," Park wrote. That structure, itself a product of human nature, nevertheless imposed itself on its inhabitants "as a crude external fact, and forms them, in turn, in accordance with the design and interests which it incorporates." For that reason, Park argued, "there is a limit to the arbitrary modifications which it is possible to make" in the physical and social organization of the city.[16]

Park's concept of urban development could lead to an acceptance of such phenomena as slums and ghettos as the inevitable results of impersonal urban processes. Park, described the metropolis as "a great sifting and sorting mechanism, which, infallibly selects out of the population as a whole the individuals best suited to live in a particular region and a particular milieu."[17] At times Park came close to blaming the poor for their poverty. In the city, he wrote,

> the poor, the vicious, and the delinquent, crushed together in an unhealthful and contagious intimacy, breed in and in, soul and body, so that it has often occurred to me that those long genealogies of the Jukes and the tribes of Ishmael would not show such a persistent and distressing uniformity of vice, crime, and poverty unless they were peculiarly fit for the environment in which they are condemned to exist.
>
> We must accept then these "moral regions" and the more or less eccentric and exceptional people who inhabit them, in a sense, at least, as part of the natural, if not the normal, life of a city.

Certainly, Park's considerable sympathy for and understanding of the urban poor and outcast and his celebration of the diversity of urban life enriched American urban thought. But his view of the city as the result of natural forces beyond conscious human control encouraged an element of fatalism in the emerging discipline of urban planning.[18]

Park's colleague Harvey Zorbaugh expressed more bluntly the fatalistic element in the urban planning perspective. Speaking to a group that included members of the Regional Plan Association of New York, Zorbaugh argued that "the city is found to be not an artifact but a natural phenomenon." Quoting Elihu Root, Zorbaugh agreed that it "'is not the result of political decrees or control.'" The city, he explained, "'is a growth responding to forces not at all political. . . . It is a growth like that of a crystal responding to forces inherent in the atoms that make it up.'"[19] Park and his students added to our understanding of the nature of the city, but at the same time they contributed to a pessimistic attitude about the possibilities of change.

The realistic perspective did not go unchallenged, and an understanding of the role of political and economic power in urban development survived into the twentieth century. In his address to professional planners cited above, Charles Beard warned that unless they exposed "to public gaze" the "various economic interests that . . . gain more money . . . by forcing anti-social development," they would simply place a veneer of public accountability and disinterested professionalism on the plans of the great capitalists.[20] In contrast, Robert Park opened his most important address to professional planners with a reference to the ecology of plant communities, thereby obscuring the unique capacity of human communities to shape consciously their own environment.[21] It was Park's view of the city as largely a result of natural urban processes and the realistic tradition that he would champion that would prove most influential in the twentieth century and that shaped the professional discipline of urban planning.

SCOPE AND PERSPECTIVE

This work began as a Ph.D. dissertation on "the origins of city planning," but it has evolved into something both more and less than that. I began the study by examining the proceedings of the national conferences on city planning between 1909 and 1934, but that material seemed to leave so much unsaid about the American city and the demand for city planning. I therefore resolved, with great ambition and too little humility, to recapture the economic, social, cultural, intellectual, and political context out of which professional planning emerged. Increasingly the urban context, rather than the city planning profession itself, became the focus of the study. Without pretending to be a complete or exhaustive study of the planning profession, the present study combines an analysis of the professionalization of planning with an argument about the development of urban thought and urban reform during a sixty-year period.

Although the scope of the study is national, most of the examples that make up the larger picture are taken from three cities: New York, Chicago, and Cincinnati. The planners themselves led me to New York and Chicago, for it was in the two largest metropolitan areas of the nation that so much of the history of planning unfolded. Although Cincinnati was a leader in the city planning movement and the first major city to give official recognition to a master plan, its inclusion in this study was, at least in part, more arbitrary—the result of my employment in that city for the past seven years. But the choice was also both fortuitous and in some ways inevitable. Cincinnati has been blessed not only with a fascinating history but with a gifted group of historians, especially Steven J. Ross and Zane L. Miller. Their work on Cincinnati in the Gilded Age and the Progressive Era, respectively, has shaped my own understanding of the evolution of urban America during that period.

As a graduate student I had read Miller's *Boss Cox's Cincinnati* just as I was beginning work on the dissertation. While not specifically about planning, *Boss Cox's Cincinnati*, with its emphasis on the spatial dynamics of urban politics, including the machine-reform conflict and its analysis of the three-dimensional aspects of city building from the location of factories and residences to the provision of public utilities, shaped my view of what rightly belonged in a history of city planning. I read Ross's *Workers on the*

Edge at a similar point in the writing of the present work. His analysis of the influence that republican ideals had on the American working class and more specifically his provocative treatment of Henry George and the United Labor party were crucial in helping me rework some of the earlier and weaker parts of the dissertation. More generally, his suggestion that if Cincinnati's "workers had united and voted along class lines in local elections, they could have dramatically altered the character of Cincinnati's development" reinforced my own conviction about the role of political choice in urban development.[22] In short the history of Cincinnati has played a more pervasive and profound role in the development of this work than the scattered references to that city might suggest.

A final word about perspective. Much of the history of city planning has been written from the perspective of the planners themselves. As Robert Fishman argues most planning historians have assumed that planning has been a progressive force in urban affairs, no more or less than the rational application of modern science, technology, and professional expertise to the design of the urban environment. As a result such history, Fishman writes, "systematically underrates the contributions that non-professionals have made to urban form and vitality; and, consciously or unconsciously, planning history supports the elitist notion that city planning is for experts, not citizens." A counter tradition has developed around such writers as Jane Jacobs and Richard Sennett, whom Fishman describes as the anti-planners. The anti-planners have come close to rejecting planning outright, Fishman argues, in insisting that the city "must have order, but that order must be truly social, built up out of the plans of thousands of individuals."[23] In radically different ways (the one questioning the competence of the citizen, the other questioning the value of planning), each perspective has obscured the potential for a democratic form of planning.

My own perspective, like Fishman's, stands somewhere between the two. The city is the greatest illustration of the potential that freedom gives to the individual, but also of the much greater

potential of average and unexceptional humans acting in cooperation. City dwellers, George recognized, "may supply themselves
with greater certainty, and in much greater variety and abundance,
than the savage; but it is by the cooperation of thousands. Even
the water they drink, and the artificial light they use, are brought
to them by elaborate machinery, requiring the constant labor and
watchfulness of many men."[24] The complexity and cooperative
character of urban life, George understood, demanded an increased application of social intelligence. As a form of cooperation
and an application of social intelligence, planning is an essential
and crucial urban activity. Its definition and practice are too important to be left to the exclusive control of experts and professionals. This work is written with the conviction that the development of a democratic form of planning is both one of most
difficult tasks we face as a society and an essential precondition to
the creation of a more humane and just urban environment. I hope
to suggest that two closely related assumptions, about the incompetence of the average citizen in the face of complex urban problems
and about the inevitability of certain forms of urban development,
stand to this day as the most serious obstacles to accomplishing
that task.

1

An Urban Republic:
Frederick Olmsted, Henry George,
and the City Building Debate

Although significant industrial development had begun in the United States by the 1850s, the large industrial city was still alien to the experience of most antebellum Americans and appeared to threaten the values of the republic.[1] In the political crisis of the 1850s, the Republican party gave expression to a free labor ideology that idealized the small-town and rural society of the Northern states. An amalgam of protestant, republican, and artisan values, the free labor ideology celebrated a wide distribution of property, economic independence, social mobility, political egalitarianism, and a virtuous and competent citizenry. Although artisans in New York and other large cities had contributed to the development of the free labor ideology, the Republican party represented small-town and rural Americans who feared the extremes of wealth and poverty and the attendant political corruption associated with large cities.[2] Yet Republican economists such as Henry Carey argued that if industrialization were carried out on a small-town and rural basis, it would preserve and complement the free labor republic. Thus the Repub-

15

lican party agreed to promote industrialization or at least to remove obstacles to it.[3]

In the forty years after 1850, the industrial city became the dominant element within the republic. Despite the hopes of many Americans, rapid urbanization was central to industrialization during that period. The spatial concentration of economic activities, economies of scale, the urban market, and the import-replacing function all made the city the most important generator of industrial development.[4] The centralizing effects of both the railroad network and commercial capital helped to create a set of dominant metropolitan areas by the end of the century.[5] Urban industrialization created considerable economic opportunity and social mobility, but it also accelerated the concentration of economic power in corporations and the expansion of the class of economically dependent wage earners, which threatened republican institutions.

As the great railroad corporations ran roughshod over the democratic process following the Civil War, many Americans feared for the integrity of the republic. "I confess that the only fear I have in regard to republican institutions is whether, in our day, any adequate remedy will be found for this incoming flood of the power of incorporated wealth," the abolitionist turned labor reformer Wendell Phillips said. Alarmed by the Republican party's subservience to corporate interests, Phillips turned to the labor movement. "The labor movement is my only hope for democracy."[6] Conversely, conservatives lamented that the labor vote had become a crucial element of the nation's politics and cited the appeals to working-class interests on the part of demagogic politicians and labor agitators as the most serious threat to the republic.[7] By the 1890s a series of industrial depressions, a rising level of labor militancy, an influx of immigrant laborers, and the proliferation of corrupt political machines had made urban industrialization the central problem facing the republic.

In the Progressive Era reformers would begin to fashion a new set of realistic values, but Gilded Age Americans debated the future of their urban civilization with reference to the values and commitments of the free labor republic.[8] In particular both Frede-

rick Law Olmsted and Henry George employed the cultural resources of free labor and republican America to imagine an alternative course for urbanization that would lead to the development
of an urban commonwealth.[9] While accepting urbanization and
embracing its possibilities, they sought to create an urban landscape that was not, in George's words, "utterly divorced from all
the genial influences of nature." Hoping to balance the advantages
of the city with those of the country, Olmsted and George sought
to inject the urban order with the political equality, economic opportunity, and social harmony they associated with small-town
and rural America.[10]

Although the debate over the future of America's urban civilization would move in different directions and reflect different assumptions in the twentieth century, it was Olmsted, George, and
their Gilded Age contemporaries who brought the debate to the
forefront of the public agenda. Much of what Olmsted and George
argued would be lost to the coming generation, but they were the
first to wrestle with a set of issues that would confront twentieth-
century urban reformers. Their concern with the spatial order and
its relation to social control and social justice, their interest in the
environmental basis of behavior and the interrelationship among
the city's parts, as well as their call for an expansion of governmental functions and a greater involvement of middle-class professionals in public service anticipated key elements of the twentieth-
century debate.[11]

CITY AND COUNTRY

The scion of a venerable New England family stretching back
to 1636, tutored by a succession of Protestant ministers, Frederick
Law Olmsted was raised in the shadow of the Puritan "city on a
hill." During his childhood he developed both a deep love of nature and an admiration for the New England way of life.[12] As a
young man he embarked on a series of practical agricultural ven-

tures, but his interest in rural life ultimately reflected the concerns of the urban romantic. With his friend Andrew Jackson Downing, Olmsted shared a belief in the beneficent influence of nature and a commitment to republicanism. From contemporary theologians and reformers, he acquired a liberal protestant faith in the perfectibility of human nature. Olmsted's celebrated accounts of the shortcomings of the slave South sharpened his commitment to the free labor and republican values of the North. Although he could not entirely dismiss the Cavalier critique of the excessive commercialism of the Yankee North and the "rowdyism" and "ruffianism" of its mudsill class, Olmsted rejected the aristocratic outlook. Describing himself as a "Socialist Democrat," Olmsted charged the government with a greater responsibility for educating and elevating the lower classes.[13]

Olmsted's urban park designs reflected all of those convictions. The urban park would provide a rural retreat for city dwellers, encourage their natural instincts for sympathy, admiration, and respect, help to perfect the Christian community, and promote a sense of civic equality. "It is republican in its very idea and tendency," Downing had said in support of a municipal appropriation for New York's Central Park, "and raises up the man of the working men to the same level of enjoyment with the man of leisure and accomplishment."[14] Municipal parks, Olmsted agreed, afforded the "opportunity for people to come together for the single purpose of enjoyment, unembarrassed by the limitations with which they are surrounded at home, or in the pursuit of their daily avocations." Such opportunities would help overcome the class divisions within the city. To the great urban parks "a body of Christians" would come, he explained, "with an evident glee in the prospect of coming together, all classes largely represented, with a common purpose . . . disposing to jealousy and spiritual or intellectual pride toward none, each individual adding by his mere presence to the pleasure of all others, all helping to the greater happiness of each." The urban park, Olmsted implied, would help to recreate the Christian commonwealth of Puritan New England within the cities of the free labor republic.[15]

Notwithstanding his admiration for the New England way of life, Olmsted was not antiurban. He eagerly accepted the challenge of developing an intelligent and humane urban culture in America. A student of the history of urban development, Olmsted acknowledged the many advantages of urbanization even as he criticized the shortcomings of the American city.[16] He understood that advances in communication, transportation, and exchange throughout the world would continue to increase both the number and the size of cities.[17] But in the future, he insisted, metropolitan development would have to be planned with reference to the needs "not of ordinary commerce only, but of humanity, religion, art, science, and scholarship." Faithful to that admonition, Olmsted's philosophy of parks grew from his study of urbanization and his critique of the American city.[18]

Sharply critical of the grid street system that had been imposed upon New York, Olmsted hoped to prevent its extension and recommended a more flexible and imaginative layout of streets. The grid facilitated the sale of real estate, but it frustrated other human activities. The standardized twenty-five by one-hundred foot lot allowed for the construction of the magnificent mansions of the wealthy, but it crowded the poor into dark, airless tenements. In "the middle parts of all these deep narrow cubes there must be a large amount of ill-ventilated space," he protested. The standardized lot was also incompatible for modest single-family dwellings for it ensured that the "ground rent would be in too large proportion to that of the betterments." Thus the grid not only condemned the poor to unsatisfactory living conditions, but it ignored the needs of the great middle ranks of clerks and mechanics, the backbone of the republican city.[19]

Overcrowding and congestion had long been central problems in metropolitan development. Citing the close connection between death rates and congestion, Olmsted argued that the improvement of urban living conditions was historically "due to the abandonment of the old-fashioned compact way of building towns, and the gradual adoption of a custom of laying them out with much larger spaces open to sun-light and fresh air." In the great commercial cities during the past century, the families of businessmen had demanded "as much of the luxuries of free air, space, and abundant vegetation as, without loss of town privileges, they can be enabled to secure." The effort to balance the advantages of city living with those of rural life had become even more important in the cities of the industrial era.[20]

Thus Olmsted's philosophy of parks addressed the particular problems of life in the industrial metropolis. Industrialization had accelerated the division of the metropolis between fast-paced, impersonal, and competitive business districts and fashionable residential areas where the fortunate found refuge from the noise, pollution, congestion, and other disagreeable aspects of industrial production. The urban park would serve as a middle ground, both clarifying the functional segregation and serving its own distinctive functions. The character of industrial production, Olmsted explained, had made "tranquilizing recreation more essential to continued health and strength than until lately it generally has been."[21] That was particularly a problem for the working class, which lacked access to a suburban or rural environment. Alleviating the stress of the competitive city of work, the park would also provide a focus for communal activities and social interaction between the classes.

Olmsted's philosophy of parks complemented his view of residential suburbs, which were designed to serve more complex functions than the twentieth century haven of domestic privacy. On the busy streets of the working city, Olmsted wrote, "to merely avoid collision with those we meet and pass upon the sidewalks, we have constantly to watch, to foresee, to guard against their movement." Consequently, "our minds are thus brought into close dealings with other minds without any friendly flowing toward them, but rather a drawing from them." For the fortunate classes Olmsted's suburbs afforded not only a domestic retreat from such tensions but a community setting where social interaction could take a positive form. The most scenic vistas, he wrote, should "be possessed by each family in common with others, at some little distance from the house, so as to afford inducement and occasion for going more out from it, and for realizing and keeping up acquaintances by the eye at least, with the community." It was just as important, Olmsted argued, for the suburb to provide opportunities for "the harmonious association and co-operation of men in a community" as to provide privacy. Unfortunately, the lower classes, trapped in the crowded tenement districts, lacked those opportunities.[22]

While Olmsted designed urban park systems in the 1860s and 1870s Henry George, another and less fortunate son of the antebellum middle class, brooded over the character of urban America. The son of a struggling middle-class Philadelphia family, George shared Olmsted's faith in a beneficent natural order and his Christian ethics. For all its detailed exposition of political economy the ultimate force of George's greatest work, *Progress and Poverty*, was moral. "Political economy and social science cannot teach any lessons," he argued, that Christ had not already taught. Combining his view of nature with his religious faith in a manner reminiscent of his political hero, Thomas Jefferson, he insisted that the "laws of nature are the decrees of the Creator." George hoped to release the instinctual capacities of all humans for sympathy, admiration and respect and to create "the city of God on earth."[23]

But George added to those convictions a commitment to artisan republicanism, inherited from his Jacksonian father and hardened both in the working-class Southwark District of Philadelphia where he grew up and in more than a decade's hard struggle on the Pacific frontier. During the depression of the 1870s, the juxtaposition of abject poverty and fabulous wealth on the Pacific frontier and in Eastern cities had fired George's imagination and left him with "haunting visions of higher possibilities."[24] He developed those visions in *Progress and Poverty*, which was perhaps more widely read than any other book in the nineteenth century save the Bible.[25] His analysis of the enigma of poverty amidst progress combined an artisan's view of political economy with a passion for social justice in order to outline an alternative vision of urban development.[26]

The young George saw a great deal of the bitter side of Ameri-

21

ca's Pacific frontier as a sailor, prospector, printer, and newspaperman. Yet he retained a love for the land and dreamed of a pastoral utopia. "Sometimes I feel sick of the fierce struggle of our high civilized life," he wrote his sister in 1861, "and think I would like to get away from cities and business, with their jostlings and strainings and cares altogether, and find some place on one of the hillsides, . . . where I could gather those I love, and live content with what Nature and our own resources would furnish; but, alas, money is wanted even for that." Conjoined with his republican ethics and increasingly tempered by the logic of the political economist, that pastoral image would remain at the center of George's response to urban America.[27]

Following Jefferson and anticipating Frederick Jackson Turner, George explained in *Progress and Poverty* that the availability of land had shaped American development.

> The general intelligence, the general comfort, the active invention, the power of adaptation and assimilation, the free independent spirit, the energy and hopefulness that have marked our people, are not causes, but results—they have sprung from unfenced land. This public domain has been the transmuting force which has turned the thriftless, unambitious European peasant into the self-reliant Western farmer; it has given a consciousness of freedom even to the dweller in crowded cities, and has been the well-spring of hope even to those who have never thought of taking refuge upon it. . . . In America, whatever his condition, there has always been the consciousness that the public domain lay behind him; and the knowledge of this fact . . . has penetrated our whole national life, giving to it generosity and independence, elasticity and ambition.

Like Turner fifteen years later, George also recognized that the "great fact which has been potent is ceasing to be" and that "the republic has entered upon a new era."[28] But unlike Turner George resolved that the availability of land and its natural opportunities must remain a central feature of the urban republic. The single tax, a confiscatory tax on the rental value of land excluding improvements, was George's solution to the problem of maintaining equal access to the land in the post-frontier, urban republic. By chang-

22

ing a single element in the political economy, George believed, the single tax would redirect the development of urban industrialization and preserve the republican commonwealth.[29]

The political philosophy that supported the single tax also owed a great deal to the Jeffersonian tradition. Jefferson's statement of natural rights, George argued, had helped to ensure America's republican experiment and its economic progress. But mere political equality could not "prevent the tendency to inequality involved in the private ownership of land," he warned. The republic might yet be preserved, George argued, if Jefferson's statement of the natural law was amended. "Nature acknowledges no ownership or control in man save as the result of exertion," he insisted; the natural law "broadly and clearly" asserted "the equal right of all men to the use and enjoyment of nature." If the monopoly of land could be broken and equal access to natural opportunities thereby secured, he concluded, then the "inequalities that continued to exist would be those of nature, not the artificial inequalities produced by the denial of natural law."[30]

Despite his Jeffersonian predilections George embraced the possibilities of the great city. The concentration of population was a stimulus to progress, George believed, and he described the single tax as "the secret which would transform the little village into the great city." Like Olmsted, George imagined a landscape and a social order that would balance the advantages of urban life with those of rural life:

> The destruction of speculative land values would tend to diffuse population where it is too dense and to concentrate it where it is too sparse; to substitute for the tenement house, homes surrounded by gardens, and to fully settle agricultural districts before people were driven far from neighbors to look for land. The people of the cities would thus get more of the pure air and sunshine of the country, the people of the country more of the economies and social life of the city.

George would combine the advantages of the country and the city and preserve respect for the rural way of life in a rapidly urbanizing society.[31]

23

LOOKING BACKWARD, LOOKING FORWARD

Both Olmsted and George struggled to square their vision of the urban future with certain aspects of their cultural inheritance. Olmsted had relatively little difficulty in abandoning the traditional American commitment to laissez-faire. In the 1850s he was already arguing that "government should have in view the encouragement of a democratic condition of society as well as of government." His difficulty was in identifying the politically virtuous agents for the reforms he proposed.[32] Olmsted's political ideals were those of the traditional middle class of independent property owners, but his reform program was eventually inherited and reshaped by a new middle class of salaried professionals who did not always share his ideals.[33]

Looking backward Olmsted recalled a time when the traditional middle class maintained its influence by virtue of personal example and the spontaneous workings of the natural order. Counteracting the influence of the promiscuous street culture of the working-class neighborhood, the milieu of the political boss and the labor agitator, his parks would help to preserve the influence of the traditional middle class in the segregated city. "By their example, and by quiet persuasion in ordinary social intercourse, they direct the action of many men of greater energy and practical ability, but of less mature taste than themselves," he wrote of the leaders of that class.[34] Looking forward he recognized that more artificial means of social control would be necessary in the growing cities, a recognition that pushed him toward a reliance on the new middle class and their professional techniques. Fortunately, Olmsted wrote, "modern science has beyond all question determined many of the causes of the special evils by which men are afflicted in towns, and placed means in our hands for guarding against them."[35] Landscape architecture was one such means. Not only the presence of the respectable classes but the professionally designed landscape, he argued, "exercises a distinctly harmonizing and refining influence upon the most unfortunate and most lawless classes of the

24

city," instilling in them the middle-class virtues of "courtesy, self-control, and temperance" and weakening their "dangerous inclinations."[36]

During the Civil War, as executive secretary of the Sanitary Commission, Olmsted had championed the cause of the scientifically educated expert and excoriated both the incompetent volunteer and the corrupt politician.[37] In the postwar period, increasingly jealous of the prerogatives of the professional landscape architect, Olmsted insisted that park planning be placed in the hands of professionally trained members of the middle class.[38] The incompetence and untrustworthiness of the average politician and the abundant opportunities for graft in the planning of parks, Olmsted argued, meant that "the ordinary organizations for municipal business are unsuitable agencies for the purpose." He advised that the acquisition of park land be "taken up efficiently by a small body of select men."[39]

The administration of the park also demanded the efforts of trained professionals. Even before Central Park opened he had worried about the "riotous and licentious habits" of park-goers at other facilities. He avoided the rugged and picturesque in Central Park so as to minimize "opportunities and temptations to shabbiness, disorder, indecorum, and indecency." He hoped the pastoral scene would afford "tranquillity and rest to the mind." But the riotous and licentious nevertheless appeared in Central Park. Disgusted by the Tweed machine's lax administration of the park and its use as a patronage mill, Olmsted demanded that control of the park be given over to an appointed board of park experts and prominent citizens which would operate like the "board of directors of a commercial corporation."[40]

In calling for a greater role for professionals and businessmen in public affairs, the forward-looking Olmsted anticipated the form much of the twentieth-century planning took; his experimentation with environmental reform anticipated something of its content.[41] In 1870 Olmsted argued that "the further progress of civilization is to depend mainly upon the influences by which men's minds and characters will be effected while living in large towns."[42] He thus anticipated the belief of many urban progressives that the key to individual regeneration and social progress lay in the design of physical and social environments, what Paul Boyer has described as "positive environmentalism." In an argument that would be repeated in Daniel Burnham's *Plan of Chicago*, Olmsted observed:

> When there has been a demolition of and rebuilding on a new ground plan of some part [of the city] which had previously been noted for the frequency of certain crimes, the prevalence of certain diseases, and the shortness of life among its inhabitants . . . , a marked improvement in all these respects has immediately followed, and has been maintained not alone in the dark parts, but in the city as a whole.

Thus in his philosophy and design of urban parks, Olmsted revealed a tension between his faith in the spontaneous workings of the natural order and the personal example of the traditional middle class and his growing reliance on the more artificial and scientific means of social control at the disposal of the new middle class.[43]

George experienced a similar difficulty in squaring the dictates of his cultural inheritance with the solutions he proposed to new problems. George struggled to justify the single tax, which to his opponents smacked of socialism, by means of his own Jeffersonian conviction that the proper role of government was simply to protect natural rights and the natural law. The "unjust and unequal distribution of wealth," he argued, transgressed the natural law, halted progress, and created other evils that would "not cure themselves." Such "evils are not imposed by natural laws," he insisted, "they spring solely from social mal-adjustments which ignore natural laws." Once the natural laws had been reinstated, George insisted, progress would resume with minimal governmental interference.[44]

Raised on the credo of limited government, yet addressing the problems of a complex urban society, George developed a profoundly ambivalent attitude toward the role of government in promoting social progress. He valued economy and simplicity in government, reinforced by his view of the deplorable state of boss-ridden machine politics. Among "the grave political difficulties" threatening the republic, he argued, was the tendency of "the proletarians of the cities" to favor large government expenditures as a way of "furnishing employment" or "putting money in circulation." Of course the single tax involved a rather dramatic intervention of government in the political economy, but George was quick to point out as one of its benefits "the great simplicity which would become possible in government." Tax collection would be streamlined, litigation concerning ownership of land ended, crime, pauperism, and other social ills arising from poverty eliminated, along with the governmental functions poverty made necessary.[45]

It was George's fear that the republican ideal of economic independence for the small producer was rapidly disappearing in urban America that drove him to the struggle with his laissez-faire proclivities, which he never fully abandoned. He would also be forced to wrestle with his belief in the harmony of the producing classes (capital and labor) within the free labor economy, a belief he probably took intact to his grave. Anxious to preserve unfettered opportunity for the small producer, George insisted that there was no fundamental conflict between labor and capital. The real conflict was between the producers and the land monopoly. The unearned increment taken in rent, a sum that reflected the social value of land and that grew with the community, was the true cause of poverty. Confiscate rent, he explained, and not only would wages and profits increase, but opportunities for the small producer would also multiply.[46]

Looking backward George clung to his Jeffersonian vision of a natural order protected by limited government and his artisan's view of the harmony of the producing classes. Looking forward he recognized that his vision of an urban commonwealth of cooperating small producers demanded a more active role for government. In the last sections of *Progress and Poverty*, he carefully dismantled the social-Darwinist view of progress and William Graham Sumner's defense of laissez-faire. Attacking the belief in heredity as the basis of individual progress, he insisted that the fate of a child "depends entirely on the social environment in which it is placed." He made a similar argument in relation to social progress. Citing the decline of every previous great civilization, he argued "that the obstacles which finally bring progress to a halt are raised by the course of progress." Only through the development and judicious application of social intelligence would our urban civilization overcome the obstacles to its own progress.[47]

Four years later in *Social Problems* (1883), George further undermined his opponents' arguments. In the development of the species, he argued, greater intelligence had necessarily accompanied greater complexity; the same held true for the progress of civilization. For uncounted generations the human species had evolved no further, while human civilization had grown infinitely more complex. "Where the development of species ends," George argued, "social development commences." The progress of civilization was due not to the evolution of the species but to the accumulation of social intelligence and its application to the problems of an increasingly complex society. To insist upon a social-Darwinist or laissez-faire approach to social development was to ignore the laws of natural development and risk catastrophe.[48] Thus George, like Olmsted, abandoned the laissez-faire element of his cultural inheritance and paved the way for a new era of reform.

Guardians of the cultural resources inherited from the free labor republic, including the utopian and perfectionist elements of protestantism, a romantic faith in a beneficent natural order, and the republican tradition in both its Jeffersonian and artisan forms, Olmsted and George might be seen as the last figures in a tradition stretching back to Jefferson, Paine, or even Winthrop. But they also grappled with the central problems of the emerging urban society. The basic contradiction between means and ends in their work, between the desire to recreate the natural order and release instinctual human emotions and the use of a manipulative social intelligence to achieve those ends, testifies to their struggle with received wisdom and new conditions.[49] Their confrontation with the new metropolitan order, which was emerging in the 1880s and 1890s, was consequently full of both irony and enduring significance.

LABOR AND THE REPUBLICAN CITY

In the 1880s the greatest support of George's ideals came from an unexpected source, the urban working class. In *Progress and Poverty* George had called for a greater role for middle-class professionals in public service, hoping to promote a spirit of altruism in the middle class and to bring "to the management of public affairs and the administration of common funds, the skill, the attention, the fidelity, and integrity that can now only be secured for private interests."[50] He had also expressed a pessimistic view of the political virtue of the urban masses. "Tortured by want and embruted by poverty," the masses were "ready to sell their votes to the highest bidder or follow the lead of the most blatant demagogue."[51] In 1880 after George had left California for New York in the hope of popularizing the single tax, he still believed that "successful [reform] efforts can come from the class above, not below."[52] Indeed, George had considerable influence among middle-class reformers, from the British Fabians and the town planner Ebenezer Howard to Benjamin Marsh, organizer of the first American city planning conference, and many other American progressives.[53] But in his own lifetime his greatest political influence ironically came at the head of a working-class political party, the United Labor party (ULP), organized in New York during 1886–87.

One of the purposes of *Progress and Poverty*, begun immediately after the railroad strikes of 1877, was to defuse the growing labor-capital conflict and to point to the overriding problem of the monopoly in land. Never a whole-hearted supporter of trade unions or strikes, George believed that "the good that can be accomplished by them is extremely limited."[54] Yet the United Labor party, as Samuel Gompers recalled, "was in inception a trade union movement."[55] Although George told one group of potential supporters that they "must accept me as the candidate of organized labor," he never fully resigned himself to the true nature of the movement he led.[56] Throughout his association with the ULP George insisted that it was not a class-based party and that class appeals had no place in American politics. In 1888, after having contributed to the ULP's rapid demise by orchestrating a purge of the socialists within it, George returned to the Democratic party of Grover Cleveland, hardly fertile ground for the radical measures he proposed.

Notwithstanding George's unease, the United Labor party was the most striking example of a class-based party in nineteenth-century America. In the wake of the May Day strikes of 1886 and the Haymarket explosion, labor organizations across the nation called for the creation of a new labor party. In New York, further inflamed by the Theiss trial in which several union negotiators had been convicted of extortion, the movement coalesced around George's mayoral candidacy. By all accounts the George-Hewitt campaign (Hewitt was the Democratic candidate and the Republican party's candidate was Theodore Roosevelt) was the most unusual and dramatic in nineteenth-century New York.[57] George's campaign mobilized the efforts of thousands of participants, the majority of them from the working class. The campaign itself consisted of a series of mass meetings, many of them in the open air. Huge crowds of working people gathered on street corners to hear George and his labor associates speak. The effort culminated in a great parade in Union Square. Despite a drenching rain a crowd of trade unionists, single-taxers, and members of the Knights of Labor, by some estimates sixty thousand strong, participated in an astonishing display of discipline and solidarity.[58]

George agreed to lead that remarkable movement for a variety of reasons. Unlike the professional city planners who followed in his wake, George saw his task as an essentially political one. He knew that his single tax threatened very powerful interests and that it could only be enacted, as Lewis Mumford later wrote, "through the initiative of the community as a whole, with an enlightened and militant working class as the spearhead."[59] When a delegation from the city's Central Labor Council asked him to run for mayor he hesitated, but he eventually accepted the challenge because he believed that a campaign centered on the single tax would "do more to popularize its discussion than years of writing."[60] Disturbed by what he saw as an increasing tendency to regard "the masses as born but for the service of their rulers," George had argued that we "cannot safely leave politics to politicians, or political economy to college professors. The people themselves must think, because the people alone must act."[61] Notwithstanding his skepticism about the political virtue of the masses, George believed the effort to create an urban republic must be a democratic one that engaged the energies and abilities of the average citizen.

George's popularity owed a great deal to his ability to express his radical proposals in the American language of republicanism. Single-taxers claimed to be virtuous citizens protecting the integrity of the republic, rather than socialists demanding the nationalization of land and other class legislation.[62] Adding labor's right to "natural opportunities for employment" to Jefferson's list of inalienable rights, George insisted that single-taxers were "Democrats and believe that political power should emanate from the people, and that in all matters that do not invade the inalienable rights of man the majority should rule."[63] "I am called a Socialist," George said during the campaign. "I am really an individualist. I believe that every individual man ought to have an individual wife, and is entitled to an individual home."[64] Thus George cast his proposals in terms of traditional American values.

Notwithstanding his protestations George seemed a dangerous radical to his opponents. His candidacy temporarily united both machine and reform politicians in condemnation of what they insisted was the politics of class. The mainstream press vilified George as a "revolutionist" and an "Apostle of anarchy and destruction." Rumors circulated that even the Republicans had tried to swing their voters to Hewitt in a last-ditch effort to defeat George. Against such odds what George insisted was a movement of "the masses against the classes" still polled more than sixty-eight thousand votes to Hewitt's ninety thousand (Roosevelt polled sixty thousand). Many believed George had been counted out illegally but the total was, nevertheless, impressive and, to his opponents, alarming. In the following year as the ULP endeavored to build a national party, machine and reform forces united across party lines to soundly defeat the fledgling movement in New York and other cities. In the face of such antagonism and a successful effort of the major parties to recruit their most effective leaders, the ULP, beset by its own internal conflicts, collapsed in 1888.[65]

In many ways George made a rather strange "revolutionist." No less than Hewitt he paid homage to the founding fathers and their constitution. "So far as we propose to treat social questions, it is solely through and by that system," he pledged.[66] Nor was he in any conventional sense a socialist. The single tax was a product of George's encounter with the agrarianism and land reform proposals of earlier labor activists and his experiences on the Pacific frontier, where manufacturing was relatively undeveloped and simple access to land could mean economic independence for the farmer or miner. "Nothing like general and protracted congestion of capital and labor could take place were this natural vent open," George argued in support of free access to land. "Nor is it true that we could not all become farmers. That is the one thing that we might all become," he added.[67] Subscribing to the conventional theory of the frontier as a safety valve for industrial discontent, George ignored the considerable capital required to set up even a self-sufficient farm and minimized the much larger problem of the concentration of industrial capital.

Labor historians as well as many of George's contemporaries have overemphasized George's ignorance of the enormous changes taking place within industry, but it is probably fair to say that he had no remedy for them. He acknowledged that the concentration of capital had made it easier "to intercept what would naturally go to labor." Yet the single tax did not directly address such late-nineteenth-century developments as the transformation of the workplace, the breaking up of traditional crafts, the growing power of the industrial corporation, and the trend towards monopoly.

Indeed, George continued to discount the growing conflict between labor and capital and its impact on the great city and to insist that the land monopolist was the one and true villain. He disappointed his trade union supporters by refusing to include basic demands on hours and wages and other labor planks in his platform.[68] He still believed that the individual, with the help of the single tax, could secure his own independence.

THE CITY BUILDING IDEAL

It was the commitment to individualism and his suspicion of socialism that prevented George from developing a comprehensive program of city planning and urban reform. The socialists within the ULP wanted to add to its platform a plank calling for the nationalization of all the means of production. Although the single tax in effect nationalized an important element of the means of production and George also favored public ownership of urban utilities, he resolutely opposed stronger measures. George saw socialism as coercive and destructive of individual initiative and feared it would "frighten away the country votes."[69] Even though he came to recognize the impact of corporate ownership and machine industry on the artisan, he clung to the ideal of the independent, small producer all the more as he saw the ideal vanishing.[70]

With his artisan's background George viewed the role of planning in the urban future in a way similar to his European contemporary, the Austrian planner Camillo Sitte. Sitte criticized the bureaucratic prescriptions of the emerging European planning profession in his *City Building* (1889). As Carl Schorske has argued, Sitte stressed actual "making" over abstract design. The city must not be "a merely mechanical bureaucratic product," Sitte wrote, but "a piece of great genuine folk art." Whereas Sitte looked to the aesthetic sensibilities of the modern artist to replace the role of the practicing artisan in urban design, George continued to place his faith in the artisan.[71]

33

In *Progress and Poverty* George had championed an active and decisive role for the average citizen in city building. "To increase the comforts, and leisure, and independence of the masses is to increase their intelligence," he wrote in a passage that echoed the artisans' defense of the eight-hour day, "it is to bring the brain to the aid of the hand; it is to engage in the common work of life the faculty which measures the animalcule and traces the orbits of the stars!" Man, George believed, "is the constructive animal; he builds, he improves, he invents, and puts together, and the greater the thing he does, the greater the thing he wants to do." Nothing illustrated this better than housing: "The beaver builds a dam, and the bird a nest, and the bee a cell; but while beavers' dams, and birds' nest, and bees' cells are always constructed on the same model, the house of the man passes from the rude hut of leaves and branches to the magnificent mansion replete with modern conveniences." It was those energies that George hope to bring to city building, and it was that ideal that provided the underlying logic for George's leadership of an artisan-dominated movement.[72]

At the heart of George's city building ideal was not only a commitment to a society of small producers but a fascination with urban homesteading and owner-built housing. The single tax would promote urban homesteading, he argued, because "the builder of a city homestead would not have to lay out as much for a small lot as for the house he puts upon it." Describing his vision of the urban future, George quoted the prophet Isaiah: "And they shall build houses and inhabit them; and they shall plant vineyards and eat the fruit of them. They shall not build and another inhabit; they shall not plant and another eat."[73] In New York, with its overwhelming majority of tenants, George continued to emphasize the issue of homeownership. Although he said little about the owner-built house, perhaps for fear of alienating members of the building trades who were the single largest contingent in his constituency, George continued to hold out the prospect of homeownership for working-class families.

Though clearly there were utopian elements in George's thought, it is not impossible to imagine the realization of even his most apparently implausible idea, the city of owner-built housing. The American invention of balloon-frame construction in the 1830s, complemented by technological improvements in sawmilling and nail-making, had already significantly lowered construction costs and brought homeownership within reach of many working-class families. Historians Olivier Zunz and James Barrett have found high rates of homeownership in working-class neighborhoods in late-nineteenth-century Detroit and Chicago. Kenneth Jackson has argued (and Zunz has documented for Detroit) that urban workers commonly built their own dwellings.[74] Such workers realized the hope of the Knights of Labor, with which both George and the ULP were closely associated, that working people "be enabled to reap the advantages conferred by the labor-saving machinery which their brains have created."[75] Moreover, the publication of house plans in magazines and pattern books proliferated in the period. "There never was a time when so many books and magazines written for the purpose of bringing the subject of architecture—its history, its theory, its practice—down to the level of popular understanding were produced as in this time of ours," wrote one contemporary art critic.[76]

The political program of the ULP, if implemented, could have reinforced and complemented those developments. The single tax was specifically designed to stabilize realty values and to make cheap land available at the urban periphery.[77] In his mayoral campaign George also advocated a free, municipally owned and operated rapid transit system that would have allowed workers to live on the periphery without sacrificing wages or excessive time. Combined with the demands for higher wages and an eight-hour day (providing "eight hours for what we will") voiced by George's labor associates—although resisted by George himself—such policies might have created just the pattern of homeownership that he envisioned.

Ultimately, nothing of the sort occurred, in part because of developments in urban America that George imperfectly understood. As Steven Ross has argued, George stood with many American workers on the edge of an industrializing society. George believed that class lines were not yet rigidly fixed and that the individual might still secure independence through initiative, hard work, and a limited set of government policies designed to protect and promote the commonwealth. But by the end of the 1880s, a significant element of the labor movement had abandoned the hope that self-reliant and independent laborers could control industrial development and preserve the republican commonwealth.[78]

Labor's new strategy owed more to the emerging realistic and pragmatic tradition than to George's republican ideals. For labor leaders such as Samuel Gompers, the ULP campaigns had proved the futility of political action and utopian dreams. Under Gompers's guidance the American Federation of Labor (AF of L) acted on the premise that America had irrevocably passed over a divide into an industrial capitalist system where the working class would have to defend its specific class interests within that system. Labor radicals who remained politically minded were drawn to scientific socialism and other revolutionary creeds that also accepted the inevitability, at least in the short run, of industrial capitalist development and that had little sympathy for or connection to republican ideals.[79]

George's own weaknesses as a leader were also partly responsible for the collapse of the movement he had done so much to create. He refused to make any accommodation to either the radicalism of the socialists, whom he purged from the ULP, or the more pragmatic strategy of the AF of L.[80] But it was not simply that he resisted all efforts to broaden the platform of the ULP to include either traditional or radical labor planks. George had also refused to place the single tax in the mainstream of labor activism stretching back to the agrarianism and land reform proposals of the National Reform Association in the 1840s. Despite the presence of veterans of that earlier movement in the ULP, George claimed the single tax as his own original contribution to the analysis of social problems. Laying claim to proprietorship of a unique piece of social technology and jealously guarding its purity, George made his own concessions to the notions of social

engineering and expert planning that would characterize the realistic tradition.[81]

Perhaps the greatest irony in George's relationship with the
ULP was the fate of the single tax at the hands of the socialists. In
1888, after George's withdrawal from the party and disappointing
results in the elections of 1887, the ULP met in Cincinnati to map
its future strategy. While a group of moderates created a new
Union Labor party, which dropped the single tax in hopes of winning the support of the urban middle class and farmers, a group
of socialists and other radicals took over what was left of the old
ULP. Edward McGlynn, once a close associate of George, explained that the ULP had rejected George but not the single tax.
During an unsuccessful effort to merge the two parties, moderates
complained that the single tax would merely increase taxes on land
and hence make it more difficult for working-class families to
achieve their most cherished goal of homeownership. Others wondered whether manufacturers, willing and able to pay a higher tax
for a desirable location, could outbid working-class families for
the land on which their houses sat and thus displace them. For the
moderates homeownership represented a crucial measure of independence that was still within reach of the working class and that
the single tax threatened. These were concerns that George could
understand, since they reflected his own values and assumptions
and he had tried to address them.[82]

It was the socialists who offered the more realistic and pragmatic argument in defense, ironically, of the single tax. They did
not deny the threat to homeownership. Instead they argued that
in the industrial capitalist system, the possibility of homeownership for the individual worker was much less important than providing adequate housing for the mass for workers now living in
unhealthy and decrepit tenements.[83] For the socialists homeownership was a chimera, or worse, an unaffordable affectation that
divided the working class between homeowners and tenants and
distracted attention from more important issues. The single tax,
on the other hand, would force speculators to build on vacant land

and also to provide needed revenues for the construction of public housing. While George had seen the single tax as a republican measure that would reestablish a harmony of interests among small, independent producers, the ULP radicals saw it as a pragmatic measure that would protect the specific interests of the working class in an antagonistic society.[84] George's legacy would continue to influence the development of urban America, but not always in ways he could have imagined.

THE SINGLE TAX AND MUNICIPAL SOCIALISM

Notwithstanding George's commitment to traditional values, an extremely radical principle was at the center of his thought, which explains the socialists' interest in his ideas. That was the principle that land values were a social product that should be used for the benefit of the community. The "immense values created by the growth of population might . . . be drawn upon to make New York the most beautiful and healthful of cities," George wrote to the trade unionists who asked him to run for mayor.[85] George's platform declared that

> the enormous value which the presence of a million and a half of people gives to the land of this city belongs properly to the whole community; that it should not go to the enrichment of individuals and corporations, but should be taken in taxation and applied to the improvement and beautifying of the city, to the promotion of the health, comfort, education, and recreation of its people, and to the providing of means of transit commensurate with the needs of a great metropolis.

In formally accepting the nomination at Cooper Union, George argued that those issues constituted "the heart of the labor question." While his socialist associates would question the exclusive emphasis on land values, even the most radical recognized it as a step in the right direction.[86]

George readily admitted that the single tax did not provide "the solution of all social problems" and that "much will remain to do."[87] But even if the single tax could not accomplish all that George predicted, it did represent the foundation for a socialist program of urban reform and city planning. It also provided a precedent for the nationalization of other forms of property, a step that George and his associates were already contemplating. In 1883 George had argued that "all businesses that involve monopoly are within the necessary province of government regulation, and businesses that are in their nature complete monopolies become properly functions of the state."[88] The municipal ownership of urban utilities, natural monopolies whose profitability grew with the community, was a logical corollary of George's critique of the land monopoly. The ULP would also call for the nationalization of all forms of communication, transportation, and natural monopolies (gas, oil, minerals).[89]

Those arguments reflected new developments in George's thought since he had written *Progress and Poverty*. The pace, complexity, and the interdependence of life in New York, in contrast to the relatively simple life on the Pacific frontier, had sharpened George's sense of the need for social intelligence and cooperation and a greater public role in urban development. "Social progress always requires greater intelligence in the management of public affairs," he argued in 1883, "but this the more as progress is rapid and change quicker."[90] He saw rapid urbanization threatening to overwhelm the natural order. Referring to the twelve thousand head of cattle butchered weekly in the city, George lamented "the elements of fertility, which, instead of being returned to the soil from which they came, are swept out through the sewers of our great cities."[91] The awesome power and vitality of the great city demanded intelligent public control.

Thus in New York during the 1880s, George's vision of the urban future took on something of the character of municipal socialism. Although he continued to believe that the republic might safely dispense with army, navy, and diplomatic corps, he argued that in an urban society "the functions which government must assume steadily increase." The "truth in socialism," he wrote, was that the government must assume the cooperative functions "which cannot be done, or cannot be so well done, by individual actions."[92] In *Progress and Poverty* George had suggested that the single tax would enable government to establish

> public baths, museums, libraries, gardens, lecture rooms, music and dancing halls, theaters, universities, technical schools, shooting galleries, play grounds, gymnasiums, etc. Heat, light, and motive power, as well as water, might be conducted through our streets at public expense; our roads be lined with fruit trees; discoverers and inventors rewarded, scientific investigations supported; and in a thousand ways the public revenues made to foster efforts for the public benefit.

Four years later he argued more emphatically that the municipal ownership and operation of public utilities was absolutely essential to ensuring "a natural distribution of population, which would give every one breathing space and neighborhood."[93] The creation of the urban republic required a strong dose of municipal socialism.

Anxious to redirect American politics and industrial development, George had argued that "a fitting and hopeful place . . . to begin is in our municipalities." George and his ULP associates had believed that "a large vote would permanently introduce into American politics the questions to which his life had been devoted."[94] Indeed they did build an influential if short-lived coalition of trade unionists and reform-minded professionals who envisioned a new urban republic and bequeathed to the nascent city planning movement a popular demand for a more just and democratic city. The coalition also outlined and popularized a practical if limited program of municipal socialism that anticipated and inspired the more effective coalitions headed by Hazen Pingree, Tom Johnson, Frederic Howe, Brand Whitlock, Herbert Bigelow, and others. Those social reformers followed George's lead in mobilizing the voting power of the urban masses, encouraging their active participation in municipal affairs, and attempting to redistribute economic and political power in their cities.[95]

THE WHITE CITY

In the summer of 1892 a very different conception of America's urban future from that suggested by either George or Olmsted began to take shape along Chicago's lakeshore. Initially authorized by an act of Congress in celebration of the four hundredth anniversary of the discovery of America, the World's Columbian Exposition provided the opportunity to create a model city of four hundred buildings covering nearly seven hundred acres. Constructed by a private corporation chartered by the Illinois state legislature, the White City, as the exposition came to be called, reflected the combined efforts of business leaders, the cultural elite, and public officials.[96] The prominent Chicago architect Daniel H. Burnham served as director of works and coordinated the activities of local businessmen, a committee of prestigious architects, and a public commission of appointed officials.

Thus the White City heralded not only a new attitude to urban development but also the emergence of a new political order. Underlying both was a deep skepticism about the competence of the average citizen to deal with public affairs. For Henry Adams that was the clearest message of the exposition. If the new urban-industrial society "were to be run at all, it must be run by capital and by capitalistic methods," he wrote in juxtaposing the exposition and the Populist revolt, "for nothing could surpass the non-sensity of trying to run so complex and so concentrated a machine by Southern and Western farmers in grotesque alliance with city day-laborers."[97] Like Turner's thesis (delivered at the meeting of the American Historical Association held at the exposition), which suggested that the frontier experience would survive as a set of disembodied national characteristics, the White City, with its plaster-like classical facades covering steel frame buildings, depicted an America where free labor and republican values would survive as outward forms for a corporate and hierarchical order. Underneath the classical and republican imagery lay the dominant reality of the marketplace, the city as a showcase for the material culture of the capitalist order.

Olmsted's participation in the planning of the exposition was a great irony. In 1870 Olmsted had expressed concern about the competitive pressures and the "conditions of corruption and of irritation, physical and mental" that held sway in the commercial districts of the city. He insisted that parks should provide "the greatest possible contrast with the streets and shops" of the working city. Twenty years later he lent his talents to the design of an exposition the primary purpose of which was the sale of industrial goods. "The underlying motive of the whole exhibition, under a sham pretense of patriotism is business," protested Edward Bellamy, "advertising with a view to individual money-making."[98]

Olmsted's participation is difficult to explain fully. Perhaps he valued it as an indication of the high regard to which he had brought landscape architecture. In his report on the exposition to the American Institute of Architects, Olmsted was concerned to vindicate the profession and to differentiate it from mere gardening.[99] Despite some hesitation, the public commission overseeing the exposition had accepted Olmsted's recommended site in Jackson Park. They accepted it, Olmsted reported, "because they could not be led to believe that we should have given this advice without having, as experts, sound reasons for doing it. The result was due to respect for professional judgment. Comparing this experience with some in my earlier professional life, I can but think that it manifests an advance in civilization." In light of his earlier clashes with venal and shortsighted municipal politicians, Olmsted was pleased with the deference to his professional expertise.[100] But the exposition planners made a very selective use of Olmsted's ideas.

The planners' refusal to provide one grand entrance at the Court of Honor especially bewildered Olmsted. In bemused explanation

42

he wrote, "I can only answer that our failure took the form of a failure of prolonged negotiations with the Illinois Central Railway." His insistence on open spaces and grand perspectives had also been frustrated by the cluttering of the grounds with too many pavilions and concession stands. Not even his woody island, which Burnham had agreed "should be free from conspicuous buildings and . . . should have a generally secluded, natural, sylvan aspect," was spared. The introduction of a Japanese temple as well as garden and horticultural exhibits, Olmsted regretted, had "much injured the island for the purpose which in our primary design it was intended to serve."[101] Consequently, the visitors to the exposition, he complained to Burnham, wore the same "businesslike, common, dull, anxious and care-worn" expressions found elsewhere in the city.[102]

Ultimately, Olmsted's confusion stemmed from his unwillingness to acknowledge the role the exposition was designed to play in the metropolis of the Midwest. His interest in community had only limited applicability in a city in which the quest for the dollar ranked second to none. Chicago, wrote William T. Stead in 1894, "knows only one common bond. Its members come here to make money."[103] Neither could his republican ideal of the park as a vehicle for the harmonious mixing of classes be transferred intact to what had become a cockpit of industrial strife. One of the more turbulent centers of urban industrialism, Chicago had been the site of a general strike and pitched battles between workers and federal troops during the railroad strikes of 1877, the Haymarket explosion in 1886, and, in the year after the exposition opened, the Pullman strike, to name only the prominent disturbances.

The planning of the White City did provide a challenging arena in which to test the forward-looking Olmsted's interest in environmental reform as a means to social control. Indeed, the explosion of violence and disorder during the Pullman strike the following year made more remarkable the order and discipline that had prevailed within the exposition. Wrote William Rainsford, "Order reigned everywhere, no boisterousness, no unseemly merriment. It seemed as though the beauty of the place brought gentleness, happiness, and self-respect to its visitors." The "restraint and discipline were remarkable," added another visitor who echoed Olmsted's interest in social control and emphasized the particular effect upon "these obscure and anonymous myriads of unknown laborers."[104] Burnham himself noted that the White City had made an impression upon the "highly educated . . . but still more perhaps upon the masses."[105] The White City offered striking support for Olmsted's faith in the transforming power of the environment, but it embodied a more manipulative conception of the role of landscape in the urban environment than the natural and spontaneous workings of Olmsted's ideal park.

Burnham's monumental, neoclassical architecture, and its dominance of Olmsted's landscapes, announced a new approach to the urban landscape. The influx of foreign-born workers, growing labor militancy, powerful and corrupt political machines, poverty and destitution, congestion and pollution, David Schuyler argues in reference to Burnham's triumph over Olmsted, "demanded not a nostalgic pastoralism or the silent influence of natural scenery but a new civic order and different urban form that would refine and civilize residents of the tumultuous cities."[106] Shorn of its republican commitments and placed in that new context, Olmsted's landscaping came to more closely resemble the English tradition of landscape architecture. Since its development in the eighteenth century, English landscape architecture had helped disguise disruptive social and economic change behind a pleasing prospect. As agricultural improvers enclosed, drained, and cleared land and thereby closed off opportunities for the middle ranks of independent cottagers, they remade the physical, social, and economic shape of rural England. Landscape architecture celebrated the new wealth that the capitalist revolution in agriculture had made possible and served as something of an antidote to the attendant social tensions, suggesting that the appreciation of natural beauty had not died and that the improvers remained in harmony with the land.[107]

In late-nineteenth-century America where the growth of corporate capitalism squeezed out the small producer and threatened republican ideals, the White City served a similar purpose. The

White City, the architect Henry Van Brunt wrote, offered "evidences that the finer instincts of humanity have not suffered complete eclipse in this grosser prosperity, and that, in this headlong race, art has not been left entirely behind." For the urban working classes, Henry Demarest Lloyd suggested, the beauty of the White City would lighten "the prosaic drudgery of their lives." Ideally, the dazzling vision of the exposition would vindicate the new urban order or, at least, discourage and deflect criticism.[108] A part of the history of the separation of production and consumption, the White City and the new urban landscape it symbolized disguised the disagreeable aspects of industrial production by celebrating its material benefits. That strategy became a central part of the realistic effort to stabilize and legitimize the new urban order.

No Mean City

The triumph of new realism, however, would never be complete. Even among admirers of the White City, alternative visions survived. Henry Demarest Lloyd, who like George criticized wasteful and chaotic patterns of city building, saw in the exposition the benefits of cooperative planning.[109] An admirer of the English Fabians, Lloyd picked up where George had left off as he struggled to create an alliance of urban workers and middle-class reformers with liberal or socialist sympathies and to turn municipal government into a staging area for a new urban republic. "The city hall represents the institution ready made for any purpose of the common good for which the common people choose to use it," Lloyd announced.[110] Like George's, Lloyd's vision of a future urban republic combined the best aspects of urban and rural life. But it also included the new element of municipal socialism, implicit in George's thought but not fully developed. Municipal socialism would become an important element in the thought and practice of those who continued to seek an alternative pattern of urban development.

In "No Mean City," Lloyd's utopian fable written in 1894, Chicagoans rose up in opposition to the dismantling of the White City. A coalition of artisans, architects, and business leaders pooled their talents and resources to save the White City. Indeed, the smoke and filth that threatened to envelop the urban oasis convinced them to try to remake all of Chicago in its image. Despite their best efforts a stark contrast between the White City and the dreariness of greater Chicago remained. "All who could emigrated to the country," Lloyd wrote, causing a "revolution in all means of rapid transit" bringing the city closer to the country. Impressed by the benefits of public transportation, Chicagoans awoke to the central role municipal socialism might play in the transformation of their city. After visiting the great cities of Europe, Chicago reformers resolved that if "the government of Paris could own and operate telephones, so could Chicago. If Glasgow could have public baths and laundries, so could Chicago. If London and Birmingham could buy land and build model blocks of model homes for the workingmen, so could Chicago." Indeed, Chicago became "a department store," Lloyd wrote in reverting to the commercial logic of the exposition, "of all the reforms which had been found to be practicable in any other city."[111]

Municipal socialism transformed not only the public life of the metropolis but the social ethics of its citizens. Urban life lost its brutal character and took on a gracious quality as an increasing array of public utilities were provided cheaply and efficiently. "With every new perfection in the equipment of city life," however, "the army of the unemployed increased." But Chicagoans were no longer willing to see their fellow citizens suffer. Moreover, they recognized that the new cooperative political economy had "proved that every man with modern means can produce many times more than he can consume." Thus the unemployed were relocated in the countryside where they lived in self-sustaining cooperatives.[112]

No Mean City, a new metropolitan order that combined municipal socialism and rural cooperation, preserved the best of industrial Chicago and the rural countryside while eliminating the worst. Both farmers beset by isolation and outmoded methods and city dwellers subjected to ugliness, cutthroat competition, and unemployment flocked to No Mean City. "Here in the same place was country for the city people, and city for the country people," Lloyd explained. Infused with a new work ethic, No Mean City was garlanded with abundant orchards and truck gardens. One hundred years after the great fire, the old inner city was destroyed and transformed into a people's park, the river and lakeshore "restored by the landscape architects to their original purity and beauty."[113] Lloyd's utopia synthesized and extended the efforts of Olmsted and George to balance the city and the country, reinvigorate protestant ethics, and preserve the republican commonwealth.

Notwithstanding Lloyd's debts to the republicans, his thought contained new elements. The province of Lloyd's expert planners went beyond what Olmsted had claimed. "Every feature of the experiment was planned by experts," Lloyd added in a nod to the coming age, "from the selection of the site to the division of the employment."[114] Moreover, his embrace of municipal socialism was forthright where George's was at best grudging; his commitment to and faith in public planning were also considerably greater. In one sense Lloyd merely updated their ideas and in doing so helped the republican vision survive into the twentieth century. But in another sense the new elements in Lloyd's thought, his embrace of the expert, his faith in public planning, and especially his fascination with the White City, were concessions to and harbingers of a new realistic approach to the urban future that was beginning to emerge. Whereas the republican tradition had employed inherited ideals in fashioning a creative response to social change, the realistic tradition developed in reaction to the profound social transformation that began in the 1870s. It was not the city of the imagination that guided the realists, but the actual city of their experience. The effort to understand the realistic tradition thus must begin with an examination of the emergence of the new metropolitan form in the thirty years after 1877.

2

The Political Economy of Suburbanization
and the Politics of Space

In the last half of the nineteenth century the United States began a long period of urban development, which by the 1930s had created a national system of metropolitan areas.[1] That period of rapid urbanization and suburbanization witnessed the growth of new and larger cities, the internal reorganization of existing cities, and the emergence of a new metropolitan form. In his pioneering statistical study, *The Growth of Cities in the Nineteenth Century* (1899), Adna Weber discovered that throughout the world urban populations were growing more rapidly at the city's periphery than at its center. The process of suburbanization, Weber suggested, was a key element in the creation of a new metropolitan form.

In contrasting metropolitan development in America to that occurring in the rest of the world, Weber pointed to the unusually low population density of American cities. Commenting on the phenomenon, Weber wrote:

> It has sometimes been urged that this is largely the result of the development of the electric street railway in America, but the

causal connection is not apparent. . . . It should rather be said that the American penchant for dwelling in cottage homes instead of business blocks after the fashion of Europe is the cause, and the trolley car the effect.

Weber recognized that suburbanization was not an inevitable response to technological developments or impersonal urban processes.[2] Nor was it a process that "conformed to biological laws," as Weber's contemporary, the urban economist Richard Hurd, asserted.[3] A product of human choice and design, suburbanization was a political process. Social conflicts, cultural values, ideological struggles, and the distribution of economic and political power shaped the process of suburbanization and the new metropolitan form it helped to create.

Kenneth Jackson has built upon Weber's insight in tracing the American penchant for suburban residences to such factors as the cult of domesticity, the relative abundance of wealth, the availability and status-conferring character of real estate, the agrarian ideal, and the fear of un-Americanized immigrants.[4] Although the suburban exodus had begun before the Civil War, it accelerated in the last quarter of the century in response to the impact of rapid industrialization. As industrial expansion undermined the stability and viability of the walking city of antebellum America, the middle class fled the noise, pollution, poverty, disease, and disorder associated with industrial production. With the middle class moving out of and immigrant laborers pouring into the inner city, the urban menace appeared greater and more unmanageable. Each new outbreak of disease, crime, and labor violence sped the flight; even in the grim depression of 1893–97 street-railway construction flourished as the exodus continued.[5]

What has not been fully recognized is that residential suburbanization was only one part of a larger reorganization of the physical and social structure of urban America in the industrial era. By the end of the nineteenth century, the functional segregation of the city had created commercial, financial, and manufacturing enclaves as well as what Hurd called a series of "residence districts divided into classes."[6] By the turn of the century, large industrial enterprises had joined the middle class in fleeing the congestion, disorder, and labor unrest of the inner city for locations on the periphery. The suburbanization of industry facilitated the transformation of the city center into a commercial and financial district and the managerial headquarters of the great national corporations. Meanwhile the increasingly foreign-born urban masses, unable to escape to the periphery because of the high cost of housing and transit or unwilling to abandon familiar neighborhoods or nearby jobs, crowded into the ring of speculative real estate surrounding the central business district where the tenement districts appeared. By 1910 a rudimentary outline of the new metropolitan form had already emerged.

Suburbanization, which entailed a complete reorganization of the city, affected the lives of all urbanites; but its costs and benefits were not equally shared. Metropolitan structure, Hurd explained, conformed to "two uniform tendencies as a city grows": "greater dispersion" at the periphery and "greater concentration" at the core.[7] Indeed inner-city populations continued to grow in absolute numbers, even as the central business districts were given over to exclusively commercial functions. While some middle-class Americans enjoyed the world's most spacious suburban communities, tenement districts such as those on the Lower East Side of New York confined the densest populations in the Western world.[8] Moreover, suburbanization and the new metropolitan form both reflected and reinforced the changing social relations of production and the larger relationship between the classes in the industrial era. Not surprisingly the sharpest political conflicts of the period centered around the arrangement and uses of urban space.

THE NEW REALISM

For a variety of reasons, the 1870s marked a turning point in American urban history. The longest uninterrupted period of economic contraction in our history, the depression of 1873–78 ushered in dramatic changes in economic practice, social structure, and political ideology. Severe downward pressure on prices created cutthroat competition and, in the longer term, the creation of pools, cartels, trusts, and oligopolies that attempted to fix prices, divide markets, and bring order to the economy. The necessity of cutting costs encouraged mechanization, increasingly powered by fossil fuels, and the substitution of unskilled for skilled labor wherever possible. The quest for economic order and stability greatly accelerated both the managerial revolution in business and the systematic application of science and technology to industrial production. By the end of the decade, the increased concentration of capital and the spread of large-scale mechanized production announced the dawning of the age of corporate capitalism; the 1880 census found four-fifths of manufacturing workers laboring in a factory setting. The economic transformation also generated important social changes. The growth of an urban, industrial proletariat would accelerate in the coming decades. Meanwhile, the managerial revolution and the application of professional expertise to economic and social problems would give rise to a new middle class by the end of the century.[9]

While to some extent immediately visible, the economic and social changes would not be fully developed until early in the next century. The most immediate impact of the depression was in the realm of politics and ideology. Widespread failure among small businesses and massive unemployment weakened the republican faith in the possibilities of social harmony within a free labor economy. At the same time labor discontent and protest alarmed the middle and upper classes and promoted a preoccupation with the defense of property rights and the status quo. The tumultuous railroad strikes during the summer of 1877 climaxed several years of industrial violence and underscored the potential explosiveness that the growing conflict between labor and capital imparted to urban disorder and violence.[10]

In the aftermath of the railroad strikes, respectable opinion was firmly if not hysterically antilabor. The *Chicago Tribune* was sanguine: "The fight with the Communists is at an end. . . . The potent argument of bullets and billies did the work.[11] The Penn-

51

sylvania Railroad's Tom Scott was less optimistic and lamented that the workers had been "allowed unfortunately to catch a glimpse of their possible power for mischief" in "what rapidly grew from a riot to an insurrection."[12] The strident tone of anti-labor opinion was often evidence of its isolation. A major factor in the scale of the disturbance was the reluctance of the state militias to fire on the crowds. In many areas militiamen put down their rifles and joined the strikers. "The sympathy of the people," explained Major General Alfred Pearson of the Pennsylvania militia, "the sympathy of the troops, my own sympathy was with the strikers. We all felt that these men were not receiving enough wages." In many parts of the country industrial capitalists were still seen as dangerous outsiders threatening the traditional order.[13]

The failure of local militias to put down the strikes alarmed the respectable classes. The state militia, wrote one Ohio journalist, "is utterly inefficient. Any hour the mob chooses, it can destroy any city in the country."[14] More analytically the *Nation* pointed out that the "militiaman to be good for anything must be a businessman, a skilled artisan, a property-holder, somebody having a stake in the country, . . . else he is as likely to fraternize with a mob as to fire on it."[15] The new realism emerged in the wake of such frank admissions of the centrality of class conflict in urban America. In the short run stability demanded punitive measures; Scott among others urged a revamping of the nation's military organization. But the *Nation* editorial pointed to a longer-range strategy of legitimating the urban-industrial order through a wider distribution of its benefits.

In the wake of the railroad strikes, business owners took the lead in transforming the state militias into the modern National Guard. In a tacit alliance with business interests, the new National Guard developed into what the *New York Times* in 1892 described as "the foremost body of citizen soldiers in the world in organization, drill, discipline, and efficiency" and took a leading role in the protection of property and the breaking of strikes. While state governments increased appropriations for the National Guard, business leaders provided the main source of additional funds. In

Chicago a secret committee of prominent businessmen raised funds to purchase Napoleon guns, gatling guns, and uniforms for the Illinois National Guard. The Commercial Club, organized in the aftermath of the 1877 strikes, donated land for Fort Sheridan while the Merchants' Club donated land for the Great Lakes Naval Station. Scott's Pennsylvania Railroad also took a leading role in building new armories and purchasing new weapons.[16] Across urban America the massive brick and stone armories provided grim reminders of the newly enhanced repressive power of the state.

Such republican visions as Olmsted's communitarian urban park now seemed hopelessly inadequate to control the explosively dangerous inclinations among the lower classes. Surrounding Central Park four new armories, symbols of the new realism, had outflanked Olmsted's masterpiece by 1892. Built to withstand "an attack from a mob," the armories were replete with "loopholes for riflemen, enfilading all approaches." Olmsted had hoped his urban parks would recreate the moral order of the village; what the *New York Times* called the "moral effect of the bayonet" seemed more appropriate to the new realism.[17] However, military force alone could not create a lasting and stable order and the realistic approach to urban problems would involve more than mere repression. Environmental reform might still prove valuable in the physical and social reorganization of the American city, but only if it reflected an awareness of the potential for violent urban conflicts.

SATELLITE CITIES

One of the more striking developments of the thirty years after 1877 was the movement of industrial production from the urban center (where it had often been the focus of mob violence) to the urban periphery. At first industrial development crept outward along the corridors of rail and water transportation. By the end of the century, giant industrial enterprises were located in outlying satellite cities. The major factors in the decentralization of industry were undoubtedly economic. Successful industrial satellites tended to grow quickly as preexisting services, such as electrical power, railroad sidings, and trucking firms, combined with cheap real estate on their edges, made them the most attractive sites for new ventures. Insurance companies, wary of multistory wooden factories that frequently burned with great loss of life and property, advocated the use of new materials and slow-burning construction designs, which demanded ample space. Industrialists who built those sprawling factories paid significantly lower premiums.[18]

As Weber pointed out the suburban town held a number of other purely economic advantages for the manufacturer:

> They include not only a great saving in rent and insurance, but economy in the handling and storing of goods. All carting is avoided by having a switch run directly into the factory; saving to machinery is effected by placing it all on solid foundations on the first floor; and plenty of space is at hand for the storing of fuel and materials, so that these may be bought when the market offers the most favorable terms.

But manufacturers favored peripheral locations for other reasons as well, including political ones. Relocation beyond the city limits allowed manufacturers to escape onerous taxation or the exactions of political bosses and to control local government. In the 1890s the Standard Oil Company created a "municipal fiefdom" in Whiting, Indiana, outside Chicago. Similarly, the incorporation of Munhall, Pennsylvania, in 1901, site of the Homestead Steel Plant, reported an investigator, "relieves the Steel Corporation from much of its responsibility as a property holder." The Ford Motor Company's notorious domination of Dearborn, Michigan, enabled it to escape responsibility for the relief of the unemployed and to resist unionization well into the 1930s.[19]

As the Ford example suggests, the decentralization of industry had also been designed at least partially for reasons of political economy, in an effort to reshape the social relations of production. Weber noted that the "suburban employer is likely to secure a high grade of employees." His "large workshops, and the prospect of a cottage and garden, and open-air life, attract operatives of the best class."[20] Such considerations influenced the planning of Pullman, Illinois; Homestead, Pennsylvania; the McCormick plant at Canalport, outside Chicago; and other industrial satellites. George Pullman, whose luxurious railroad cars had discouraged the abusive tendencies of the "rougher element" of the train-riding public, hoped that a more attractive work environment would similarly promote a loyal and efficient work force. Thus he built the model community of Pullman where he provided his workers with company housing and other services and surrounded them with beauty and culture, all at a 6 percent profit.[21] The Carnegie company, acting on the belief that homeownership was a force for conservatism and stability, provided low-interest mortgage loans and built some housing for sale to its employees.[22] Ironically, Pullman and Homestead were the scenes of two of the larger and more bitter strikes in the 1890s.

The difficulty with the Pullman and Homestead experiments, as a later industrial planner understood, was that the provision of company housing "superimposed the landlord-tenant strife on the capital-labor antagonism."[23] An artificial division between the discontents of work and the problems of the local community has characterized much of American urban political history, a division which the company town tended to erase. In the company town the employers' normal but often disguised interest in living arrangements, where capitalist values and habits are inculcated and the discontents of work alleviated, became more visible. Without the usual mediating buffers such as a separate landlord class, a multifarious wholesale and retail sector, and government social services and public utilities, both work-related and community-related frustrations were charged to the employer.[24]

Pullman's efforts to uplift his workers and exclude saloons had already created considerable animosity when his policy of deducting rents from wages even as those wages were slashed precipitated the bitter strike of 1894. Moreover, while urban politics were generally organized around ethnic and neighborhood divisions rather than economic ones, often to the benefit of employers, company policies became central to local politics in Pullman. The residents of Pullman elected the first socialist alderman to serve in Chicago's city council.[25] In Homestead the workers displayed a disturbingly proprietary interest in both the town and the company's works. During the 1892 strike the Advisory Committee of the Amalgamated Association of Iron and Steel Workers not only patrolled the works and unceremoniously escorted both deputy sheriffs and Pinkertons out of town, but it acted as the legal authority in the town, closing saloons, keeping the peace, and issuing ad hoc laws.[26] Such developments were not what paternalistic employers had had in mind.

In the wake of the Homestead and Pullman strikes, industrial decentralization continued and even accelerated. In 1904 Weber reported that "manufacturing no longer centers in the great commercial cities, but is developing smaller cities of its own."[27] By 1915 when Graham R. Taylor published his study of satellite cities, large industrial plants operated in East St. Louis, Granite City, and National City outside St. Louis; Garfield, Lodi, Kearney, Yonkers, and Long Island City surrounding New York; Argo, Hawthorne, and Gary in the Chicago region; as well as in Flint, Lackawanna, West Milwaukee, South Saint Paul, and other peripheral sites.[28] But even before the Homestead and Pullman strikes and increasingly after them the industrial satellite was taking on a different form.

Many industrialists had come to doubt the wisdom of Pullman's efforts, and Pullman himself had had second thoughts. In 1883 the Cincinnati firm of Procter and Gamble employed Pullman's architect, S. S. Beman, to build their new plant in suburban Saint Bernard. When young Harley Procter expressed an interest in building housing for workers, a colleague suggested he speak to Pullman who, complaining of difficulties with maintenance, rent collection, and evictions, recommended against the idea. Procter's new factory was designed with an "eye for beauty as well as utility. . . . A broad lawn separated the factory from the street, trees were planted, flower beds set." But there was no provision

56

for company housing and no model town. Taylor reported, "Autocratic control is now generally dismissed from consideration."[29]

In St. Bernard as well as in nearby Norwood and Oakley and in many other industrial satellites across the country, the day ended, Taylor wrote, as the worker "rushed out of a factory set in a landscape of open fields and wooded hillsides, scrambled for a seat in a street car or grimy train and clattered back to the region of brick and pavement, of soot and noise and jostle." Residents of tenement districts like Cincinnati's West End could not afford the suburban housing found in or near the satellite cities. The admirable efficiency and even beauty of the suburban plants prompted Taylor to ask whether "similar skill and ingenuity have been applied to the community life, to town planning, housing, health, and recreation." He found that they clearly had not.[30] Pullman's form of paternalism had been rejected, but less intrusive forms of labor control were still of interest to employers.

At Gary, Indiana, strategically situated between Minnesota iron ore and Pennsylvania coal, the U.S. Steel Corporation had spared no expense to streamline production. To perfect the site the corporation leveled sand dunes, filled in swamps, and moved three railroads and the Grand Calumet River. But for those industrialists and most others, Taylor found, city building remained at best "a side issue." The control of labor, however, remained a crucial concern. Taylor discounted the rumors that Gary's Grand Calumet River was relocated to serve as a "moat against mob violence" and that the corporation thus commanded a position "impregnable to mob attack and so calculated to withstand a prolonged siege." But he did conclude that the "Steel Corporation's triumphs in the economics of production are only less impressive than its complete command over the army of workers it commands." And the strike of 1919 would illustrate that the corporation's control of the lakefront did indeed facilitate the importation of strikebreakers from cities on the Great Lakes.[31]

Employers believed that the suburban plant would keep the social discontent and labor disturbances of the inner city from disrupting their operations. In the 1880s the secretary of the largest machine tool firm in heavily unionized Cincinnati blamed the "fe-ver of excitement" when striking machinists paraded through the factory district for causing his own employees to strike. In 1905 the machine-tool industry began its move to suburban Oakley, where it successfully resisted both strikes and unionization.[32] At the turn of the century, a Chicago industrialist complained that his city was a "hotbed of trades unionism" and that strikes were chas-ing away the largest corporations. As new investment came into the region, another explained, it was "the smaller towns [that] are getting these manufacturing plants." When asked if employers had constructed suburban plants to escape unions, the chairman of the New York State Board of Mediation and Arbitration laconically replied, "They have been located with that end in view."[33]

Industrialists expressed similar concerns to Taylor. One ex-plained that during a street-car strike "every time the strikers pa-raded past his plant a veritable fever seemed to spread among" his employees. Others credited decentralization for keeping "trade unionism weak," Taylor reported, probably because suburban workers had "less opportunity to learn of new jobs" or to "com-pare work conditions and wages."[34] Weber, too, had noted the greater strength of trade unions in large cities. He explained, "Even when wages rule the same, many employers have aban-doned the great city to escape other exactions of the labor unions."[35] Similar considerations influenced the location of the massive coal-fired, electricity-generating plants that often pow-ered the suburban industries. In a 1906 *Engineering Magazine* article, an industrial designer argued that "suburban locations, slightly out of the large centers of population, are desirable owing to the fact that labor troubles are not so liable to occur, and should they arise they can be handled better when located outside the lime light." The use of strikebreakers, he added, was especially facili-tated "when considerable space is available around the industry on which temporary shelters can be erected."[36] The labor problem was an important factor in the decentralization of industry, but it also dictated that industry not move too far from the great city. The suburban plants were generally only slightly beyond the large population centers because, as both Weber and Taylor noted, the great city retained at least one advantage, an abundance of cheap labor. "The great city contains a large population that is uneducated, unskilled and poverty-stricken," Weber observed. "Incapable of organization, it sells its energies to the bidder at starvation wages." In Pullman the tracks of the Illinois Central Railroad served as a cautionary reminder of the closeness of the reserve army of the unemployed. At the newer suburban plants, Taylor noted, it was the "persistent efforts of plant superintendents" to secure extensions of the electric street railway system that allowed employers to draw on the urban labor pool. As long as the plants remained near a big city, strikes and other labor disturbances would be handled, he explained, "by temporarily drawing upon the large surplus of labor" in the nearby center. By tying the industrial satellite to the tenement districts, the street railway served to facilitate the decentralization of industry.[37]

THE SOCIAL ORDER OF THE METROPOLIS

Residential arrangements reflected the new realism as well. Those members of the upper classes who remained in the inner city endeavored to shut out the disorder of the streets. A resident of Cincinnati's once-fashionable West End recalled that the "nightly battening-down of the house increased our sense of siege."[38] In Chicago Potter Palmer's "turreted Wisconsin granite fortress" rose above the street like an "angry Gothic castle."[39] H. H. Richardson's famous Glessner house in Chicago, focused on an interior courtyard, represented the artistic triumph of this architecture. With its recessed doorway the Glessner house presented a blank face to the street. Such houses, architectural critic Montgomery Schuyler quipped, "were not defensible except in a military sense." They eased the "patron's anxiety to have a seat of refuge against the uneasy proletariat."[40] For those with less courage, the residential retreat to the suburbs was a more typical response to urban disorder and to the rise in class tensions.

59

During the 1850s Alexander Jackson Davis's design for the elegant suburb Llewelyn Park, New Jersey, had used curvilinear streets, garden designs, open spaces, and restrictive covenants to keep urban disorder at arm's length. Although the escape from urban disorder continued to be a prime element in the suburban ideal, Olmsted's Riverside initiated a series of postwar efforts to combine the advantages of the rural retreat with all the conveniences of city life. In the 1870s A. T. Stewart, the pioneer of the department store, designed Garden City, Long Island, which Kenneth Jackson has described as the "most ambitiously planned suburb of the nineteenth century." Lavishly provided with sylvan landscapes, Garden City, the *New York World* reported, was also to have "all the appliances of municipal life."[41] Even as its importance as a refuge and a haven from the city became more pronounced, the suburban residence became dependent on a plethora of mass-produced goods and public utilities (gas, water, electricity, transportation) provided by the city.

Stewart's role was more than coincidental. Just as the department store retailed the consumer benefits of industrialization in a setting free of the mundane and disagreeable elements of industrial production, suburbs like Garden City, Riverside, Lake Forest, Brookline and others enabled the suburbanite to enjoy the amenities of metropolitan life without the inconvenience of living near the noise, pollution, and poverty associated with industrial production.[42] In a fashion that paralleled and reinforced the function of the department store, suburbanization disguised links between a rising standard of living and the urban modes of production (and the impoverished urban masses) that made the rise possible.[43] Moreover, in mutually supporting ways the suburb, the department store, and the advertisement taught styles of consumption and domestic habits that served to distinguish the middle class from "the other half."[44]

The new suburban life style was an important element in the emergence and consciousness of the new middle class at the end of the nineteenth century.[45] Before the Civil War the ownership of property and a measure of economic independence characterized a large American middle class that included farmers and the multifarious small producers and retailers of the towns. By the turn of the century, a new middle class of salaried employees and professional servants of the national corporations had begun to emerge. As economic independence became less of a defining characteristic of the middle class, protection from the insecurities of the new urban industrial order became a more important one. Such protection took the form not only of corporate connections and professional status, but also of the suburban haven from the violence, disease, and squalor of the inner city.

The tenement was the center of the very different world of "the other half." By the 1890s tenement construction had "polluted" much of Manhattan and the Bronx, Jacob Riis reported, and represented the social and physical "boundary line" between rich and poor.[46] If the granite houses of the rich who continued to brave the inner city seemed like fortresses, the tenements resembled prisons. A typical New York City tenement, six to eight stories tall, incarcerated one hundred or more people. Lacking sufficient light and air and often without sanitary plumbing or even running water, the tenement was a breeding ground for a variety of diseases including typhus fever, smallpox, and pulmonary tuberculosis. In 1879 the dumbbell tenement, which in Lewis Mumford's view "raised bad housing to an art," won a contest for the best-designed model tenement sponsored by *Plumber and Sanitary Engineer*. The dumbbell's pathetically narrow and completely enclosed air shaft let in little light and no fresh air and served primarily as a receptacle for rotting garbage. In their study of the tenement house problem, DeForest and Veiller recommended it be renamed the "foul air shaft." It worked most effectively as a flue in tenement house fires.[47]

Although New York had the most severe tenement house problem, Boston, Cincinnati, Chicago and other cities faced their own serious housing problems. Only New York and Boston had a worse housing problem than Cincinnati, Veiller reported. Cincinnati harbored almost every type of bad housing imaginable from "large block buildings housing hundreds of people, to the small

dilapidated wooden house occupied by two or three families."
Cincinnati was spared only the infamous dumbbell tenement. But
Cincinnati had its own notorious accommodations, including the
one-hundred-room Rat Row along the riverfront.[48] In the "Big
Missouri," a converted spice mill just outside the central business
district described by a local health officer as "an outrage against
decency and humanity," three hundred tenants shared a single outdoor water hydrant.[49] The speculatively built tenement made a
rather late appearance in Chicago. But industrialization after 1880
and a huge influx of immigrants had caused "a dangerous overcrowding in all the poor districts," and the "building of tenements
on speculation" had become "a regular and profitable means of
investing capital," the city health commissioner reported.[50] While
Chicago never suffered from the solid blocks of five- and six-story
tenements found in other cities, the expansion of the central business district and rising realty values led to the overcrowding of
lots with ramshackle buildings.[51]

HOW THE OTHER HALF SHOULD LIVE

Suburbanization thus clarified and sharpened class divisions. As
the physical and social distance widened between the classes, a combination of fear and envy, manipulation and resentment marked
the relationship between the middle class and the poor. The spec-
ter of "fraternization" between the classes or middle-class sympathy for political radicals and labor agitators became a thing of the
past.[52] Of course the respectable middle class had always questioned the propriety of their social inferiors. "They love to clan
together . . . in filth and disorder," charity leader Robert Hartley
said of the urban poor in 1851, "provided they can drink, and
smoke, and gossip, and enjoy their balls, and wakes, and frolics
without molestation." But the pristine environment of the well-
equipped suburb lent a sharper edge and new imagery to such attitudes. Fulminating against the Tammany Hall and its inner-city
minions, the Reverend Charles Parkhurst blamed "the slimy, oozy

62

soil of Tammany Hall" for turning the city into an "open cess-pool." Political reform thus became an exercise in "municipal sewerage" that served to "drain that political quagmire, and . . . get rid of the odor, the mire, and the fever germs."[53]

The segregated social order of the metropolis also generated a new approach to moral reform. In 1870 Olmsted was already con-trasting the promiscuous culture of the poor with the middle-class ideal of domesticity. He hoped his urban parks would be sufficient to break up the "young men in knots" he saw in the tenement districts and to encourage the emulation of middle-class mores among the poor.[54] By the 1880s the leaders of the Charity Orga-nization Society confronted what they believed to be a much more serious problem. In 1887 the society's Charles Kellogg feared that "the classes which wealth and poverty and occupation make have drifted apart, and are more monotonously uniform. . . . There is no solvent of social ties like urban life," he concluded. In response the society launched an organized system of friendly visiting in the belief that "if we do not furnish the poor with elevating influences, they will rule us by degrading ones."[55]

The Charity Organization Society's policy of friendly visiting was superficially similar to the work of Olmsted's close friend Charles Loring Brace. A critic of those institutional reformers who had "discovered the asylum" a generation earlier, Brace cre-ated the Children's Aid Society in the 1850s in the hope of combin-ing the natural and spontaneous forms of social control associated with the family and the small town with a modicum of formal organization and structure. While the notion of friendly visiting paid homage to Brace's ideal, the charity reformers, both physi-cally and psychically distant from the lives of the poor and fearful of their potential for mischief, laid much greater stress on formal organization and structure. Sending detailed reports to employers, landlords, bankers, the police, as well as to a host of relief and charitable agencies, the "friendly" visitor was part of a highly or-ganized and bureaucratic effort to control the poor.[56]

The conflict between the reformer and the machine politician was thus in part the result of a clash between the culture of the suburbs and that of the tenement districts.[57] The friendly visitor,

Jane Addams wrote, "obligated to lay all stress . . . upon the industrial virtues, and to treat members of the family almost exclusively as factors in the industrial system," could not recreate "the emotional kindness with which relief is given by one poor neighbor to another." The poorhouse always stood behind the friendly visitor; if moral uplift failed to pay the rent, the destitute would be dragged off as he or she "squealed shrilly like a frightened animal in a trap," as Jane Addams recalled. Only those who witnessed poverty arise from the "loss of work, or for other guiltless and inevitable reasons" could fully understand the culture of the poor, Addams concluded.[58] In contrast machine politicians imitated the cooperative spirit of their constituents. Holding "beefsteak suppers, chowder parties, picnics, and balls," the machine spread "an immense amount of charity work, and an immense amount of geniality and relative comfort among the poor," Hutchins Hapgood noted.[59] Though machine politicians failed to provide alternatives to the inequities of suburbanization and grafted for their own pockets, they also distributed a portion of the tribute they exacted from the powerful magnates who shaped the city.

THE COSTS OF SPECULATION

The usual stamping ground of the magnate and the focus of power in the metropolis was the central business district. The grand railroad terminals that symbolized metropolitan power and the trolley lines that crisscrossed the central business district underscored its crucial role as the hub of inter- and intracity rail transport. Warehousing and storage facilities and light industry often clustered near the terminals. But the most expensive real estate in the central business district was reserved for financial and commercial functions. Skyscraping office buildings accommodated banks, insurance companies, and other financial institutions; the administrative apparatus of the national corporations that coordinated far-flung systems of production, marketing, and distribution; and the offices of professionals, especially those with ties to the great corporations. Nearby fashionable shopping, hotel, and entertainment districts provided a showcase for the consumer culture of the new corporate order.[60]

Thus the reorganization of the central business district must be added to the decentralization of industry and the creation of suburban retreats for the new middle class as the rational forces that shaped the new metropolitan form. Those elements of the metropolitan order also foreshadowed what would become the central concerns of the city planning profession, specifically a system of zoning to codify the functional segregation of the city and improved means of transit to unify the metropolis. But the metropolis was by no means fully the product of rational forces, a fact of which the tenement residents were perhaps most painfully aware. In a variety of forms, economic speculation and its irrational consequences had a great deal to do with the most disagreeable aspects of metropolitan life.

The major focus of financial manipulation was the new urban utilities. Essential to the expanding city and the quality of life, the new technologies of transportation and communication were vast and profitable enterprises. "Many men regard the city as an economic necessity—a thing to be used but not to be loved—as a means to riches, power, and pleasure," Delos Wilcox wrote in reference to the great utility magnates. "In haste to be rich," he charged, they are "careless of the city they build so far as its fitness for a permanent habitation of men is concerned." The new transportation and communication technologies have "given men a certain apparent, though partly superficial, independence of locality." But their construction and the financial manipulation that surrounded them left the city "fit only for transients" such that the "well-to-do get away from it as much as they can." For working families that could not or would not leave the city, Wilcox concluded, "locality persistently asserts itself, and the faster distance is abolished the more rapidly the price of standing room rises."[61] The cost and accessibility of the new utilities, especially mass transit, divided suburbanites from the other half.

In the 1890s the expansion and electrification of the street railway system was heralded as a way to bring the suburban residence within the reach of the working class. Even before electrification Boston's Henry M. Whitney spoke of the "moral influence" of the five-cent fare in defense of his monopoly of Boston's horse railways.[62] Electrification, extension, and low uniform fares brought "suburban residence within reach of large classes of the poorest people," argued sociologist Charles H. Cooley in 1891. Street railway expansion acted "as a safety valve to relieve the congested districts," reported another student of municipal traction the same year. Three years later the labor economist John R. Commons credited low fares with allowing workingmen to escape the slum.[63]

Certainly the street railway brought home ownership within the reach of many of the better-paid, skilled workers. But even those who escaped the inner city found that overcrowding and congestion often followed them to the periphery. Residential districts such as the Bronx in New York or Roxbury in Boston that were opened by street railway extensions were quickly crowded with tenements and multiple-unit dwellings. Street railway extensions were speculative undertakings; profitability demanded full streetcars and hence dense neighborhoods. Moreover, street railway expansion increased the accessibility but also the cost of peripheral real estate. Those struggling into the middle class competed for real estate with thousands of other potential home owners as well as with industrial and commercial interests and speculators. Speculative realty values soared even higher in the inner city served by multiple railway lines. There the very poor, the recent immigrant, and the unskilled competed for the worst housing on the most expensive real estate.[64]

Thus, even as it opened the urban periphery, the street railway intensified congestion in many residential districts and especially in the central business district.[65] A great deal of speculation centered on the deteriorating residential properties on land just outside the central business district that might rise precipitously in value with a business district expansion. As its value rose and until it was actually converted to commercial use, such property had to generate large rental incomes, generally secured by squeezing more tenants into the existing buildings. Speculative owners had little incentive to maintain their properties while they waited for them to be demolished in favor of a commercial use.[66] Of course not all tenement owners were speculators. Skilled workers and small tradesmen often owned tenements and lived in the buildings. With limited financial resources and often having paid too much for the building, such landlords also generally crowded in tenants and neglected maintenance.[67] Inflating the costs of real estate, construction, and rents, speculation in all its forms remained the largest part of the tenement problem.

Lawrence Veiller, an advocate of tenement reform familiar with conditions across the country and coauthor of the New York State Tenement House Commission report, argued that major improvements in housing would result if buildings were "erected directly as an investment on cash," thereby eliminating speculative profits. "Hardly one of these houses is erected as an investment, but in nine cases out of ten is built purely as speculation," Veiller reported. At the top of the speculative pyramid was the building loan operator "whose business is the buying up of land in certain portions of the city as opportunity offers, and holding such land until some builder desires to build in that neighborhood," and then selling "at a greatly increased valuation." Even the conservative *Commercial Advertiser* agreed that the "building loan operator adds nothing to the value of the property. . . . On the contrary their general plan is to inflate prices by every trick, device, scheme, practice, that is known to the business."[68]

Most of the builders themselves were also speculators. Tenements were seldom erected singly but in groups. As a respected New York builder explained:

> The average speculator who erects a tenement house knows practically nothing of building. He purchases the raw materials, in the case of brickwork, and awards the contract for putting up the masonry to what is termed a 'lumper,' who furnished him the labor at a certain price per thousand for laying the brick. A similar system prevails in some of the finishing trades. . . . The

various lumpers who are interested in doing this class of work are often irresponsible men who have no interest in the building. . . . The result is that, in the average house built under this system, the workmanship is woefully bad. . . . The product is a miserably built structure . . . and one that will deteriorate very rapidly.

The speculative builder then either sold at an inflated price (in which case an overextended purchaser might watch helplessly as the building deteriorated) or held the property in the hope that the value of the land would increase while he rented it out.[69]

At the intersection of the speculation in land, housing construction, and urban utilities was the street railway. In the late 1880s hundreds of independent horse-drawn railways crisscrossed the nation's cities. But after Frank Sprague's successful experiments in Richmond, Virginia, in 1887, the electrification of street railways quickly followed. By 1902 94 percent of street railways had been electrified. Between 1890 and 1902 track mileage had tripled and the number of passengers doubled in the $2 billion industry. Electrification demanded investments in huge generators. The great "gaunt, many stacked structures" devoured hundreds of tons of coal daily and contributed to a doubling in fixed costs.[70] Once a method had been found, with the aid of the Vanderbilt fortune, of using "one central producer and distributor of power," a wave of merges swept the industry.[71]

The electrification and consolidation of street railways offered great profits, and it attracted powerful investors. While nearly every city had its traction millionaires, the Widener-Elkins-Whitney-Ryan syndicate dominated all others. Those Philadelphia and New York speculators and financiers, with ties to commercial and industrial capital from Morgan to Rockefeller, controlled $1 billion in street railways, the centerpiece of a financial empire.[72] Although street railway magnates were not the wealthy, one-dimensional malefactors of popular mythology, financial speculation figured more prominently in their calculations than the public interest. The payment of dividends on watered stock and the failure to retire stock based on depreciated if not decrepit capital weakened the industry, made the lowering of fares problematic, and undermined the entire public transit system by the early twentieth century.

Real estate speculation was inextricably related to the industry as well. While many extensions exploited existing residential areas, other extensions were aimed at opening areas in which the magnates owned tracts of land.[73] New York's first surface line extended to "the suburban villages of Yorkville and Harlem, passing through the woods and wild lands of Upper Manhattan, which this very line was to transform into a flourishing and continuous suburb." Such developmental schemes were replicated throughout the country; in 1902 the Census Bureau reported that track mileage was expanding more rapidly than traffic. Professional managers such as Herbert Vreeland of New York's Metropolitan lines assured their employers that the traffic would come. In the meantime real estate speculation could be as important to transit magnates as the billions of nickels collected annually.[74] Although such speculation ultimately opened the periphery to suburban residences, it also played a role in inner-city congestion. The speculative withholding of peripheral land increased its ultimate cost to suburban builders and added to the pressure on inner-city real estate.[75] In deciding against certain extensions, the magnates also limited the accessibility of suburban real estate. Cincinnati's Kilgour syndicate, heavily invested in suburban real estate in Hyde Park and Mt. Lookout, quickly extended service to those areas while denying service to rival developments in Oakley and Madisonville.[76]

THE STREET RAILWAY: SYMBOL OF THE METROPOLIS

By the turn of the century, the outlines of the new metropolitan form had taken shape. The city of concentric circles or what Hurd more accurately called the star-shaped city was the product of the decisions of industrial capitalists, suburban developers and their clients, public utility entrepreneurs, speculators of all sorts, and of the more limited choices of ordinary urbanites. As Weber had understood, the street railway was not the driving force behind metropolitan development; but as the key to the new spatial arrangements it did serve as the most visible symbol of a transformation whose precise delineation was not yet clear. With good reason Theodore Dreiser made a street railway financier the central character in his epic trilogy of life in metropolitan America. In *The Titan*, Dreiser's Cowperwood (closely modeled on Charles Yerkes) arrived in Chicago having "gone through a great life struggle in one metropolis and tested all the phases of human duplicity, decency, sympathy, and chicanery that one invariably finds in every American city." Ineluctably drawn to the seat of power in his adopted city, Cowperwood "loved the thought of streetcars and the vast manipulative life it suggested." Dreiser and others may have exaggerated the power and conspiratorial genius of the street railway financier, but he was a central figure in the new city.[77]

Although the magnates were not omnipotent conspirators, their control of enormous financial resources gave them considerable power to influence metropolitan development. By 1907 Thomas Ryan, for example, held the Equitable Life Assurance Society and "the controlling influence in a large number of banks, trust companies, and railroad and industrial corporations."[78] Such resources not only helped finance the construction of skyscrapers and tenements, the twin towers of metropolitan congestion, but allowed the magnates to influence the development of the central business district and the placement of industry.[79] Not only through the control of investment capital but in the extension and curtailment of lines and in their fare and transfer policies, the magnates influenced urban development. Indeed, the particular physical arrangement of at least one city seemed well designed to produce a "traction bonanza." On the lines between suburban Norwood and Cincinnati's West End tenements, Taylor discovered, the "same cars which carry factory workers out at 7:30 each morning are loaded on the way back with Cincinnati office workers going into the city. The reverse happens each afternoon."[80] Although the development of urban transportation followed a pattern set by the sub-urbanization of industry, the residential exodus, and the reorganization of the central business district, it appeared as the most visible factor in the city's transformation.[81]

While they were not an independent cause of the reorganization of the city, the street railways became an easily recognizable and, for some, a hated symbol of the new metropolitan order. "Grave misunderstandings often arise between street railway companies and the public," Edward Higgins noted. The fare structure generated mistrust as the "public is largely composed of the working classes to whom the daily 5 or 10-cent fare forms a material burden." The public widely perceived that the companies were reaping windfall profits. The electrification of street railways, Edward Durand argued, "meant, first and foremost, economy," yet "there has been no lowering of fares in most of our great urban communities for several decades." But another source of animosity was what Higgins called the "inevitable" accidents ranging "from the running down of a peddler's cart to the killing and maiming of a carload of passengers." The speed of the trolley's careening around New York's Union Square inspired the epitaph "Dead Man's Corner."[82]

With fares too high and its employees' wages too low, surrounded by corruption, bribery, and public scandal, the cause of a growing number of accidents and injuries, the street railway was an essential but nevertheless vulnerable link in the metropolitan order. A "street-car strike in a great city," Wilcox understood, "brings to light the enormous power involved in the control of city car lines." The street railway had "so fashioned the growth of our cities and so changed the habits of their citizens that a tie-up of the lines means a very serious paralysis of city life."[83] Street railway lines such as Chicago's West Side lines passed through tenement districts dotted, as the *New York Times* put it, with "scores of choice spots for mob violence" where "capital is cordially hated."[84] Street railway strikes beset metropolitan America, disrupting normal business for days or even weeks at a time. With few resources other than a profound frustration, the lower classes realized, at least for brief periods, Wilcox's adage that the "control of the streets means the control of the city."[85]

Although it was fitful and often unsuccessful efforts at unionization that precipitated street railway strikes, their scale depended on the largely spontaneous participation of the tenement districts. An 1886 strike in New York gathered support in the tenement districts around Grand Street, the *New York Times* reported, where the "entire neighborhood . . . took no pains to conceal its sympathy with the employees. . . . Everybody in the neighborhood . . . seemed to harbor a grievance against the railroad." The strikers directed the crowds in a "methodical and orderly" tie-up of the cars.[86] In 1899 a crowd estimated at fifty thousand from the "thickly populated tenement districts" stopped the cars along New York's Second Avenue in support of a strike of only two hundred men.[87] In Dreiser's *Sister Carrie* the end of Hurstwood's harrowing experience as a scab "came with a real mob" in "an exceedingly poor-looking neighborhood."[88] Such crowds soaped tracks, dynamited supports, overturned and burned cars, and threatened strikebreakers.

The strikes were not, however, confined to the tenement districts. The success of the strike and the focusing of attention on the grievances which animated the crowds depended upon disrupting the business of the city. When the disorder reached the business districts, the conflicting interests of the poor and the commuting middle class became clear. When the Grand Street cars in New York's 1886 strike reached Broadway, white collar workers, presumably commuters, leaned out of office windows "to applaud the police," while shirt-making women from nearby sweatshops jeered.[89] An 1888 strike in Chicago left North Side commuters "at the mercy" of the strikers. During the strike the few passengers braving the cars "were surrounded by angry groups" as they got off. Soon "business men, clerks, women bent on shopping" all sought alternative means of transit.[90] In many strikes, like an 1895 strike in Brooklyn which ended only after National Guard troops entered the city, the cars ran completely "empty because of the fear of further violence."[91] The effectiveness of the horse militia in that strike, firing into open windows and crashing through saloons frequented by strikers, convinced one journalist that "we must have more cavalry."[92] Such incidents revealed that the heavy use of force remained an important part of the metropolitan order.

At best street railway strikes won higher wages for some workers and vented the frustrations of the tenement dwellers. At worst they degenerated into crime, senseless violence, and the wanton destruction of property. They did little to illuminate the actual forces remaking the late-nineteenth-century city and even less to suggest alternative paths of development. But they do provide evidence of the conflicts inherent in the process of suburbanization and of the energy that would animate a much more positive and serious challenge to metropolitan development. In his 1886 mayoralty campaign, Henry George's juxtaposition of transit manipulation and the tenement problem proved the most effective part of his contest with Abram Hewitt. Although George did not illuminate all the forces remaking the metropolis, he exposed the irrational consequences of speculation and suggested a more rational and just path of urban development. Moreover, his condemnation of land speculation focused attention on a key element in the political economy of the metropolis, specifically the arrangement and uses of urban space, in a way that every citizen could understand.

POVERTY AND PROGRESS

In one sense the contrast between George's fall campaign and the street railway strikes that had occurred the previous spring could not have been more pronounced. Louis Post recalled the great Union Square Parade:

> The police arrangements were the worst possible. In the Bowery and Fourth Avenue the procession was every now and again tangled up with horse-cars, and no policeman was at hand. It appears that large squads of police were massed at different points,

in readiness to break up a riot, but there were few to be seen at any point where they might have prevented a riot. The horse-car drivers and the paraders were, however, upon excellent terms with each other, and although the confusion was exasperating to both, the utmost good feeling prevailed.

In its more peaceful and positive way, however, the George campaign addressed the same issues that underlay the strikes.[93] George's platform stated "that existing means of transit should not be left in the hands of corporations which, gaining enormous profits from the growth of population, oppress their employees and provoke strikes that interrupt travel and imperil the public peace, but should by lawful process be assumed by the city and operated for public benefit." During the campaign George explained, "We could take those railroads and run them free, let everybody ride who would, and we could pay for it out of the increased value of the people's property in consequence."[94] Such arguments prepared the way for the more explosive rhetoric George employed in discussing the issue of home ownership, which he placed at the center of his campaign.

George insisted that the private manipulation of socially created wealth in the form of transit franchises and land values was responsible for New York's housing problem. At Cooper Union in early October, George referred to this "great central fact":

> The vast majority of men and women and children in New York have no legal right to live here at all. Most of us—ninety-nine per cent at least—must pay the other one per cent by the week or month or quarter for the privilege of staying here and working like slaves. . . . Nowhere else in the civilized world are men and women and children packed together so closely. As for children, they die almost as soon as they enter the world.

Comparing the density of New York's Lower East Side to both London and Canton and citing New York's own health commissioner's estimate of a 65 percent infant mortality rate in the Mulberry Bend tenement district, George prepared to turn the crowd's outrage to positive effect. "Now, is there any reason for such overcrowding," he asked. "There is plenty of room on this island.

74

There are miles and miles and miles of land all around this nucleus. Why cannot we take that and build houses upon it for our accommodation." Only financial speculation and the land monopoly stood in the way. He continued, "There is no good reason whatever why every citizen of New York should not have his own separate house and home; and the aim of this movement is to secure it."[95]

In a city where more than 90 percent of the residents were tenants, his frequent condemnation of "that monstrous injustice which crowds families into tenement rooms" proved effective.[96] George's opponent Abram Hewitt could neither ignore those arguments nor dismiss them as anarchistic bombast. New York's respectable classes had appealed to Hewitt to run against George precisely because Hewitt seemed to personify the very same values (individualism, the self-made man, economic independence, and social mobility through honest, hard work) with which George promoted the single tax. Indeed Hewitt's only hope of defeating George was in attracting the votes of those workers who aspired to move up into the middle class through their own initiative.[97] George's doctrine of "confiscation," Hewitt argued, could never succeed in a city where "a large majority" of people owned their own homes. Hewitt outrageously exaggerated the extent of home ownership in the city, but aside from appealing to his reputation as a liberal friend of labor and of trade unions and predicting a new era of conciliation in labor relations (all of which he did) it is not clear what else he could have done. Uncontested, George's arguments undermined the basis of Hewitt's campaign.[98]

In a much broader fashion Hewitt challenged George's philosophy and proposals in a campaign reprint of Hewitt's own 1883 speech at the opening ceremonies of the Brooklyn Bridge.[99] That same year, in a variation on the theme of progress and poverty, George had argued that the bridge project illustrated the failure of political morality and ethics to keep pace with technological innovation. In reference to a recent scandal involving the suspension bridge's steel cables, George wrote, "The skill of the engineer could not prevent condemned wire from being smuggled into the cable."[100] In his speech and campaign reprint, Hewitt also addressed the theme of progress and poverty. In a comparison of the wages of the slaves who built the pyramids to those of the laborers on the bridge, Hewitt argued that the "effect of discoveries of new methods, tools and laws of force has been to raise the wages of labor more than an hundredfold." Progress steadily eliminated poverty, he argued in opposition to George, as "the distribution of the fruits of labor is approaching from age to age more equitable, and must, at last reach the plane of absolute justice between man and man."[101] In promoting the development of commerce, Hewitt concluded, great public projects like the Brooklyn Bridge sped the city toward that ideal.

Hewitt's use of those arguments during the campaign is ironic. It is not only that the secret history of the bridge would later reveal Hewitt's own cynical role in the weaving of defective wire into the cable. It is also that both the Brooklyn Bridge and another great public project, the subway system that Mayor Hewitt would propose in 1888, actually exacerbated the pattern of speculation and high rents that George condemned. The bridge, as the *New York Tribune* noted in an 1882 editorial, was a major focus of the sort of speculation so endemic to the metropolis.

> It is understood that certain men expect to make large sums out of real estate operations in connection with the bridge. They believe that when completed it will increase the value of property on the line, and adjacent to it, to a degree which will make delay a source of profit. They are in no hurry to have their work finished. They wish to perfect all their plans and get hold of the property which they desire first.

Just as the extension, electrification, and acceleration of transit in Manhattan would increase rents, so too would the bridge bring high rents to Brooklyn. In support of rapid transit across the bridge, the *Railroad Gazette* predicted that the "building lots in Brooklyn, now 30 minutes or more from Fulton Ferry, would probably double in price—much more, very likely—should rapid transit between the two cities be provided." With the increase in rent, the *Gazette* concluded, the first "really great usefulness" of the bridge would result. By the end of the century, DeForest and Veiller reported, high rents had "debarred the smallest home seeker" from Brooklyn.[102]

PUBLIC TRANSIT, PRIVATE PLANNING

The same conflict between property values and community values beset the planning of New York's subway system. Despite George's proposals, and although Hewitt had spoken in favor of a municipally built rapid transit system as early as 1873, Hewitt avoided the transit issue during the campaign. In 1888, however, the new mayor issued a special message on rapid transit that proposed the construction with municipal funds of two electrically powered subways. Although rejected in 1888 Hewitt's proposal later provided the foundation for the construction of New York's first subways.[103] In contrast to George's, Hewitt's proposal reflected a greater passion for economic development than for social justice.

In its Annual Report of 1887, the Chamber of Commerce had warned that congestion was dangerously increasing the cost of doing business in the city. Hewitt's special message added to that a concern for the future of the city's tax base. "Our rate of taxation depends upon the growth of the unoccupied portion of the city," Hewitt explained. Without rapid transit, population would be driven out to Long Island or New Jersey, outside the city's taxing authority. A rapid transit system serving the Annexed District (the Bronx) would enable the city "to get the benefit of taxation upon the increased value of property, which according to the best authority, increases as the square of the velocity of travel." But increased tax revenues would not justify a subsidy for public transit; Hewitt's system would be operated by a private firm and based on a profitable five-cent fare.[104]

Hewitt's proposal did not meet with immediate success, but between 1890 and 1894 the *Real Estate Record and Builders' Guide* led a successful campaign to unite business interests behind it. Pointing to the development of municipal ownership under business auspices in Europe, the *Record and Guide* allayed fears that the subway would increase the city's tax burden in insisting that "we want the city of New York to go into the rapid transit business largely because it is so profitable." A committee of real estate developers, anxious to see their properties rise in value, defended the city's legal right to enter the transportation field. They pointed to municipal ownership of park, water, harborfront, and dock systems in support of a similar investment in subways. During the same period labor leaders formed their own rapid transit committee and initiated a petition drive in favor of a municipal subway. Forty-seven labor organizations, as well as George and Samuel Gompers, backed the proposal of the social reformer Charles Stover that the "new rapid transit system be built BY THE PEOPLE AND FOR THE PEOPLE." The proposal included a crucial provision that the subway "shall be operated by and at the expense of the city." [105] While all parties agreed the city should finance the construction of the subway system, the questions of municipal operation and user fees remained open.

In 1894 a new rapid transit bill, largely the work of Hewitt, passed the state legislature and created a new rapid transit commission with the power to construct a subway with municipal funds. In light of the public scandal over the Brooklyn Bridge contracts and the widespread distrust of both private economic interests and public officials that he shared, Hewitt had warned against simply lending the city's credit to private investors who might then bleed the treasury. [106] He also vehemently opposed handing the rapid transit project over to elected officials; "Spare us that horror!" he pleaded in 1894. [107] The new commission reflected his belief that the city's leading men acting for and through the municipality could accomplish this great public work. Unlike previous commissions composed largely of elected officials and mayoral appointees, the 1894 commission by law consisted of the mayor, the comptroller, the president of the chamber of commerce, and five leading businessmen. The commission also enjoyed the power to fill any vacancies that occurred. [108]

78

The new commission insulated rapid transit planning from labor's demand for a municipal subsidy. Before 1894 business interests were careful not to ignore working-class concerns. A "cheap, well-located system of rapid transit would do much to relieve the congestion of the slums," the *Record and Guide* editorialized, and would allow "poor people to live in a small house rather than in a small part of a big house." Tempering its enthusiasm for a profitable municipally operated system, the *Record and Guide* had agreed that "even should dividends be earned, it would be more profitable for the city to spend the excess in betterments and . . . in reduction of the fare than to put it in the treasury." Civic leaders echoed those same points.[109] Despite the objections of Hewitt and others who saw it as "anarchical," labor had secured a provision in the 1894 bill providing for a referendum on municipal operation, apparently establishing the principle of public participation in transit planning.[110] But labor's failure to win representation on the new commission limited the applicability of that principle and left rapid transit planning in the hands of the city's business elite.[111]

Nevertheless, New Yorkers watched the work of the new commission with great expectations. The East River, one journalist explained, had been "cramping the flow of the human tides between workshop and bedroom into one narrow stream" across the Brooklyn Bridge. New rapid transit facilities, he added, would facilitate the realization of the Pennsylvania Railroad's long-term plan for the great development of Long Island, "not only as a truck garden for the great city, but as a residential suburb."[112] Under the supervision of the rapid transit commissioners, another journalist reported, "private enterprise has planned and is executing works of great magnitude." The new subways and the construction at public expense of a tunnel under the East River for the exclusive use of the Long Island Railroad (owned by the Pennsylvania Railroad) were "enabling New Yorkers to devote Manhattan Island almost entirely to business." Other benefits were expected as well. With improved transit "country residences," the journalist added, "will become the privilege of the poor." Rapid transit would mean "that the men with the dinner-pail, as well as the men with the check book" could enjoy suburban living and return refreshed "to their work each morning to renew the struggle for existence . . . in the most intense city in the world."[113] Yet rapid transit not only failed to realize those social benefits, but it seemed to exacerbate the problem of congestion. By 1907 the crush of traffic at the Brooklyn Bridge had made it what one journalist called "a place of discontent." Still, the public grasped desperately at every new rapid transit proposal even when it meant turning planning power entirely over to private interests.[114]

Two years earlier in 1905, a group of commercial and industrial leaders in Brooklyn had formed the Citizen's Central Committee to promote the construction of more bridges and tunnels. Under the leadership of the future city planner Edward Bassett, the committee supported Bassett's boyhood friend Charles Hughes for governor. One of the first acts of Governor Hughes was to create a new and extraordinarily powerful public service commission. The new commission had no official connection to the city government or its electorate except the power to pay its bills with municipal funds. The municipal reformer Henry Bruere termed it "absolutely irresponsible to the community whose interest it is intended to conserve." The new commission, Bruere continued, made "community control over its utilities seem remote" and thus further insulated transit planning from the demand for municipal ownership and operation.[115] Transit corporations recognized the commission was their "best defense against dangerous legislation," one journalist reported, and accepted it "graciously."[116] By 1917 the public service commission had secured the construction of new railroad tunnels under the East and Hudson rivers, increased trolley service over the Brooklyn and Williamsburg bridges, completion of the new Manhattan and Queensborough bridges, and a doubling of the rapid transit system to more than six hundred miles.[117]

Still the new subway system did not realize the great social benefits that had once been associated with it. In order to secure the extraordinary expansion of transit facilities, the public service commission had assured "the operating companies a continuation of large profits and placed the burden of carrying deficits from operation upon the city," explained an early historian of rapid transit.[118] Bassett had insisted on a subway "that would allow the riders to pay the expense of operation, interest and amortization" and had opposed proposals "to build on a large scale, placing part of the future burden on the taxpayers."[119] The new subways did prove an immediate boon to propertied interests and to the business development of Greater New York.

But the new subways also seemed to confirm the fears of the architect and housing reformer Henry Wright that too little attention had been paid to transit's relation to social problems. At the very least, he suggested, fares must be "sufficiently low to induce the workingman to move to outlying sections." Raising the issue of a municipal subsidy, Wright argued that "operating costs are secondary to acceptable living conditions" and urged city officials to recognize transit as a legitimate "municipal function."[120] At least one public service commissioner, Milo Maltbie, was also concerned that the demands of social reform had been ignored. Addressing the 1913 national conference on city planning, Maltbie warned that without careful planning rapid transit would lead only to an extension of the tenement districts. Without some control over realty values, it would be impossible, he explained, "to have subways unless at the same time they are content to have congestion—tenement houses, solidly built blocks and not separate dwellings."[121] But the dominant role of private interests in transportation planning made it difficult if not impossible to realize rapid transit's public promise.

Insulating transit planning from public debate and political conflicts, New York elites had dramatically extended the city's transportation facilities. But at the same time they had minimized its potential to inject the suburbanization process with a greater measure of social justice. Transit improvements unquestionably accelerated suburban development, but the benefits of suburban development would continue to be unequally shared. More than any other issue, rapid transit raised questions about the arrangement and uses of urban space. The answers to those questions constituted a dividing line between the public aspirations of various

81

groups of reformers and the reality of what private development would create in the city. In the Progressive Era the rapid transit debate served as the battleground where those committed to the republican vision of what the American city might be confronted the new urban realists who pragmatically accepted what the new metropolitan order had to offer. As a result of that debate, a new urban discipline would emerge, a new boundary line between the public and private cities that defined both the responsibilities of municipal government and the limits of urban reform.

3

From Rapid Transit to City Planning: Social Efficiency and the New Urban Discipline

Humanity demands that men should have sunlight, fresh air, the sight of grass and trees. It demands these things for the man himself, and it demands them still more urgently for his wife and children. No child has a fair chance in the world who is condemned to grow up in the dirt and confinement, the dreariness, ugliness and vice of the poorer quarters of a great city. It is impossible to think with patience of any future condition of things in which such a childhood shall fall to the lot of any large part of the human race. Whatever struggles manhood must endure, childhood should have room and opportunity for healthy moral and physical growth. Fair play and the welfare of the human race alike demand it. There is, then, a permanent conflict between the needs of industry and the needs of humanity. Industry says men must aggregate. Humanity says they must not, or if they must, let it be only during working hours and let the necessity not extend to their wives and children. *It is the office of the city railways to reconcile these conflicting requirements* [emphasis in original].

Charles H. Cooley, 1894

In the Progressive Era a series of questions surrounding public transportation, from municipal ownership and fare structures to the unionization of transit workers, proved to be the most explosive issues facing municipal politicians. The republican ideal of balancing the advantages of urban life with those of rural life had generated a widespread and intense interest in rapid transit; as early as the 1840s journalists had lauded

the "levelling and democratic Omnibus" and its essential "republicanism." But by the turn of the century, at least in part due to
Henry George's dream of relocating inner city populations in garden cities, Americans saw rapid transit as nothing less than a pana-
cea for a wide range of urban problems. Cooley's assertion that
rapid transit would do nothing less than resolve the conflicting
demands of industry and humanity reflected the unrealistic hopes
Americans attached to rapid transit in the 1890s.[1]

In 1892 Carroll Wright, U.S. commissioner of labor, argued
that "as municipal governments undertake to solve the problems
that are pressing upon them," they looked to rapid transit to "distribute the population of congested districts through country districts." Cheap, rapid transit was an "ethical consideration" and a
key to "the improvement of the condition of the masses." Regarding municipal ownership Wright believed that if "the spirit of
altruism . . . among our millionaires" did not provide rapid transit, then the people would "insist upon a public solution of the
question."[2] In 1898 Adna Weber warned that Americans would
not "become reconciled to the idea of bringing up their children
in hot dusty, germ-producing tenements and streets. But a solution of the problem is now in sight, the suburb unites the advantages of city and country. . . . More rapid transit is urgently
needed for metropolitan populations and is the only solution of
their problem." Pointing to England's 1883 Cheap Trains Act and
its $2 million annual subsidy, Weber suggested the need for a
similar subsidy. Social reformers, settlement workers, and labor
unions joined in the chorus recommending rapid transit as a solution to urban problems.[3]

The hopes associated with rapid transit were exaggerated. Such
factors as racial and ethnic prejudice, the cost of new housing, and
habit vitiated rapid transit's capacity to disperse population.[4] So
too did the demands of profitability. Elevated and underground
rapid transit facilities opened new middle-class residential districts, but to the extent that they dispersed population they undermined their own profitability. Private control of transit went hand
in hand with the concentration of population simply because, in the

transit magnate Charles Yerkes's unfortunate phrase, "the strap-hangers pay the dividends."[5]

But cheap rapid transit nevertheless represented a potentially important social reform in metropolitan America. Even without dispersing population, rapid transit widened employment opportunities which, in turn, enabled families to afford better housing. The nationwide movement for three-cent fares or special workingmen's tickets enlisted the support of labor organizations and reflected the importance of public transit to working families.[6] If rapid transit systems were to be publically owned and operated, then they potentially promised even greater benefits. Public franchises, as both George and a number of social reformers he had influenced argued, were a form of socially created wealth that grew with the community. If a transit system was to be run on a profitable basis, they insisted, the profits rightfully belonged to the community. The capitalized value of public franchises, Frederic Howe argued, "would adorn the city with school houses, parks, and playgrounds; it would pave streets, build sewers, and beautify the city with works of art."[7] Urban experts such as Wright and Weber suggested that public ownership would bring lower fares and equal access to the suburban periphery.[8]

Public control of rapid transit might also have provided an important tool for directing the city's growth and for encouraging greater public participation in municipal affairs. A municipal subsidy would have overcome the contradiction between the demands of profitability and the desire to disperse population and might have enabled urban governments to ease congestion. Moreover, municipal ownership of public utilities that touched the average citizen on a daily basis, Howe argued, would "convert every citizen into an effective critic" and "create a public sense, a social conscience, a belief in the city and an interest in it." Voter turnout for referenda on municipal ownership and other transit issues reflected public interest in transit planning. In 1904 more than 170,000 Chicago voters participated in a referendum on municipal ownership. Howe argued, "It is this democratic flavor of reform in Chicago that makes for its permanence."[9]

Yet relatively little came of the grand hopes associated with rapid transit. Indeed, only a few cities actually built rapid transit systems and few of these were municipally owned and operated. The proponents of municipal ownership, who rarely advocated a municipal subsidy for mass transit and encouraged the belief that municipal ownership could simultaneously lower taxes and fares while dispersing population, were themselves partly to blame. "Instead of dealing with public ownership as a necessary addition to the responsibilities of city government," advocates of municipal ownership too often "described it as something of a free ride," as Paul Barrett has said of Chicago's Edward Dunne. The rise of professional city planning in the twentieth century failed to revive interest in rapid transit; if anything professional planners contributed to its demise. Instead, the dream of breaking up the slums and dispersing urban population once attached to public transit became associated with the private automobile.[10]

Barrett has done more than anyone to clarify how that happened. Paradoxically, Americans believed that public transportation should be provided by regulated private enterprise, while private transportation in the form of the automobile deserved (and in fact benefited from) lavish public subsidies. The frequent condemnation of the huge profits of greedy transit entrepreneurs, although not without justification, reinforced the belief that mass transit could and should be profitable even as it dispersed population.[11] While mass transit suffered from constant political controversy, the automobile, James Flink has suggested, seemed "an especially attractive reform to Americans because it did not involve collective political action."[12] The American preference for individualistic and technological solutions to social problems as opposed to those that were collective and political undermined support for rapid transit. But the demise of rapid transit also involved the development of the realistic approach to urban problems during the Progressive Era.

Social reformers who advocated rapid transit perpetuated the republican effort to use municipal government as a vehicle for transforming the city in the interest of the commonwealth. By the

end of the Progressive Era, however, a new set of realistic reformers had wrested the reform mantle from the republicans. Though
responding in part to the public aspirations kindled by the republicans, the realists charged municipal government with a different
responsibility. "Social efficiency," a phrase that reflected an important shift in urban thought, became the watchword of the realistic reformers. Uniting the image of the well-organized corporation and the well-managed factory with the growing prestige of
social science and social engineering, the drive for social efficiency
implicated municipal government in the effort to create an urban
environment conducive to maximizing production and accumu-
lating capital.

Creating such an environment entailed not only an efficient economic infrastructure but at least a measure of social harmony. By
securing needed physical improvements and protecting the consumer's interest in a bevy of urban utilities and services, reformers
would secure social efficiency. The logic of social efficiency thus
also demanded an enhanced role in municipal governance for a
variety of professionally trained experts at the expense of the machine politician and the ignorant voter.[13] Despite its great cost,
rapid transit could be (and in New York was) defended as a necessary infrastructural improvement and an important public service. It was as an impediment to the other elements of social efficiency that its fate was sealed. As a source of graft and as a
patronage mill, it provided too many opportunities for the corrupt
and incompetent politician. More importantly, advocates of rapid
transit seemed intent on using it to raise divisive economic questions. Chicago alderman William Dever suggested that rapid transit involved nothing less than "the more equal distribution of the
great wealth of this country."[14] Rousing the masses, exacerbating
class tensions, and drowning out the rational logic of the expert,
the rapid transit debate frustrated the drive for social efficiency.
Further burdened with frequent labor controversies, rapid transit
seemed to create more problems than it solved.

The realists' rejection of rapid transit was part of the development of the new urban discipline. A set of principles and practices

that defined both the responsibilities of municipal government and the limits of urban reform, the new urban discipline represented the realistic reformers' program for dealing with the physical and social problems of the metropolis. While some realists were emphatic about keeping costs low, most were willing to support reforms that promoted economic and social efficiency; and municipal expenditures generally increased under their tenure.[15] But realists consistently shunned reforms that raised divisive economic questions or threatened social harmony.[16] Their program would serve as the municipal wing of a national effort to stabilize, rationalize, and legitimate the corporate order.[17]

Before the realists could supplant the republicans, however, they had to offer some alternative to rapid transit and the tremendous hopes it raised. As an integral part of the new urban discipline, city planning represented the realists' response to the problem. City planning worked within the existing political economy not only to make the metropolis more efficient but also ideally to ameliorate its social problems and to promote social harmony. At the First National Conference on City Planning, the realtor Henry Morgenthau called on planners to attack congestion, which he described as "an evil that breeds physical diseases, moral depravity, discontent, and socialism."[18] At the same conference the landscape architect Robert Pope emphasized the importance of city planning in "lessening class strain, of ameliorating the struggle between labor and capital."[19] Improved sanitation and sewerage, better street paving, and traffic regulations would improve public health and safety and ease congestion. Above all exclusionary zoning, essentially a system of building restrictions, promised to improve residential conditions and even, the most optimistic predicted, to depopulate the tenement districts. Best of all, in the realists' view, city planning would do all that without raising troublesome questions about the urban political economy.[20] Thus the journey from rapid transit to city planning illuminates a larger transformation of urban politics around the turn of the century, a transformation based on a changing perception of the city itself.

THE MUNICIPAL REVOLUTION AND THE CITY TRENCHES

In proposing the confiscation of the rental value of land and the use of that social wealth in the interest of the commonwealth, George and the United Labor party had challenged the contemporary perception of municipal government and of the city. Drawing on an artisanal politics that had been common in the late eighteenth century, George and the ULP treated the city as a republican commonwealth. In the eighteenth century the municipal corporation, threatened by scarcity and prodded by the commonwealth ideal (stressing the government's responsibility to promote the common good) and the mutualist and producerist traditions of the crafts, had carefully regulated the local economy in the interests of economic justice.[21] Although increasingly marginal, that practice had continued into the nineteenth century.

By 1825, however, municipal governments had begun to focus less on controlling commerce, prices, and crafts than on enhancing the health, safety, and convenience of the urban environment. The shift in municipal functions occurred for a variety of reasons. In part, municipal officials simply responded to a growing demand for clean water, basic sanitation, fire and police protection, and other public goods. At the same time a declining threat of economic scarcity and the liberal faith in the invisible hand of the market made regulation seem unnecessary and unwise; if municipal government was to have any economic function at all, it would be to facilitate individual initiative rather than to regulate in the public's interest. The development of political democracy simultaneously introduced residence, property, and age, rather than membership in a guild or other agency of the economic community, as the new criteria for citizenship. With broader political participation and increasing partisan affiliation, residential proximity rather than common economic interests appeared to be the basis of the urban community.[22]

The rise of the political machine coincided with, reflected, and reinforced the new conception of municipal politics. The machine emerged just as urbanites began to view the city as a residential, as opposed to an economic, community; and the machines organized voters on a residential basis.[23] As cities spent increasing amounts in providing police, fire, and health protection, building schools and streets, and providing charity and other social services, the municipal revolution placed substantial economic resources (jobs, contracts, and services) in the hands of local officials who used those resources to organize their machines. But the rise of the machine and the changing perception of municipal politics were also closely linked to the emergence of industrial conflict.[24]

Industrialization eroded both the commonwealth ideal and the traditions of the crafts upon which the perception of the city as an economic community had been based. Amy Bridges writes:

> In 1828, New York's artisans believed in the interdependence of economic pursuits, that there was a concrete and identifiable common good, and that government's proper concerns included facilitating prosperity by assisting economic development. By the election of Lincoln, few in the city dared claim that the interests of capital and labor were the same, and few citizens believed that any set of government policies could ensure prosperity and comfort.

Thus the municipal revolution served to remove divisive economic questions from urban politics and provided the machine with an arena in which the conflict between capital and labor might be accommodated.[25] Rather than organizing workers on the basis of common economic interests, the machine engaged workers as residents of neighborhoods in a competition for an expanding array of public goods and services.[26]

Standing between labor and capital, the machine channeled class conflict into what Ira Katznelson has called a system of "city trenches" that prevented a direct confrontation between antagonistic economic groups. When George and the ULP threatened the system of city trenches, good-government reformers temporarily shelved their condemnation of corrupt and grafting politicians and stood with the machine in defense of the city trenches. Submerging his differences with Tammany, Abram Hewitt accepted the machine's nomination in order to defeat the attempt "to organize one class of our citizens against all other classes. . . . The idea which underlies this movement," he protested, "is at war with the fundamental principles upon which our government was organized and rests."[27] In Cincinnati a "Republican-Democratic-capitalist" alliance condemned the ULP leaders as foreign rabble rousers "without any understanding of our institutions." A similar fusion of machine and reform forces across party lines in Chicago condemned the ULP as "anarchists and cutthroats."[28] Those coalitions defeated the ULP but they were not able to preserve the system of city trenches intact.

George had hoped to inaugurate a new era in American politics and to inject his principles of political economy into urban politics. The new system of urban politics that emerged in the Progressive Era was certainly not what he had envisioned. But George and the ULP had had an important impact on urban politics.[29] Their most important legacy was a group of social reformers who united the tactics of machine politics with the strategy of the ULP.[30] Such social reformers as Detroit's Pingree, Cleveland's Johnson and Howe, Toledo's Jones and Whitlock, Cincinnati's Bigelow, and New York's Wagner mobilized the voting power of the urban masses, encouraged their active participation in municipal affairs, and attempted to redistribute economic and political power in their cities. Rapid transit and municipal ownership served as their most important organizing issues.

MUNICIPAL OWNERSHIP AND THE CITY REPUBLIC

Mayor of Detroit during the 1890s Hazen Pinegree was among the first and more imaginative of the social reformers. In his fight with Detroit's transit corporations for a three-cent fare, Pingree mobilized mass support by exposing bribes paid to corrupt alder-men, organizing boycotts, encouraging petition drives, and even personally directing what was essentially a three-day riot against the city's street railways. Similar events occurred in other cities. "For the greater part of nine years, Cleveland was an armed camp," wrote Frederic Howe of Tom Johnson's struggle with the street railways. "There was but one line of division." [31] The debate over rapid transit and municipal ownership proved both so explosive and such an effective organizing tool because it raised fundamental questions about the political economy of the metropolis.

The 1898 Chicago municipal elections provide one example of the issue's impact. When the transit magnate Charles Yerkes tried to secure a fifty-year extension of his franchises with the help of corrupt councilmen and state legislators, Mayor Carter Harrison mobilized his constituency against the scheme. When Harrison promised to secure 10 percent of gross receipts for the city as a way to lower property taxes, former governor John Altgeld joined the fray to accuse Harrison of ignoring the needs of the poor and favoring wealthy taxpayers. Recommending municipal ownership and operation of the street cars with a four-cent fare, Altgeld broadened the terms of the debate. In turn Harrison took his case to the people in a volatile series of neighborhood debates with local aldermen. When the election went against Yerkes, the in-transigent magnate tried to force his new franchises through the lame-duck council. Citizens inflamed by the rhetoric of the recent campaign held protest meetings, staged angry marches, and sur-rounded city hall on the night of the crucial vote, carrying nooses and guns and threatening to hang any aldermen who voted for Yerkes's franchises. Harrison recalled "I seriously doubt whether any American community has ever been as completely aroused on an economic issue as was Chicago in those days." [32]

The rapid transit debate, social reformers found, led naturally to larger issues, especially the connection between realty values and the housing problem, the benefits of the single tax, and the plausibility of the garden city ideal. In a 1904 article ostensibly about the decentralization of industry, Adna Weber stumbled upon these issues. "We have learned that the packing of human beings into tenement barracks devoid of light and air is not due to the necessity of any natural law, but to the greed of man. The city, even the largest city, can now be made as healthful as the country, because cheap rapid transit enables city workers to live many miles away from their work-places." The unrealized potential of rapid transit, Weber argued, demanded "a strict control of franchise privileges by the public authorities."[33] Weber went on to illustrate the persistent association of rapid transit with the single tax. Commenting on Ebenezer Howard's garden city experiment, Weber noted that "the title to the land is transferred to the whole community, the aim thus being to preserve to the city as a whole the unearned increment due to the mere growth of the city." If the experiment succeeded in "abolishing ground-rents and appropriating to the communal treasury the increase in land values," he concluded, "it would open unlimited possibilities for the reconstruction of urban centers."[34] Coming from as respectable a figure as Weber, such statements suggested why banks, trust companies, and other powerful economic institutions with vested interests in metropolitan realty values vehemently opposed republican supporters of municipal ownership such as Tom Johnson.[35] But they also reveal why the transit debate was central to the strategy of the social reformers. Rapid transit and municipal ownership remained both prominent and volatile issues because they were so inextricably linked to questions about the impact of economic and political power on urban life.

Social reformers found referenda on municipal ownership and other transit issues an effective way of promoting working-class participation in municipal affairs. New York's Robert Wagner recalled that his fight for a five-cent fare to Coney Island "readily commended the support of the urban masses" and quickly became the "most discussed topic in the metropolis."[36] Cleveland's Johnson seemed to thrive on the controversy surrounding the transit issue. A long-time transit entrepreneur himself, Johnson seemed vulnerable to popular attack. Howe recalled:

> Frequently his meetings were on the verge of riot; in the east end where feeling was most vindictive and but a handful of his friends would be present he would stand on the edge of a jeering, sometimes a hissing crowd that packed the tent far out to the street lines, smilingly leaning on the edge of the table until the uproar quieted. Then he would frequently win the meeting by a simple story or sweet appeal . . . He seemed to court this kind of exposure to attack.

Johnson directed the anger less on the corrupt alderman than on the forces that corrupted the alderman and especially on "the kind of big business that deals in and profits from public service grants and taxation injustices." Wagner, Harrison, Pingree, Johnson, Howe, Jones, Whitlock, and Bigelow all used transit issues to mobilize working-class constituencies and to focus attention on questions of power.[37]

The transit issue provided social reformers a base from which to alter the distribution of political and economic power in the city. In his study of the evolution of municipal functions, Milo Maltbie argued that the non-taxpaying citizen "recognizes that there are certain limits to his demands for greater municipal activity," but social reformers worked hard to extend the activities of municipal government to the benefit of their poorer constituents.[38] Borrowing money for poor relief, sponsoring municipal gardens, opposing wage cuts for municipal workers, financing large public works projects while canceling orders for labor-saving machinery, pressuring private utilities to launch new projects and hire new workers, and threatening to erect a municipal bakery unless bread prices were lowered, Detroit's Pingree administration developed a program of "municipal stewardship" that broadened the municipal government's social responsibility.[39]

Elsewhere social reformers and urban liberals extended the effort to redistribute economic and political power by strengthening unions, regulating business, and creating a more equitable system of taxation. Pingree had led the way in trying to shift a greater proportion of the city's tax burden onto large corporations and realty interests.[40] Urban liberals secured lower utility rates, shorter hours and better wages for city workers, and a variety of services from education and public housing to improved sanitation and unemployment relief for their working-class constituents.[41] From their electoral bases in the cities, social reformers and urban liberals also advocated broad-based state and national reform programs, addressing inequities in both the workplace and the living space.[42] Thus the rapid transit and municipal ownership issues not only gave rise to movements that expanded the agenda of municipal government into the realm of political economy, but they generated an attack on economic inequality on the state and national level.

It was Frederic Howe who articulated the theory of municipal governance that underlay those efforts by stressing "industrial democracy" as the key to municipal reform.[43] City building, he argued, involved far more than the paving of streets and the laying of sewers. It involved the development of "a city-consciousness, that instinct which is willingness to struggle for the common weal, and suffer for the common woe,—then, and not until then does the city spring into life." The municipal ownership of public utilities, Howe insisted, was the key to the creation of that city-consciousness.[44] Arguing that the city was potentially the most democratic of our political units, Howe called for "a new sort of sovereignty" in the form of a "city republic." The key element of this new sovereignty would be the authorization of "the people of a city to call a constitutional convention, made up of delegates from the several wards, with power to adopt, alter, or amend the fundamental laws of the community; to determine what powers may be exercised, as well as the means of raising and expending revenue." Thus Howe saw municipal government as the basis for a revitalized and more democratic republic. Howe quite consciously built on George's efforts.[45] "If we have gained nothing else," George had announced after the 1886 mayoral election, "we have given the powers that be a very sincere respect for the working-man's vote."[46] Indeed, George and the ULP had helped to turn the working-class vote into a potent force in municipal politics, one that generated new strategies and new initiatives in urban politics among elite reformers.

The Moral Equivalent of the Machine

The efforts of George and the ULP and of the social reformers to revive the perception of the city as a republican commonwealth did not ultimately succeed. But neither did the competing view of the city as a single, cohesive residential community survive intact the political upheavals of the period. Rapid spatial expansion and the functional segregation that accompanied it were creating a network of discrete neighborhoods within the metropolis. While interdependent, those neighborhoods were divided not only by geography but also by social and economic differences that gave to each a distinct set of needs, functions, and attitudes. As neighborhood divisions increasingly paralleled social and economic ones, the segregation of rich and poor not only threatened the natural bonds of the social order and spontaneous forms of social control, but also the artificial political accommodations defended by the machine, the system of city trenches.[47] Hence social reformers and urban liberals had been able to use the machine's own tactics to storm those city trenches.

But even before that happened, elite reformers, who had once grudgingly accepted machine politics as necessary to social order, began to see the machine as a potential threat. Two years after George's mayoralty campaign, the political scientist Frank Goodnow traced New York's political crisis to the process whereby the "middle class, which had thus far controlled the municipal government, were displaced by an ignorant proletariat."[48] Some reformers called for mass disenfranchisement or radical structural changes to minimize working-class influence.[49] Those drastic solutions to urban problems, however, proved unacceptable to much of the American public and even to many elite reformers. Slowly, a less drastic and more influential approach to municipal reform, one that saw the city as an interconnected organism and the central business district (rich with business and professional talent) as its brains, began to emerge.

In a series of speeches and articles between 1887 and 1892, the

96

Brooklyn reformer Seth Low outlined the new approach. Low addressed two closely related questions: "First, what ought a city undertake to do?" and second, "what form of organization" ought municipal government take? In answering the first question, Low pointed out "that a city has not a single attribute of sovereignty." He flatly rejected the republican position in arguing that rather than a political commonwealth, the municipal government was simply a business corporation supplying certain public services. Municipal politics concerned only the "best means of conducting this business" rather than the larger issue of "the liberties of the people."[50] But neither did Low accept the view of the structural reformers who blamed everything on the ignorant or corrupt voter. Low defended universal manhood suffrage because "it Americanizes our foreign-born citizens more rapidly than any other system possibly could."[51] In a strange amalgam of the concerns of the structural reformers and the republican vision, Low explored the role municipal government might play as an agency of both social control and social justice.

As befit a future president of the National Civic Federation, an agency dedicated to mediating the labor-capital conflict and stabilizing the corporate order, Low saw a threat to American civilization in the rising level of urban conflict. Anticipating the new urban discipline, Low argued that the American city faced a choice between social efficiency and obsolescence.[52] The federal system of divided authority and checks and balances, he argued, should not have been extended to municipal government. Such procedures paralyzed bureaucratic efficiency and allowed machine politicians and backroom bosses to control municipal affairs without accepting responsibility. He argued that the representative legislature in the city should really be seen as "a board of directors." Authority and hence responsibility should be centralized in the mayor, he added, as the chief executive officer of the city.[53]

Such reforms promised great results. "If we could only have more confidence in our city governments," he told a group of Philadelphia reformers, "how much more they might do for us than now they do. Think of what has been done in some of the best cities of Europe; bad neighborhoods have been renovated through the action of the authorities; unwholesome buildings have given way to open spaces and small parks; public baths have been erected and maintained for the public benefit." Low even raised the issue of the municipal ownership of public utilities but quickly added that "few American cities have manifested so great competency in other directions as to justify a very strong inference that they would administer successfully business of this kind." He deeply regretted that such incompetence prevented the assumption of additional responsibilities. "Losses of this character fall almost entirely on the poor," he argued.[54] Here was the crux: if controlled and administered by the right men according to business principles, municipal government could become a powerful force for social harmony and economic development.[55]

The program of municipal reform paralleled in many ways the pattern of machine politics. Rejecting mass disenfranchisement, Low recognized a need to develop neighborhood organizations similar to the machine's.[56] Municipal reform had failed in the past, Low's associate Carl Schurz explained, because reformers lost "contact with the masses of the people, while the representatives and agents of Tammany Hall remained constantly among the classes of population which furnish the most votes."[57] By the 1890s social settlements like New York's University Settlement, which Low actively supported, had begun to create neighborhood organizations rivaling those of the machine's.[58] Settlement leaders like Boston's Robert Woods pledged to remain "in natural, continuous association with the humblest citizens." "Neighborliness is at the basis of even bad politics," Woods professed, "and sound government can be built on no other foundation." Developing an "accurate and minute familiarity with the local pattern of streets, houses, and institutions," he concluded, the settlements would develop "the same exhaustive acquaintance and knowledge of personal minutia" as the machine.[59]

Although many settlement leaders appreciated the positive features of the machine, they still saw it as a major obstacle to more important reforms. The local alderman understood the poor and their problems, Jane Addams admitted, "better than the big guns who are always talking about civil service and reform." James Reynolds of New York's University Settlement also recognized why the poor looked more to the ward leader than to "the moral leaders of standing, whose abodes are remote from them." But the machine's "municipal program was limited," Reynolds charged, and lacking in "intelligent purpose and . . . moral ideas." The "positive evils of corrupt government . . . fall heaviest upon the poorest," Addams wrote in echoing a point made by both Low and Reynolds. A purified government could reverse that equation and do a great deal for the poor. "Go into politics. Every force that believes in making righteousness pervasive should do the same," Reynolds implored his colleagues. "Political reform is the great moral opportunity of our day, and let us be wise enough to seize it." The settlements' view of municipal reform as essentially a moral problem complemented the realists' efforts to de-emphasize economic issues.[60]

In alliance with the realists, settlement leaders would take over the machine's role in mediating class conflict. The Haymarket explosion and its political repercussions had alerted Woods to the dangerous development of a class system "based predominantly on income." As spearheads of reform, settlement leaders would build up "the state at the precise point of its greatest disintegration," the working-class neighborhood.[61] A rising level of class conflict worried Jane Addams also. Although she supported the labor movement, she envisioned it in moral terms and criticized labor leaders for turning it into an adversarial agency and for being "apathetic to higher motives." When "class interest becomes the governing and motive power," she warned, "the settlement can logically be of no value to either side."[62] Admiring Addams's effort to mediate between "the suburb and the city center," Graham Taylor, the founder of the Chicago Commons settlement, hoped that the settlements would "stand in between" organized capital and organized labor "before the lines of difference became rigidly set for conflict."[63]

The settlements also borrowed the machine's strategy of engaging neighborhood constituencies in a competition for public goods and services. Settlement leaders came to recognize, as Woods put it, that the machine and the boss's "ever-present philanthropy" met "important and legitimate needs and yearnings."[64] But municipal reformers could provide those services more efficiently and without the corruption and immorality associated with the machine. Woods urged his neighbors to "come together as consumers" to procure the "professional services they need."[65] Replacing "the variety of casual services" that the machine offered in "voluntary but calculating ways" with similar services dispensed by "municipal and philanthropic institutions with high professional standards," the settlements would provide a moral equivalent of the machine.[66]

The actual political power of the settlements in the neighborhoods, however, rarely matched their rhetoric. Their would-be constituents often saw the settlements as a "bunch of people planning for us and deciding what is good for us without consulting us."[67] In a series of electoral contests in the 1890s, settlement candidates, Woods admitted, "far from being welcomed, were scorned or resented." The settlements' program for municipal government, "taking thought for its bookkeeping, safeguarding its finances, and enhancing its administrative efficiency," he lamented, made "but a sorry appeal" among their neighbors.[68] Addams wondered, "What headway can the notion of civic purity, of honesty of administration make against this big manifestation of human friendliness, this stalking survival of village kindness?"[69] Addams recognized that the poor did not lack moral and ethical standards, but that they had to "balance their opinions by their living" and the machine was often the only thing standing between them and destitution.[70] Woods understood that the poor dreamed of "a broadly and humanly serviceable city, powerful, generous, considerate" and the machine, despite its often cynical motivations, came closest to that ideal.[71]

In his own neighborhood Woods elected to cooperate with the "Honorable Jim" Donovan, a machine politician dedicated to social reform. But elsewhere the failure to defeat corrupt aldermen convinced the settlements of the need, Woods recalled, to go "over the heads of both machine and electorate" to secure municipal reform.[72] Fortunately, the electoral campaigns, Addams noted, had created "a sense of identification with public-spirited men throughout the city who contributed time and money."[73] The alliance between commercial and industrial leaders and the settlements strengthened with the turn of the century.[74] The settlements brought to the alliance "a rival body of knowledge capable of being used to create a political substructure and superstructure analogous but superior to the machine," Woods explained, while commercial and industrial leaders supplied financial resources that allowed settlements to create "a system of public services often far in advance of what district political leaders are capable of achieving."[75] But the effort to "institutionalize the welfare program," as Amos Pinchot put it, and to replace the machine's social role in the neighborhood was only a secondary aim. In helping to create "a new type of city-wide public spirit," the settlements encouraged the development of a program of municipal reform that transcended both the machine and its neighborhood constituency.[76]

THE NEW URBAN DISCIPLINE

The new reform program and the settlements' role in it was multifarious. Among the residents of Greenwich House, for example, were the municipal reformer Carl Schurz; Crystal Eastman, who later worked on the Russell Sage Foundation's Pittsburgh survey; the labor reformer and future New Dealer Frances Perkins; Benjamin Marsh, organizer of the city planners' first national conference; and fellow planner George Ford. When Seth Low became mayor of Greater New York, James Reynolds of the University Settlement became his personal secretary. The tenement reformer Lawrence Veiller had also resided at the University Settlement in the 1890s. Graham Taylor, head of the Chicago Commons, served on the Municipal Voters League and at least two of his residents, John Smulski and William Dever, became municipal reformers. His son, Graham R. Taylor, contributed a study of industrial decentralization to the city planning movement.[77]

The active participation of business leaders was a key element in this new city-wide program of municipal reform. The growing potential of the working-class vote, the persistent volatility of urban politics, as well as the increasing complexity and cost of the city's infrastructure convinced business leaders, many of whom had once supported the machine, of their own interest in municipal reform. As Cincinnati's Walter Draper put it, "the problems that confront us will not be settled by the radical nor by the standpatter, but by the progressive conservative." Reform-minded businessmen recognized, Draper argued, that a "new order of things must prevail . . . [and] have determined that the knife that will perform the operation must not cut deeply enough to kill."[78] By the end of the Progressive Era, the combined efforts of business leaders and moral reformers (and increasingly of technically trained professionals) would coalesce into the new urban discipline.

In the interests of social harmony, the proponents of the new urban discipline often supported a wide range of useful improvements, including the municipal playgrounds, gymnasiums, libraries, and baths for which social reformers campaigned. Settlement leaders in particular often cooperated directly with social reformers and voiced republican attitudes. Lambasting commercial recreation "which ministers to pleasure in order to drag it into excess because excess is more profitable," Jane Addams called for municipally sponsored alternatives. "We are only beginning to understand what might be done through the festival, the street procession, the band of marching musicians, orchestral music in public squares and parks."[79] But the logic of their support would change subtly as the new urban discipline took shape.

Moral reformers with ties to the traditional middle class had often expressed anticorporate attitudes. Blaming starvation wages and crumbling tenements for urban immorality, Benjamin Flower, the crusading editor of *Arena*, called for "radical economic changes" and an end to the "vicious class legislation" of "a soulless plutocracy." But the reverse side of moral reform was the condemnation of the immorality of the poor, their search for "bestial gratifications" as Flower put it, and the call for individual and social regeneration.[80] The moral reformers' association with business leaders would result in a greater emphasis on moral effect than on economic cause and on social efficiency than on social justice.

That pattern was particularly pronounced in regard to the city's congested tenement districts. Henry Foreman, president of Chicago's South Park Commission, explained that neighborhood parks would reduce "poverty, intemperance, immorality, crime, and sickness" and hence were "not merely humane" but "imperative for reasons of public safety."[81] In Chicago's parks, settlement resident Ernest Poole noted, "play has become a deep, wholesome Americanizing force." Poole particularly lauded the shower rooms where young boys benefited from "cleansing under official eyes."[82] Graham Taylor rejoiced, the "city which has made its reputation by killing hogs has awakened to the fact that manufacturing good and sturdy citizenship is even more important."[83] Were the parks orderly? asked the recreation planner J. Horace McFarland. "Yes," he answered in affirming their function as a new means of social control, "and without blue-coated restraint."[84] Neighborhood parks, McFarland recognized, and a carefully planned physical and social environment might take the place of force in regulating the behavior of the lower classes.

On a grander scale proponents of the city beautiful movement predicted similar results. "Mean streets make mean people," argued Charles Mulford Robinson. The dreary lives of tenement dwellers who descended from "dismal rooms to sadder streets," Robinson wrote, explained why "lights and music sometimes lure them into dangerous places, or that the voice of the agitator alone awakens in them an echo in dull ears." The "improved street," he advised, "has, in short, an improved population."[85] Robinson urged the erection of civic centers that would "visibly dominate" the city: "To them the community would look up, seeing them lording over it at every turn, as, in fact, the government ought to do."[86] Broader streets, impressive civic centers, neighborhood parks, and other improvements would create not only a more beautiful but also a more orderly city.

But it was not the greater emphasis on social efficiency and social control than on social justice alone that distinguished the proponents of the new urban discipline from social reformers. It was also a difference between democracy and paternalism (as Robinson's view of the civic center suggests). Where social reform relied on the organized voting power of the urban electorate to demand reform, the new urban discipline relied on the rational analysis of the urban expert and the enlightened self-interest of the progressive businessman to institute reform from above. Those municipal issues that raised divisive questions, exacerbated class tensions, and encouraged mass participation and popular debate thus undermined both the means and the ends of the new urban discipline. New municipal functions that addressed the needs of urban consumers served the realists' program well; those that addressed problems associated with urban modes of production proved troublesome.

Unfortunately for the realists, it was precisely those conflicts endemic to the political economy of the metropolis, between landlord and tenant, factory worker and employer, labor and capital, that had created the demand for new municipal functions in the first place. After his year-long study of the evolution of municipal functions, Milo Maltbie reported, "There is hardly a municipal function which has not been made necessary" by an increase in such conflicts.[87] Even something as seemingly innocuous as the creation of Chicago's system of neighborhood parks might raise divisive questions. Watching park attendants "endlessly sweeping and mopping in an effort to keep off the dark coating of sticky, greasy soot that settles down from" the nearby stockyards led the settlement resident and future socialist Ernest Poole to contemplate the stark contrast between Chicago's brand-new parks and its slum neighborhoods. It was a contrast, he concluded, that raised such troubling "questions as wages and rents, city charters, inheritance taxes," and the municipal ownership of public utilities.[88] This was made all the more problematic when social reformers such as Howe called for a constitutional convention to extend municipal powers. The proponents of the new urban discipline had to assert their own expertise in prescribing the proper functions of municipal government and to instruct the voting public. In that sense the new urban discipline was literally an academic discipline, the discipline of political science.[89]

MUNICIPAL INNOVATION AND THE FUNCTIONS
OF CITY GOVERNMENT

In his study of municipal functions, Maltbie found a clear division between the taxpaying and non-taxpaying electorates on how municipal services should be financed. Taxpayers wanted new services financed by user fees while a larger and growing group of non-taxpayers, supported by labor organizations, wanted increased property taxes to subsidize user fees. At the center of the controversy was the public utility corporation. Maltbie reported that the "citizen learns from the political economist that in certain industries an increasing density of population is invariably accompanied by increased consumption and decreased cost per unit." Appropriating that "unearned increment," Maltbie continued, the public utility "corporation thus receives most of the benefits from conditions which it has little or no hand in creating."[90] Most urbanites came to agree that the corporations should be forced to pay a greater share of their profits to the city; the issue was whether the result should be lower taxes or lower user fees.

Particular attention focused on the transit corporation. "The proposition that municipal street railways ought to be supported by taxes or loans meets with no approval," Maltbie observed. "Everyone recognizes that free transportation at present would be unjust."[91] It is true that relatively few voices called for free, subsidized transit; but there were plenty of voices demanding that excessive profits be taxed as means to lowering fares. Pingree led a nationwide movement for the three-cent fare based on the proposition that compensation from transit corporations should benefit the unpropertied majority of citizens in the form of lower fares rather than the propertied minority through lower property taxes.[92] Nor did the appeal to professional expertise generally quiet popular demands. In certain fields such as public health and sanitation, technically trained professionals had been able to assert that their particular expertise placed them above politics. But the long history of controversy in regards to transit, the public's familiarity with the service, and the profit-basis of the enterprise made it difficult to abstract expert opinion from the political context.[93]

Early in the 1890s New York business interests had expressed enthusiasm for a municipally constructed subway and defended it as a proper function of municipal government. But once the provision of public transit was accepted as a legitimate municipal function, New York businessmen learned to their dismay, it was extremely difficult to control public debate.[94] The creation of New York's rapid transit commission, which placed planning power in private hands and insulated it from popular demands, suggested one way that rapid transit might have become an important part of the new urban discipline. "It is obvious," the *Real Estate Record and Guide* argued in defense of the subway and other such public improvements, "that without an orderly, dignified, and splendid city the highest type of citizen if impossible." Settlement leaders and elite reformers in New York similarly saw rapid transit as a way of extending the benefits of the middle-class life to at least the aristocracy of labor and thus of stabilizing the urban order.[95] Other cities created commissions similar to New York's; but because rapid transit never could be completely divorced from divisive economic issues, it did not become an integral part of the new urban discipline.

In the early twentieth century, neither transit corporations nor transit engineers exhibited much enthusiasm for either municipal ownership or operation. Since it was the pressure exerted by business interests and professional organizations, the "extra-legal molders of municipal rule," that often tipped the balance in favor of new functions, a lack of enthusiasm on their part could help to keep the issue entirely off the municipal agenda.[96] Neither did such reform organizations as the National Civic Federation (NCF) and the National Municipal League (NML) show much enthusiasm for municipal ownership of public transit; after careful study of the transportation question, neither would endorse municipal ownership.[97] The NCF and NML, which forged links between business leaders and professionals on a national scale, reflected the growing disenchantment with the municipal ownership of transit among the proponents of the new urban discipline.

During the same period a group of urban reformers, experts, and academics whom Kenneth Fox has described as "municipal innovators" developed a functional prescription for city government widely adopted by city administrations. The combined effort of officials with the NML, the Census Bureau, and academic political scientists, this functional prescription codified the lack of enthusiasm for either the municipal ownership of transit facilities or a municipal subsidy of transit fares. Although the prescription left open the possibility of municipal ownership, it effectively discouraged it. The municipal innovators defined as legitimate municipal functions

[those] activities which are performed for all citizens alike without compensation, the expense being met by revenue obtained without regard to the benefits which the contributors may individually derive from any or all municipal activities. . . . Most of them are essential to the existence and development of government and to the performance of the governmental duty of protecting life and property and of maintaining a high standard of *social efficiency* [emphasis added].

Public transit, which some citizens did not use at all and which was financed directly through user fees, did not fit that description.[98]

Moreover, the intense controversy that surrounded public transit and its association with the incompetent boss and corrupt machine violated the principles of social efficiency and hence disqualified it as a proper municipal function. Municipal ownership of transit was theoretically a possibility under a separate category, quasi-private or commercial undertakings, but the definition of such functions—"those activities from which a revenue is derived that represents a partial or full compensation or return for the privileges granted, commodity or property sold, or specific service rendered"—precluded free transportation and discouraged a municipal subsidy.[99] Adopted by reform administrations across the country, this functional prescription discouraged consideration of municipal ownership of transit facilities as a proper function of city government. Instead, municipal governments limited their involvement with public transit to the regulation of private corporations in the consumers' interest.

The municipal innovators expressed a genuine concern about the conflict between efficiency and democracy. Yet for all their insistence on the importance of the democratic control of municipal government they (unlike the social reformers) precluded debate over the proper tasks of city government from their conception of municipal democracy. Leo Rowe, a political scientist and municipal innovator, predicted that the "democracy toward which we are approaching will be a democracy of pleasures and enjoyments rather than the democracy of the suffrage." Rowe's statement was a fair description of the realists' program of municipal reform. Fulfilling Low's desire that municipal government focus on the business of providing public services rather than the liberties of the people, the realists excluded the larger issues of economic and political power from municipal debate.[100]

Notwithstanding the work of the municipal innovators, popular interest in rapid transit died hard; and its persistence helped the republican program of social reform survive. It was only the rise of the automobile and the development of city planning, less controversial means of inspiring at least some of the same hopes associated with rapid transit, that allowed the new urban discipline to emerge triumphant. By the end of the Progressive Era, as Paul Barrett has clearly shown in the case of Chicago, the dream of perfecting urban transportation and emptying the slums had become attached to the automobile and the city planning profession that developed around it. Of course the dream did not turn out as planned. Improved roads, traffic regulations, and zoning resolutions won middle-class support and indeed benefited the middle class; but they did little either to solve the transportation problem or to empty the slums. Moreover, the streetcar system, the essential means of transportation that determined the employment, shopping, and entertainment opportunities for the working class, deteriorated as public funds were invested in the automobile infrastructure. Yet working-class Chicagoans, transfixed by the promise of the automobile, supported or at least acquiesced in the triumph of city planning.[101] Similar stories occurred across metropolitan America. The history of Cincinnati's ill-fated rapid transit beltway illustrates the role of the new urban discipline in the journey from rapid transit to city planning.

CINCINNATI'S HOLE IN THE GROUND

In 1913 Maltbie addressed the national conference on city planning on the relationship between public transit and city planning:

> In the discussions of city planning there has been a noticeable lack of consideration of transportation facilities. Volumes have been written on the relative advantages of street plans, and the ingenuity of engineers, landscape architects and municipal experts has been taxed to discover the most attractive design. But with the exception of this one factor, the public highway, so little consideration has been given to transportation that it is almost a virgin field from the standpoint of city planning. Yet I venture to assert that there is no one factor, with the possible exception of topography, which has a greater influence not only upon the direction of city development but upon the character of the city from every standpoint.

After Maltbie's address Alfred Bettman, city solicitor of Cincinnati, related public transit to his city's housing problem. In Cincinnati the "working people as a rule travel enormous distances over the surface system, going from factories which lie more or less in the outlying portions of the city into tenement houses or congested districts," he explained. Aside from easing the daily commute and increasing the range of employment opportunities, he argued, rapid transit would encourage the development of "new residential localities which may help to solve the housing problem" and distribute "population into more healthful surroundings." The administration of Democratic Mayor Henry Hunt of Cincinnati, Bettman concluded, was developing plans for a rapid transit beltway that would achieve those goals.[102] Hunt's plan reflected his conflicting commitments to social efficiency and social reform and proved to be a major factor in the demise of his administration. Throughout 1913 a bitter street railway strike (which ironically began just as Bettman returned from the planning conference) and an acrimonious debate over municipal ownership beset discussions of rapid transit, severely strained Hunt's tenuous coalition of elite Republican reformers and insurgent Democrats, and helped to defeat his reelection effort.

Twelve years later the beltway was still uncompleted. Municipal reformers, who had not elected a mayor since Hunt, blamed the corruption and inefficiency of the Republican political machine for the notorious "hole in the ground" and urged abandonment of the project. Bettman, now a nationally renown planner, argued that comprehensive city planning offered the best means of addressing the city's social and economic problems. In 1925 the city's reformers, having secured a new municipal charter and an official master plan, organized themselves as the Charter party, elected Murray Seasongood mayor, and went on to control city government for the next decade. The reformers' abandonment of rapid transit and their embrace of city planning was a crucial factor in the triumph of reform in Cincinnati.[103]

During 1912 Hunt had been negotiating with the city's traction monopoly to effect a compromise favorable to his rapid transit plan. The delicate negotiations were pursued behind closed doors, but it proved impossible to keep them there. When Hunt, in an effort to revive the central business district, ease congestion and the daily commute, depopulate the tenement districts, and bring suburban homes within reach of Cincinnati's workers, introduced his plan late in 1912 he found himself embroiled in a volatile debate he could not control.[104] Inextricably linked to profound social and economic changes in the city and burdened with a legacy of political controversy and great expectations of social reform, rapid transit invited controversy. Still, in January 1913 Hunt seemed on the verge of winning agreement for a $29 million valuation for the properties on which regulated profits would be figured. But the contentious single-taxer Herbert Bigelow, fearing that an inflated valuation would destroy any hope for eventual municipal ownership, introduced state legislation that would revoke the franchise and substitute an indeterminate permit based on a three-cent fare. Although the bill died in committee, it disrupted Hunt's negotiations and inflamed public opinion.[105]

By the end of April, it again seemed as though an agreement might be reached with the traction monopoly when the city's street car workers entered the debate. While an international union attempted to organize a Cincinnati local, a delegation of labor leaders called on Mayor Hunt. They suggested, the *Cincinnati Post* reported, "that motormen and conductors be given some share, through higher wages, in the benefits of the proposed $29,000,000 traction settlement."[106] The men saw the negotiations as an opportune time to press their demands for a ten-hour day, half pay for waiting crews, and a five-cent raise in pay. In an effort to strengthen their position they also adopted a resolution demanding municipal ownership and formed a Citizen's Municipal Ownership League.[107] When the traction monopoly remained intransigent, the streetcar employees' municipal ownership league gained the support of the city's major labor organizations and was rechristened the Trades Union Municipal Ownership League.[108] At the same time Bigelow launched a People's Street Railway League with the aim of securing a referendum on municipal ownership that would repudiate Hunt's traction settlement.[109]

Meanwhile the city braced for what one newspaper feared would be "the greatest strike in the history of this city."[110] The crisis quickly became, the *Times-Star* reported, "the most exacting through which the city officials have had to pass since the begin-

111

ning of the Hunt administration."[111] At the end of the first full week of the strike, a crowd of several thousand clashed with police downtown where the streetcars converged at Fountain Square. At midnight Hunt requested troops from the governor and was refused.[112] The next day, insisting that the city was beset by rioting and mob violence, Hunt renewed his call for troops but was again rebuffed.[113]

A municipal takeover of the transit system now appeared to be the only remaining course of action. Later that same day city solicitor Bettman filed suit against the company, asking the court to take charge of the properties, appoint a receiver, and initiate condemnation proceedings.[114] Pressured on all sides the traction company recognized the union on Monday. The biggest loser in the whole affair, however, was Hunt. Despite his effort to remain neutral and to secure a just settlement, his call for troops had earned him the enmity of many of his erstwhile labor supporters. On the other hand, one traction company stockholder expressed privately an attitude probably shared by many elites in the city. The "politicians in both parties are trying to take advantage of the situation to play the so-called labor vote," he complained. Bettman's suit, he added, was "a disgrace to any lawyer."[115] Hunt's reform coalition could not survive in that atmosphere. His negotiations with the traction company and his hopes for the rapid transit beltway were also in shambles. Nor were his troubles yet over.

At the end of the same week in which the strike ended, Bigelow stepped up his campaign to secure a referendum on municipal ownership.[116] Speaking to large crowds in the city's working-class neighborhoods, areas which were the most tenuous part of Hunt's coalition, Bigelow vowed to bring municipal ownership and the three-cent fare to Cincinnati. Criticizing his opponents for trying to "scare the little property owners . . . as though municipal ownership would increase the debt of the city and raise the taxes of the citizens," Bigelow painted an overly rosy picture of municipal ownership that included a three-cent fare, higher wages, and enough profits to finance the construction of the beltway.[117] Bigelow raised expectations that Hunt could not possibly fulfill and convinced many voters that Hunt had made too many compromises with the traction monopoly. In July a Hunt-backed slate of commissioners was elected to write a new charter that would facilitate his rapid transit plans, but the voters rejected the charter in the fall.[118] The turbulent summer also cost Hunt his reelection bid in November when the Republican machine returned to power.[119]

In the aftermath of Hunt's defeat the Republican machine picked up the rapid transit plan as its own.[120] During the next ten years, a new machine-appointed Rapid Transit Commission, dominated by leading business interests and insulated from public debate, resolutely pushed forward the plan.[121] The city's reformers, however, abandoned rapid transit. The transit imbroglios of 1913 had contributed to a year of social tensions and political controversy unlike anything the city had experienced since the ULP campaigns of the 1880s. The charter campaign of 1913, the reformers' *Citizens' Bulletin* lamented, had been marred by "demagogism," "sensationalism," and "the indulgence of hysterics." What was needed, the *Bulletin* added, was an atmosphere conducive to "cool judgement . . . seasoned with temperate thought and accurate and precise reasoning."[122] Without such an atmosphere the proponents of the new urban discipline failed to solve much of anything.[123]

FROM RAPID TRANSIT TO CITY PLANNING

During the next decade Cincinnati's reformers embraced city planning as a way of addressing the same problems that had bedeviled Hunt. Bettman led the effort with the organization of the United City Planning Committee (UCPC) in 1915. The passage of a state city-planning enabling bill in 1915 and the creation of an official city planning commission in 1918 were among the major accomplishments of the UCPC. City planning, Bettman argued, was central to a city-wide and comprehensive assault on the city's physical problems. The comprehensive approach, which included a master plan for the city, city-wide housing codes, and zoning, would bring improved housing, community development, and economic efficiency, Bettman concluded.[124] The Better Housing League (which Hunt had helped to create and of which Bettman was a member) announced, "There is every reason to believe that zoning will have the effect of hastening the provision of transportation facilities to new districts and of encouraging the construction of workingmen's homes near factory sections so that workers may live nearer to their work and be spared the necessity of traveling long distances." Securing the same benefits as rapid transit zoning would also prevent the sort of "violent controversy" that resulted from the commercial and industrial invasion of residential districts and thus serve to ease rather than exacerbate social tensions.[125]

In 1921 the UCPC issued a report critical of the rapid transit plan, urging the abandonment of the project and that the $3 million already spent be charged off as a "dead loss." In 1923 the Technical Advisory Corporation, a group of consultants hired by the City Planning Commission to prepare a comprehensive master plan, recommended that construction of the beltway be halted and that the remaining funds be used in a comprehensive street repaving program. The following year a survey of the city's municipal government estimated that $11 million would be needed to complete the beltway and warned that, due to the increased use of automobiles and declining ridership, "the taxpayers rather than the car riders will be required to pay for practically the entire improvement." In 1925 the UCPC urged that the remaining beltway funds be spent in "developing main radial thoroughfares."[126] Indeed, the "hole in the ground" was now more valuable to reformers as a club with which to beat the inefficient and corrupt Republican machine than as a major social reform.[127]

Cincinnati's master plan, adopted in 1925, completed the estrangement of the city's reformers from rapid transit and their embrace of the automobile. Downtown congestion, the master plan suggested, could be relieved through the rerouting of street cars, the widening of some streets, extensive creation of one-way streets, restriction of heavy trucking and deliveries, parking restrictions,

114

and other traffic regulations. Outside the central business district the plan called for an extensive program of widening, extending, and repaving existing thoroughfares. The plan pronounced rapid transit "financially undesirable" and added that the money "that would have to be spent in completing the loop could be far more profitably spent in developing main radial thoroughfares." [128]

The hopes for housing reform once attached to rapid transit were now tied to zoning and the regulation of subdivisions (and effectively limited to the middle class). [129] Zoning, which established building districts with height, bulk, and use restrictions, prevented the spread of the tenement districts, but it provided no solution to existing slums. By excluding low-income housing from the choice residential districts, zoning probably exacerbated the problem. Although the Better Housing League had predicted improved housing conditions for all residents, other supporters of the zoning resolution were less optimistic. The city's health commissioner admitted, "Zoning is not a cure for present ills, but it does safeguard the future against a repetition all over the city, of evils which now prevail in certain sections." [130]

The master plan reflected a similar pessimism. Noting that 30 percent of the city's population paid escalating rents to live in increasingly overcrowded tenements, the master plan concluded that the tenement problem was "bound to remain a problem for several decades to come," especially in light of the recent influx of blacks into the city. The costs of constructing single-family and even four-family and row houses drove rents above what "the vast majority of colored families and a great many white wage earners" could afford. "This means that it is not feasible now to give any consideration as a part of the City Plan to providing housing for low-wage earners," the plan stated. The provision of housing for higher income groups might ease congestion somewhat, but beyond that the plan provided only for "the amelioration of living conditions in the older parts of the town by zoning protection and by provision of parks, playgrounds, community centers and open spaces." [131] In reference to the city's sixty-five hundred existing tenements, the Public Health Federation reported that "practically

none promote health, comfort and good standards of citizenship."
Describing the tenement problem as "practically hopeless," the
federation called for more supervised playgrounds to teach "the
lessons of self-control." Such playgrounds were needed, added
one reformer, "to counter-balance the evils of this industrial period."[132] Reformers now faced the unenviable task of managing a
housing problem that they had little hope of solving.

Unquestionably, the shift from rapid transit to city planning
reflected the growing significance of the automobile and the pressure it placed on municipal officials.[133] It also reflected an important redefinition of the housing and other urban problems. Referring to the rapid transit plan as part of the city's "patchwork
planning," Bettman argued that comprehensive city planning recognized a "close organic relationship between each city improvement and every other city improvement." City planning defined
urban problems in terms of the interdependent parts of an organic
metropolitan community rather than focusing exclusively on the
poor. The immediate problems of the poor were deferred in the
belief that with the general improvement of metropolitan conditions, the poor would ultimately benefit.[134] But the reformers' embrace of city planning also revealed the influence of the new urban
discipline and a commitment to social efficiency.

Whereas the campaign for rapid transit had brought the city only
divisiveness and recrimination, city planning promised economic
efficiency and social harmony. Planning would improve the efficiency of civil engineering, testified the president of the Ohio Mechanics' Institute. Zoning, Bettman argued, "will promote building by the protection it affords to investments in buildings and
preserve land values." As a force for social harmony, planning
would fight juvenile delinquency, explained a charity worker, and
"promote peace and contentment among" the citizenry. Zoning,
explained a labor leader, meant that "the man anxious to own a
home would be assured that his property would not depreciate in
value," a principle that "holds good for the wage earner as well as
the man of independent means." Addressing the same theme, another zoning supporter argued that the "worker who retires in his

modest home surrounded by plots of verdure and foliage, and whose nostrils are filled with pure ozone during his nocturnal rest will certainly show fewer nihilistic tendencies than the worker" living amidst the noise, filth, and overcrowding of the tenement districts.[135]

The statement of one medical expert and zoning proponent most clearly established the close connection between city planning and the new urban discipline. Referring to the noise, pollution, and congestion associated with large factories, he cautioned that "of economic disturbances and inequalities I am not speaking; it is only from the standpoint of health and particularly of 'nervousness' that I desire to write these few remarks."[136] Distancing themselves from demands for broad social change and avoiding political controversies, city planning proponents created an environment in which the rational arguments of the expert would dominate public debate.

To be sure zoning and city planning proved far less controversial than rapid transit, winning widespread if sometimes lukewarm support and generating very little opposition. In that sense they did contribute to social tranquility. But they also failed, as Cincinnati's master plan had predicted, to solve the housing problems of the city's poorer residents and probably exacerbated them.[137] Of course rapid transit proponents too had promised more than they could deliver, even in the best of circumstances. But the rapid transit debate had at least raised larger questions about economic and political power in the city.

In contrast city planning left untouched the larger economic inequalities that had created urban problems in the first place.[138] "If long hours, low wages, and extensive periods of unemployment" were the prime causes of congestion and urban misery, Charles Beard had asked in reference to city planning in 1912, "how can a municipal government hope to make any radical changes when the underlying economic forces are beyond its reach."[139] Although he wrote before the emergence of the city planning profession and while a wide-ranging public debate over the province of city planning was still taking place, Beard's question anticipated the limitations of professional planning. In the 1920s an acceptance of the political economy of the metropolis and the veneration of the expert would become the hallmarks of the city planning profession. When the city planning debate began early in the century, however, nothing was inevitable about the direction it would take. The development of the city planning debate and the subsequent professionalization of city planning is an important and complex story in its own right.

The depression of 1873 created widespread suffering. In New York the Tammany machine distributed free coal to the poor during the winter of 1877. From *New York in the Nineteenth Century*, Dover Publications.

Labor demonstration in Union Square, 1882. One banner at left reads "Pay No Rent." In 1886 Henry George briefly united this constituency with middle-class reformers behind the single tax. From *New York in the Nineteenth Century*, Dover Publications.

Tammany-sponsored barbecue, 1884. Although they were corrupt defenders of the status quo, machine politicians distributed
a portion of the tribute they exacted from the powerful magnates
who shaped the city. From *New York in the Nineteenth Century*,
Dover Publications.

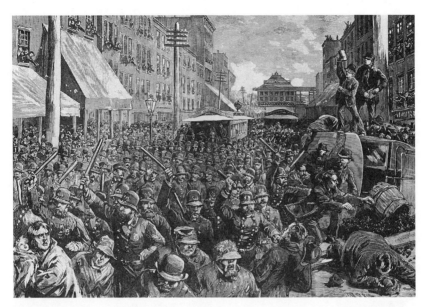

Street railway strike in lower Manhattan, 1886. Essential to the reorganization of the city, the street railway became for many a vulnerable and hated symbol of the new metropolitan order. From *New York in the Nineteenth Century*, Dover Publications.

Court of Honor, looking west from the Peristyle, World's Columbian Exposition, 1893. Disguising the disagreeable aspects of industrialism behind a pleasing prospect, the exposition heralded a new realistic approach to urban development. Courtesy of the Chicago Historical Society (ICHi-02524).

Potter Palmer residence, Lake Shore Drive, Chicago, 1888. Palmer's "angry Gothic castle" represented the new realism in residential arrangements. Such architecture, quipped Montgomery Schulyer, was "not defensible except in a military sense." Photograph by J. W. Taylor. Courtesy of the Chicago Historical Society (ICHi-01256).

Procter and Gamble's Ivorydale plant, ca. 1890, was an early example of the suburbanization of industry. George Pullman warned young Harley Procter of the dangers of providing company housing or a model town, neither of which existed at Ivorydale. Courtesy of the Cincinnati Historical Society.

With the suburbanization of industry, Graham Taylor wrote, the worker's day ended with a streetcar ride back to "the region of brick and pavement, of soot and noise and jostle," like this West End neighborhood in Cincinnati, ca. 1900. Courtesy of the Cincinnati Historical Society.

Brooklyn Terminal, Brooklyn Bridge, 1903. Divorced from the single tax and other social reform initiatives, rapid transit across the bridge handsomely rewarded land speculators and brought high rents and overcrowding to Brooklyn. Courtesy of the Library of Congress (LC-D401-16664).

Cincinnati's hole in the ground, ca. 1920. A series of controversies and the rise of the automobile undermined the city's plans for a rapid transit beltway. Courtesy of the Cincinnati Historical Society.

Lewis Hine's unconventional and humane view of New York's real estate boom included this photograph of a construction worker on the Empire State Building. The skyscraper was completed in 1930. Courtesy of the National Archives (American City List, #79, 69-RH-4K-1).

Congestion at the intersection of Fifth Avenue and 42nd Street, Manhattan. The first step in the scientific management of urban space, George Ford suggested, would be to calculate "the money value of the time of the people involved and . . . the time interest on the capital tied up in vehicles and their load." From the *Regional Plan of New York and its Environs, Vol. 1, The Graphic Regional Plan*, 1929. Courtesy of the New York Regional Plan Association.

Burnham's *Plan of Chicago* was designed to allow the Loop to handle "many times" its current traffic. This photograph of Dearborn Street looking south from Randolph, ca. 1909, was probably staged. By 1911 eighty-five officers directed traffic in the Loop, the first of a series of lavish public subsidies that would promote automobile use. Courtesy of the Chicago Historical Society (ICHi-04191).

New York's Carnegie Playground, ca. 1908–15. Their experience with the organized play movement encouraged the Chicago sociologists to explore new forms of social control for an urban population. Courtesy of the Library of Congress (LC-USZ62-71919).

Deputies attacking a crowd of pickets at a plant near Pittsburgh, 1933. A wave of strikes in the mid-1930s made urban America what the federal report *Our Cities: Their Role in the National Economy* called the "great battleground of the Nation." Labor unrest probably played an important role in encouraging the report's scathing critique of urban life. Courtesy of the Library of Congress (LC-USZ62-38114).

4

The Professionalization of City Planning and the Scientific Management of Urban Space

From high atop the American Railway Building that he had designed, Daniel Burnham surveyed his beloved Chicago. The beautiful watercolor prints that adorned his *Plan of Chicago* and the plan itself reflected a similar lofty perspective of the city's commercial and financial elite. Perhaps better than anyone this "architect of capitalism" understood the enormous pressures exerted by rising realty values in the city. One of his central concerns was to protect those values while eliminating the economic inefficiency with which they were associated. Burnham warned that planless growth was "neither economical nor satisfactory" and that both "overcrowding and congestion of traffic paralyzed" the city's economy. Yet Burnham's interests extended far beyond the central business district.[1]

Just as Jules Guerin's watercolors offered an idealized view of Chicago's future, Burnham too envisioned a harmonious and orderly city. Although Guerin's paintings revealed nothing of the physical squalor and social chaos of metropolitan Chicago, those conditions were very much on Burnham's mind. The view from the city's skyscrapers took in not only the costly congestion in the central business district, but also such reminders of political conflict and social disorder as the Halsted railway yards, Haymarket square, the west side tenement districts, and the distant Pullman. Rapid growth and the influx of "many nationalities without common traditions or habits of life," Burnham knew, had created a demand for a "well-ordered" city.[2] Social efficiency as much as economic efficiency characterized Burnham's plan for Chicago.

THE BEAUTIFICATION OF CONGESTION

In addressing the problem of congestion, Burnham faced the nearly impossible task of easing congestion without threatening the realty values based on that congestion. Between 1877 and 1892, as Chicago dominated an ever-larger region, the value of real estate in the central business district had increased by 700 percent. The extension of mass transit, the construction of the elevated Loop, and the spread of the skyscraper spurred another increase of more than 100 percent between 1894 and 1910.[3] Burnham's patrons in the Commercial Club had no desire to see that trend reversed. The enhanced realty values that resulted from Burnham's lakefront park plans had played an important role in the Commercial Club's commissioning of the *Plan of Chicago*. Nor did Burnham himself have any desire to slow the aggrandizement of what he called the "Metropolis of the Middle West." In the broad prairie surrounding Chicago, Burnham saw an "illimitable space now occupied by a population capable of illimitable expansion."[4] Admiring Haussmann's decision to drive Parisian boulevards far into the surrounding region, Burnham proposed a series of concentric highways encircling the region and a system of arterial roads connecting every nearby town to the metropolis. Chicago officials, he argued, would have to oversee the planning of areas throughout the region "to care for the traffic that will be imposed upon them by reason of their location in relation to the

business district."⁵ Burnham's plan would ensure that the metropolis dominated an ever-larger region.

The pressure on central Chicago, Burnham recognized, would
"increase in geometrical ratio" with the expansion of the metropolitan region. Congestion would strangle Chicago unless it was
redesigned with an eye to efficient circulation. In speeding the
movement of people, the automobile and street improvements
rather than public transit held pride of place in Burnham's plan.⁶
Where congestion reigned, Burnham advised, "new streets must
be created at whatever present cost." The "remorseless cutting of
main lines through the district to be developed" would prove the
most economical in the long run. Even his boulevards, which
were to beautify the city and to serve other social purposes, would
be designed so "that circulation shall be everywhere promoted but
never impeded."⁷ To facilitate the transportation of goods, central
Chicago would be transformed into "a traffic clearing house." A
giant freight-handling center on the southwest side would encourage the decentralization of industry and allow through freight to
be diverted around the city. For handling materials destined for
the city itself, the freight center would mesh with two harbors and
an underground connecting system to "form one complete machine." Those improvements would enable the central business
district to handle "many times" its current traffic, Burnham explained, and protect the interests of Chicago's commercial and financial elites.⁸

Burnham's plan also included benefits to the city's industrial interests. The new freight center would well serve industrialists already located on the southwest side and encourage others to move
there. Burnham's suggestion that the city's freight be handled "as
largely as possibly by machinery" must have pleased industrialists
harried by the city's notoriously militant teamsters.⁹ Beauty would
benefit industrialists as well. Labor productivity necessarily improved in a work force whose "nerves cease to be wracked by
irritating conditions," Burnham explained. Light industries located along the boulevards would benefit from increased sunlight
and fresh air, which would enable labor to "work with greatest

effectiveness." Civic improvements, which Burnham was quick to point out would encourage the wealthy to spend more time and money in the city, would also make Chicago "a good labor market in the sense that labor is sufficiently comfortable to be efficient and content." [10]

Burnham's concern for working people extended beyond the workplace and the demands of economic efficiency to a concern with both social justice and social order. The "lakefront by right belongs to the people," Burnham insisted; recreational opportunities in lakefront parks and wooded preserves would enable wage-earners to "take up the burden of life in our crowded streets and endless stretches of buildings with renewed vigor and hopefulness." Broad boulevards and spacious parks would accommodate "parades and pageants" and "give charm and brightness to the life of people who must of necessity pass long summers in the city." [11] Beauty might even ease class antagonisms. Railway and utility buildings (frequent targets of mob attacks), Burnham advised, should present "a smiling face to the public." A "well-arranged grass plot will often turn away wrath from a public service corporation." [12] Beauty served in the struggle for social efficiency.

In his innovative responses to the problems of capital accumulation, Burnham contributed to the realistic approach to metropolitan development. His response to the social problems of the metropolis, however, still reflected the moral attitudes of the small-town America of his youth. [13] The realistic Burnham argued that beauty "has always paid better than any other commodity, and always will," but the moralistic Burnham insisted that "cities which truly exercise dominion rule by reason of the appeal to the higher emotions of the human mind." [14] A religious man of generous instincts, Burnham valued his plan above all else for its ability to create a moral order in the city. "After all has been said," he argued, "good citizenship is the prime object of good city planning." [15] In this Burnham reflected the larger city beautiful movement, which had its origin in the host of village improvement associations that sought to recapture the sense of community associated with small-town America. [16] City beautiful advocates predicted a moral reawakening as a result of their efforts. Charles Mulford Robinson, for example, called for a city "more prideworthy . . . , more majestic, [and] better worth the devotion and service of its citizens."[17]

In that vein Burnham saw the tenement districts essentially as a moral problem. Fearing that the municipality might some day have to provide housing for those "so degraded by long life in the slums that they have lost all power of caring for themselves," Burnham offered street improvements as an alternative solution.[18] By narrowing residential streets grassy plots could be provided that would induce "habits of neatness and comfort" and bring "people from cellars and dark rooms out into the light, thus contributing to good order and higher humanity." Burnham lauded Haussmann's remaking of old Paris with "its dirty, crowded, ill-smelling, narrow, winding streets, the hotbeds of vice and crime" and advocated similar measures for Chicago. Some districts, like the Halsted-Chicago Avenue district where the 1877 railroad strikes had exploded into violence, represented "a menace to the moral and physical health of the community" and demanded drastic measures. The "cutting of broad thoroughfares through the unwholesome district," Burnham prescribed, would serve to lance the moral inflammation.[19]

A monumental civic center, which was never built, was to be the centerpiece of Burnham's moral order. The civic center would evoke civic loyalty, promote good citizenship, and provide a focus for public life. The "right of the people to assemble for discussion is fundamental," he maintained in a republican vein, and appropriate public spaces must be provided even if at the expense of efficient circulation. Yet Burnham's design seemed to confuse imperial awe with republican virtue. Combining city, county, and federal offices, the civic center would reflect the "dignity and importance of the city," Burnham wrote, and promote the "good order . . . essential to material advancement." The impressive grouping of public buildings would represent "a long step toward cementing together the [city's] heterogeneous elements." In particular the court house would teach Chicago's disorderly masses "the lesson that 'obedience to law is liberty.'" Soaring to an "impressive height, to be seen and felt by the people," the central administration building would serve as a symbol of "civic order and unity."[20] The civic center reflected the uneasy mixture of realistic, moralistic, and even republican elements in Burnham's thought.

The richness of the *Plan of Chicago*, despite its occasional excesses and contradictions, attests to the breadth of vision and largeness of purpose of its author. At first it seems difficult to associate the work of Burnham with the profession of city planning that was just beginning to emerge when the plan was published. His interest in moral order seems to place him closer to Olmsted than to the professional advocates of zoning. His assertion of the rights of the people (to the lakefront, parks, and public spaces) is rather more reminiscent of George and his followers than to the proponents of the city efficient. Moreover, Burnham, like other members of the city beautiful movement, understood the city as a complex social organism for living and working rather than in the more limited terms of the economic machinery of the city efficient.[21]

But unlike other city beautiful advocates, Burnham had a firm grasp of the economic logic of the city efficient.[22] Thus he anticipated the outlook and orientation of the new profession in his championing of metropolitan dominance of the region, his concern with efficient circulation, street improvements, and highway design, and in his working relationship with metropolitan elites. More importantly, he suggested how planning might be divorced from the most controversial issues of the day (low-income housing and mass transit, for example, neither of which figure prominently in his work) and still have a significant impact on urban development. In 1909 when the Commercial Club presented the *Plan of Chicago* to the public, however, the view of a noncontroversial program of city planning was still only a suggestion and not yet a reality. At that time city planning was still part of a wide-ranging political debate about the course of metropolitan development.

THE PLANNING DEBATE

The city planning debate was part of a larger struggle concerning the proper role of government in promoting social progress. As Robert Wiebe and others have argued, both middle-class professionals and businessmen played prominent roles in overturning the laissez-faire and social Darwinist attitudes to economic and social development.[23] Business support for government regulation and public planning often stemmed from a desire to stabilize and legitimate industrial capitalism.[24] The members of the new technical and managerial professions, from medicine to engineering, often provided the personnel for that "search for order" and contributed their own concerns with rationality, order, and social efficiency.

City planning was in part a result of the search for order. At the Second National Conference on City Planning in 1910, Frederick Law Olmsted, Jr., delivered a ringing condemnation of laissez-faire and the unhealthy and wasteful urban environments it created. He argued, "Mankind will not be content with such an attitude after the imagination has grasped the larger possibility of control."[25] Professionals were particularly intrigued by the possibilities of physical and social planning. John Dewey, the philosopher of the reform-minded professionals, argued that the most effective reformation of society depended on "the intelligent selection and determination of the environments in which we act."[26] City planning reflected the effort to reshape the physical and hence the social environment of the American city.

Though some sort of planning was crucial to any effective program of urban reform and a clear advance over the non-policy of laissez-faire, it created problems of its own. Many conservatives opposed planning because they doubted it could be reconciled with a commitment to liberty and free market capitalism. On the left radicals asked whether an effective form of planning demanded some control over economic as well as physical and social development. Even more problematic was the question of whether planning and a reliance on a bevy of experts could be made compatible with democracy. The potential conflict between efficiency and democracy raised the question of who would exercise the "larger possibilities of control," who would select the proper environment for whom.[27] Despite the political nature of such questions, professional planners came to see themselves as disinterested and to see planning as a technical and managerial activity that was above politics. Many believed, in the luckless phrase of the city planner George Ford, that in "almost every case there is one and only one, logical and convincing solution of the problem involved."[28] Whether professionals acknowledged it, however, planning remained a profoundly political undertaking. Moreover, their's was not the only view of the planning province.

The origins of many elements of progressive reform are to be found in the mass discontent organized by Gilded Age radicals as much as in the middle- and upper-class search for order.[29] That was certainly true of the movement for city planning. The republican critique of land speculation and of the costs of congestion and the alternative vision of an urban commonwealth played a major role in undermining the laissez-faire defense of the unplanned city and continued to influence the city planning debate in the Progressive Era. The republican view particularly found expression in the Committee on the Congestion of Population (CCP), whose members organized the First National Conference on City Planning in 1909. Benjamin Marsh, the young secretary of the CCP, was particularly well acquainted with Henry George's work.

An important part of the criticism of the city beautiful movement came from a republican perspective. Marsh, for example, argued:

> [The] grouping of public buildings, and the installation of speedways, parks and drives, which affect only moderately the daily lives of the city's toilers, are important, but vastly more so is the securing of decent home conditions for the countless thousands who otherwise can but occasionally escape from their squalid, confining surroundings . . . to experience the aesthetic delights of the remote improvements.[30]

At the 1909 conference the landscape architect Robert Pope complained that "we have rushed to plan showy civic centers of gigantic cost . . . when pressing hard-by, we see the almost unbelievable congestion with its hideous brood of evil; filth, disease, degeneracy, pauperism, and crime. What external adornment can make truly beautiful such a city?" Is "not external splendor a mockery when cloaking congested slums," Pope asked; the main task of city planning, he insisted, was "to remedy congestion." Those criticisms were overly harsh and, worse, they probably alienated republican sympathizers and potential allies within the city beautiful movement. They certainly aided the realistic proponents of the city efficient who, from a very different perspective, attacked the city beautiful for its extravagance and neglect of economic efficiency.[31] But those criticisms do suggest that an awareness of mass discontent and a desire for social reform played an important role in the origins of the national conference on city planning.[32]

In 1907 a group of settlement leaders, convinced that congestion was a leading cause of distress in their neighborhoods, had organized the Committee on Congestion of Population and launched a campaign to bring relief to the tenement districts. Under the chairmanship of Mary Simkhovitch, the CCP developed an exhibit, including maps, diagrams, charts, statistics, models, and photographs, which toured the country highlighting the social costs of congestion and its connection to realty values. Although parts of the exhibit reflected antiurban attitudes, Simkhovitch developed a positive concept of regional planning that owed a great deal to republican ideals. Speaking before the national conference on city planning, Simkhovitch called for "a rational, conscious suburbanization," that would bring the advantages of urban civilization to the countryside and preserve the advantages of the vibrant urban neighborhood while eliminating dangerous congestion.[33]

The CCP also resembled the republicans in its willingness to tackle the controversial political problems associated with congestion. Citing the social costs of congestion in terms of tuberculosis and infant mortality, Simkhovitch called for a legal limit on population density:

> We can reduce the number of persons to an acre by lowering the limit on the height of tenement houses. This will in some cases result in its being unprofitable to build tenements on very valuable land, and will serve to force people out of cities. It may be that this is unconstitutional, that the society which has created land values can not constitutionally do away with those values. This is a serious question demanding the most careful consideration.

Marsh was even more forthright in his *Introduction to City Planning*, which served as a companion volume to the exhibition. Like Simkhovitch, Marsh linked congestion to death and disease and argued that in an urban community "bulling the real estate market is tantamount to murder of its poorer citizens."[34] At the national conference Marsh continued that line of attack, arguing that "the enormous tribute of disease due to land speculation and exploitation must be checked by the only competent power—the Government." He called for "a commission on land values in our great cities, similar to the Interstate Commerce Commission." Marsh concluded, "It is not my province to determine what is a fair profit on real estate, but it is needless to state that a profit of three or four fold in a few years is prohibitive, is essentially unsafe and unnecessary and undemocratic."[35] In the view of the CPP, political and economic issues were central to an effective program of city planning.

Simkhovitch and Marsh also treated city planning as a democratic process. In a different context Simkhovitch argued that it was "unsound to divorce politics from a passionate interest and turn it into a cold-blooded art for the intellectual"; the CCP exhibit was designed to stimulate public opinion towards a passionate and democratic assault on the problem of congestion. She also understood that an effective program of city planning would have to take into account her neighbors' very real love for urban life.[36] Lillian Wald, another member of the CCP, knew that "not only the East Side 'intellectuals' but the alert proletariat may furnish propagandists of important social reforms."[37] Marsh referred to city planning as the "challenge to democracy" and argued that the problem of inflated land values demanded a "radical change in the attitude of citizens toward government and the functions of government."[38] The members of the CCP understood that their radical proposals demanded a mass democratic movement.

New York City's Commission on Congestion of Population, created in response to the work of the CCP, provided a blueprint for putting those ideas into practice. Adding the overcrowding of factories, low wages, and long hours to land speculation as the prime causes of congestion, the commission urged a coordinated attack on the problem that included stronger factory legislation and enforcement, support for the hour and wage demands of labor unions, the taxation of land at a higher rate than buildings, and the creation of garden cities. In his review of the commission's report, Charles Beard argued that precisely that sort of mixture of economic and physical reconstruction offered the most promising model for a democratic program of city planning.[39] Soon after the commission's report was issued, the 1911 Triangle Shirtwaist Company factory fire, in which one hundred forty-six female employees died, provided the impetus for a democratic assault on the physical and social problems of the metropolis. Unfortunately, the nascent city planning profession was already moving in other directions.

A PARTING OF WAYS

The tragic factory fire focused public opinion on the problems of the industrial working class and spurred the Tammany machine, with the urging of Robert Wagner and Al Smith, to create the New York State Factory Investigating Commission. After holding more than twenty public hearings and making exhaustive and first-hand investigations, the commission successfully recommended passage of fifty-six separate laws related to problems ranging from factory safety, fire and sanitation regulations to minimum wages.[40] In calling for the building of a safer and more healthy city, the commission addressed some of the same issues as did city planners; it also faced some of the same obstacles.

The demand for stricter safety codes for factory buildings and the elimination of tenement sweatshops raised the ire of powerful realty interests. "You can no longer distinguish the real estate owner by the smile of prosperity," complained the counsel of New York's Real Estate Board, "because his property is now a burden and a liability instead of a comfort and source of income."[41] But a powerful Democratic majority in the state legislature, backed by strong public support, overcame such objections. In basing their recommended legislation on the police power and relating their objectives to the health, safety, and welfare of the community, the commissioners frustrated efforts to overturn the legislation in court.

The work of the CCP, the report of the New York City Commission on Congestion of Population, and the success of the Factory Investigating Commission illustrated the potential for a democratic program of city planning linked to a broad agenda of social reform. In fact the Triangle factory fire did play an important role in the development of New York's pioneer zoning resolution. Yet zoning, which became the city planning profession's most important tool, ironically served to separate city planners from the mass discontent and the program of social reform that had given rise to the First National Conference on City Planning.[42] The widening gap between social reformers and professional city planners would illustrate Sam Bass Warner's contention that "the late development of the labor movement, legitimatized only in the mid-thirties, and the consequent failure of the labor and urban reform movements to coalesce have contributed to the heavy middle-class bias of our urban programs—and weakened all attempts to serve the lowest third of our population." Yet the work of the Factory Investigating Commission did contribute to the development of an important alternative to the realistic vision of the city planning profession, an alternative that carried republican ideals into the 1920s.[43]

Strengthening Tammany Hall's support among the city's working class and poor and improving its reputation among reformers, the Factory Investigating Commission catapulted both Smith and Wagner to state and national prominence. As governor of New York, Smith created a New York State Commission of Housing and Regional Planning (CHRP) in 1923.[44] In creating the CHRP Smith reached out to the dissenting architects and planners who had organized the Regional Planning Association of America (RPAA). Lewis Mumford, the intellectual leader of the RPAA, was a prominent critic of metropolitan aggrandizement who urged planners to recognize the "interdependence of city and country." That interdependence led Mumford and his colleagues to embrace the garden city ideal.[45] The garden city ideal, based on a balancing of the advantages of urban life with those of rural life, a limitation on the size of cities, and the communal ownership of land, owed a great deal to republican ideals and especially to Henry George. Placing the garden city in the larger context of regional planning, the RPAA extended the republicans' political approach to urban development.[46]

Recognizing the political determinants of urban development, Mumford and his colleagues proposed a new set of political priorities as the key to implementing regional planning and creating garden cities.[47] In a critique of metropolitan aggrandizement, Mumford explained, "Regional planning asks not how wide an area can be brought under the aegis of the metropolis, but how the population and civic facilities can be distributed so as to promote and stimulate a vivid creative life throughout the whole region."[48] Clarence Stein (a member of the RPAA and chairman of the CHRP) added, "To the few the great city gives all. To the millions it gives annually less and less."[49] Regional planning would redress that balance. New York State, Smith argued, "must be planned to serve the interests of every man, woman, and child and to give opportunity for a fuller and finer life, and not for the benefit of privileged groups."[50] Thus Governor Smith endorsed the view of planning as part of a larger program of social reform.

In an extensive survey of New York City's housing stock conducted in 1925, the CHRP found that for the two-thirds of the city's families with income less than twenty-five hundred dollars, not even the minimum standards of the 1901 tenement law could be met. Thousands of the old-law tenements had been destroyed, but the slow pace and high cost of new construction had forced even more people into those remaining. The fifty thousand new tenement apartments built since 1901 rented at twice what the average family could afford. Since financing represented as much as 55 percent of the expense in the costs of commercial construction, the CHRP argued that "responsible officers of financial institutions should recognize a social responsibility" to provide low-cost mortgages for low-income housing. The public should "insist on the realization of the social trust as well." The CHRP harbored no "real hopes" for the private market, however, and concluded that public credit, tax exemptions, and innovative land-use planning were necessary to solve the housing problem.[51]

The philanthropic, limited-dividend housing corporation might possibly provide low-income housing, but the CHRP regretted that such ventures "cannot get adequate capital." Granting tax exemptions for new housing, as provided for in New York's 1920 tax law, attracted capital to the field; but the law had failed to provide for minimum standards and maximum profits.[52] In New York City, Roy Lubove argues, the law had subsidized speculative builders rather than tenants.[53] At the urging of the CHRP, the legislature amended the law in 1926 to exempt only limited-dividend corporations from state taxes and authorized municipalities to similarly waive local taxes.

To illustrate the usefulness of the law, the RPAA, in cooperation with the philanthropist Alexander Bing, organized the City Housing Corporation, which built the model communities of Sunnyside in Queens and Radburn, New Jersey. Stein and fellow architect Henry Wright illustrated the advantages of cooperative residential planning in their design for Sunnyside. Using the block rather than the individual lot as the unit of planning, their one-, two-, and three-family row houses covered only 28 percent of the total block; speculative projects covered from 50 to 90 percent.

Collecting the remaining open space into an interior commons on each block, Stein and Wright provided both a parentally supervised play area for children and a focus for neighborliness. But the experiment also revealed that serious obstacles to community planning and to the solution of the housing problem remained. Burdened at Sunnyside with New York's excessive and wasteful grid of streets and utilities, Wright insisted that the comprehensive planning of streets and utilities as well as housing was crucial to proper community development.[54] More troublesome, the Sunnyside experience proved that even under the best conditions, philanthropy could provide decent housing only at a cost above what New York's poorer two-thirds could pay.

The work of the CHRP and the Sunnyside experiment convinced Mumford that the housing question was not simply a problem of minimum standards. It concerned nothing less than the question of "how the great mass of people with an income below a decent subsistence level can purchase for themselves the necessities of life." A solution to the problem, he insisted, depended on a society "willing to distribute the income of industry with some relation to the biological needs of the worker."[55] Governor Smith agreed that building housing "for wage earners of small income is unprofitable under the existing system." In 1926 Smith and the CHRP called for the creation of a state housing bank, armed with the power of condemnation, to provide funds and building sites at a nonspeculative cost for limited-dividend corporations.[56]

Although the New York state legislature failed to act on those recommendations, Mumford attended the 1927 national conference on city planning in order to impress the seriousness of the problem on professional planners. If planners were to improve living conditions, they could no longer plan on the basis of past trends with an eye to "limitless growth and expansion" and grand financial returns, Mumford told the conferees. Better housing and a more healthful distribution of population would have to become their primary concerns. If the speculative cost of real estate and of investment capital stood in the way of those goals, he concluded, then these too must be subjected to "intelligent social control."[57]

Mumford pleaded for a program of city planning with social reform as its primary goal. He spoke to a profession, however,
which since its inception had moved steadily away from social
reform and into close partnership with the dominant economic
interests.

THE PROFESSIONALIZATION OF PLANNING

Benjamin Marsh, who worked as hard as anyone to make city
planning a vehicle for social reform, later charged that "speculators and bankers had captured the city planning movement."
Marsh knew what he was talking about. In a series of efforts to
shift the burden of taxation in New York from buildings to land
values, he earned the ill will of some of the city's most powerful
institutions from the New York Real Estate Board to the Catholic
church. By the time of the CCP exhibit, his reputation was secure.
"I don't believe you know how radical that man Marsh is," Standard Oil executive Charles Pratt explained to a CCP representative in refusing to contribute to its work. Upon meeting Marsh
and learning of his enthusiasm for the single tax, Robert DeForest
had warned him that "if you touch the land problem in New York,
you probably won't last here two years."[58] Marsh lasted longer
than two years, but the pressure on him took its toll.

By 1910, when he testified before Congress on the city planning
movement, Marsh had begun to make concessions to the powerful
opposition he faced. Although he continued to insist that low
wages were part of the housing problem, he assured the politicians
that he was not a single-taxer.[59] Six years later when leading planners such as John Nolen were urging their colleagues to remember
that the "controlling purpose of land subdivision is profit" and the
younger Olmsted was acknowledging that the basis of the American city "must inevitably be in private ownership," Marsh had
already abandoned the movement to pursue other initiatives.[60]
Five years later New York's city engineer would warn planners at

the national conference against "throttling the speculative instinct and vision of the real estate developer to which, if kept within reasonable bounds, every city owes so much in what spells progress."[61] Whether or not speculators, bankers and other powerful economic interests actually controlled the city planning movement, they certainly had a profound influence on its development. The arcane process of professionalization, however, also had its impact.

At the First National Conference on City Planning, Robert Pope advocated the creation of "a profession equipped to make city planning the social and economic factor it ought to be."[62] The organizing committee created at that conference included representatives of the Committee on Congestion of Population, the American Institute of Architects, the League of American Municipalities, the American Society of Landscape Architects, the American Civic Association, and the National Conference of Charities and Corrections. The composition of the organizing committee, argued civil engineer George Swain in 1912, reflected the belief that city planning was primarily an architectural and sociological problem. Swain lauded the multifaceted approach to planning, but he protested that the role of the engineer had been neglected. While illustrating the eclectic nature of the profession's origins, Swain overestimated the extent to which the engineering perspective had been excluded from the early movement.[63]

As early as 1910 Olmsted had noted the paramount importance of "treating all the means of circulation in a city as a single connected system, and at the same time of recognizing clearly the differentiation of all its parts, so that each shall fit its function simply but without waste, from the biggest terminal down to the smallest alley." The influence of the engineering perspective grew in the years following Swain's protest.[64] In 1913 George Ford boasted that "city planning is becoming as definite a science as pure engineering."[65] Three years later New York's chief engineer Nelson Lewis argued that "the fundamental problems of city planning are, and from their very nature must be, engineering problems." Social issues such as low-income housing and public health,

Lewis concluded, "were matters of administration rather than planning."[66] As the profession donned scientific pretensions, the engineering perspective tended to crowd out the interest in social reform.

Professionalization also narrowed the occupational composition of the city planning movement and the educational background of its members. Representatives of five occupations (landscape architects, engineers, attorneys, architects, and realtors) accounted for nearly three-fourths of the charter members of the American City Planning Institute, the planners' professional organization creation in 1917. At least ten of the charter members were graduates or employees of Harvard, where the profession edited its own journal beginning in 1917 and created the nation's first school of city planning in 1929.[67] Of the eighteen contributors to John Nolen's professional handbook published in 1916, nine had received a degree from Harvard.[68]

The scientific pretensions and elite education of planners won them a measure of professional recognition, but it tended to divorce planning from the social and political forces that had originally given rise to the demand for city planning. Professional planners lost sight of the very people in whose interests they claimed to plan. The hopes, fears, and aspirations of local neighborhoods and communities became increasingly marginal factors in professional planning. As early as 1913 George Ford had complained that "our best laid plans may be interfered with by some political or local prejudice," ignoring the possibility that the planners' own proposals represented political choices or that local traditions were based on sound reasoning.[69] Six years later Bruno Lasker charged that planners knew only the "viewpoint of the master class" and urged them to acquaint themselves with the viewpoint of the neighborhood.[70]

A lingering concern with social reform survived within the profession even into the 1920s, but it was a decidedly minor theme. In 1921 the national conference adopted a resolution "that every city should create conditions that will make one-family detached houses possible for people with small incomes." The planner's first responsibility was "to protect those who cannot protect themselves," argued Robert Whitten at the same conference. In 1927 no less a figure than Henry Hubbard, editor of the profession's journal and founding director of the Harvard School of City Planning, still saw city planning as a powerful instrument for social reform. Meeting head-on those skeptics who doubted whether city planning constituted a true profession "distinct from architecture, engineering, law, or some other already existing and recognized profession," Hubbard argued that city planning synthesized "all the fields of human endeavor that concern themselves with the bettering of the surroundings of civilized humanity." City planning was not only a legitimate profession, he concluded, but a profoundly humanistic one.[71] Hubbard's ideal, however, worked against the trend toward specialization within the profession.

THE STRANGE CAREER OF EXCLUSIONARY ZONING

The most important factor in the early development of the city planning profession was zoning. Essentially a legal device, zoning divided the city into districts with specified uses and limitations on the height and bulk of buildings. The legal and technical problems associated with zoning helped planners to lay claim to expert status. E. M. Bassett, eager to establish city planning as a recognized profession, explained that he had tried to "separate city planning from architecture, landscape architecture, and cognate callings." Defining planning as the legal platting of the city and its zoning districts, Bassett warned that any effort to "broaden" planning beyond that would make it "meaningless." The limited and specific objectives of zoning served to isolate the profession from controversial discussions of social reform.[72]

To be sure some saw zoning as the high road to social reform, free of the divisiveness and uncertainties of earlier efforts. The mechanical aspects of the city, wrote architect John Taylor Boyd, "function more efficiently, and reach higher standards than do the

137

non-mechanical activities of political administration and of social and economic relationships." Zoning's transformation of the city into a smooth-running mechanism would not only be easier than previous efforts at social reform, but it would provide unexpected benefits. With the perfection of the city's mechanical organization, Boyd concluded, "the political and social side of the city, with all its human relationships, might become more wholesome."[73] While this view had very little impact on the city planning profession in the 1920s, it does suggest the lingering association of zoning and social reform and the complex origins of zoning.

The original enthusiasm for zoning had grown out of the larger planning debate. In his *Introduction to City Planning*, Marsh described zoning as a key to the success of German city planning and to the future health of the American city. What particularly attracted Marsh and other planning advocates to German zoning was its association with the public ownership of land and a progressive land tax policy. In German cities where as much as 60 percent of urban real estate was publically owned and up to 10 percent of speculative realty values were taken in taxation, zoning gave the municipality considerable control over urban development. At the first national conference several participants spoke glowingly of the German city and the promise of zoning.[74]

Social reformers, especially Frederic Howe, were also fascinated with the German example of zoning's promise.[75] In fact the history of social reform intersected at several points with the origins of zoning. The Triangle factory fire spurred the zoning movement, when public outrage was directed at the serious overcrowding of the garment industry's multi-story lofts. The enthusiasm for rapid transit also had its impact on the zoning movement. In 1912 public service commissioner Bassett, concerned that new subway extensions would exacerbate the already critical problem of congestion among lower Manhattan's skyscrapers, began exploring new building regulations with Manhattan Borough president McAneny and other city officials. Their concerns would soon become an important reason for the appointment of a new commission.[76]

The composition of New York City's Heights of Buildings

Commission (HBC), appointed by Mayor William J. Gaynor in 1913, reflected those diverse origins. The HBC included Abram I. Elkus, a prominent and reform-minded lawyer who had served as counsel to the Factory Investigating Committee, and Lawson Purdy, president of the city's tax commission who had at one time promoted Georgist tax reforms from a soapbox in Madison Square. The HBC also included the foremost authority on the tenement problem, Lawrence Veiller.[77] Befitting its origins, zoning seemed to be in the hands of a group of men interested in social reform. Even HBC chairman Bassett, not known as a crusading social reformer, professed a commitment to the decentralization of population and the single-family home. Despite his own role in gutting the reformist potential of New York's subways, he would continue to argue that rapid transit was "the only thing that will bring low rent and sunny homes to working people in great cities."[78]

The city's financial and commercial interests, however, were also well represented on the commission. The HBC included four major realtors, two large commercial builders, two manufacturers, and two members of the Fifth Avenue Association of merchants. Despite the diversity of zoning's origins and the membership of the HBC, the commissioners gave relatively little attention to the problems of industrial safety and housing that had contributed to the original interest in zoning. Their 1913 report emphasized "first, regulation of high buildings, second, districting, and third, Fifth Avenue conditions. No specific recommendations were made on factories and residences."[79] The dominant perspective of the Heights of Buildings Commission, as its official name suggests, was that of the city's skyscraping financial and commercial elite.[80]

The issue of height limitations had first been raised in 1912 by the quasi-official Fifth Avenue Commission, created at the request of the Fifth Avenue Association of merchants and composed of six of its members and the city's chief engineer. Recommending a height limitation of 125 feet in the Fifth Avenue area, the merchants hoped to exclude the lofts and especially the immigrant labor force of the garment industry from their fashionable shopping district. They became the most vocal supporters of zoning. But height limitations also concerned the skyscraping business district of lower Manhattan. City officials facing improved rapid transit feared that the concentration of population had already overwhelmed their ability to deal with a serious fire or other catastrophe. The HBC observed, "This being the situation to-day, the question arises as to what might happen in case of a general panic should the entire district be solidly built up with buildings of the present extreme heights."[81]

The tendency of skyscrapers to rob the air and sunlight from surrounding buildings created additional problems, not only for the health of office workers but for the stability of realty values.[82] Bassett later explained that the "real estate owners were at a loss to know what to do with their property. They were looking at any angle as a talking point and they were more inclined to help along a promising plan like zoning."[83] The instability of realty values, which began with the financial panic of 1907 and was exacerbated by the expansion of transit facilities and skyscraper construction, won over the downtown property owners to modest height limitations (three hundred feet with the mandatory use of setbacks above that height). With the support of those powerful interests, the HBC successfully recommended state legislation granting the city the power to establish building zones.

The HBC proved conservative, however, even in its approach to building controls. Reformers from George to Marsh had pointed to the need for public control of land to limit the role of speculation in city building. But Purdy, who was well acquainted with such arguments, promised to "pay reasonable regard to the character of buildings in making its zoning regulations in order to enhance the value of land and conserve the value of buildings."[84] As Purdy's case suggests, the imperative of allaying the fears of the city's realty interests shaped many of the commissioners' decisions. They rejected the acquisition of city land through the power of eminent domain, their 1913 report explained, precisely because the "expense and burden of condemnation proceedings and litigation in multitudinous cases would create a tax burden that would increase rather than compensate for injury to property interests."[85] Instead the HBC relied on the city's police power to protect the health, safety, and welfare of its citizens. The police power provided the city with a relatively cost-free method of limiting the height, bulk, and uses of buildings; but the commissioners used that power cautiously. They decided against dealing retroactively with inappropriate buildings (a power upheld by the Supreme Court in 1915) because, as Bassett later explained, "the purpose of zoning was to stabilize and protect lawful investment and not to injure assessed valuations or existing uses."[86] The influence of financial and commercial interests had transformed zoning into an effective defense of their interests.

The greatest long-term impact of zoning, however, stemmed from its role in preserving suburban residential districts from invasion by industry or low-income housing. That aspect of zoning had been foreshadowed in the HBC's 1913 report. The interest in exclusive residential districts stemmed from the same principle as the Fifth Avenue merchants' desire for exclusive shopping districts. Both were predicated on the need to divorce the alluring consumer benefits of industrial society from the disagreeable aspects of industrial production. Robert Cooke of the Fifth Avenue Association complained of the "appalling" invasion of the fashionable shopping district by the workers of the nearby garment district: "Nothing so blasting to the best class of business and property interests has ever been seen or known in any great retail district as this vast flood of workers which sweeps down the pavements at noontime every day and literally overwhelms and engulfs shops, shopkeeper and the shopping public." For J. Howes Burton, also of the Fifth Avenue Association, the exclusionary principle concerned not just Fifth Avenue but "the very heart of New York, and comprised all that makes the city worth while as a place to shop, play, work, and live in."[87] Residential developers, the HBC noted, used restrictive covenants to exclude "apartments, stores or factories" and ensure "the creation and maintenance of a residence section of a certain desired type."[88] But restrictive covenants created legal and practical problems; zoning would provide a more effective and legally sound method of protecting the residential suburb.[89]

The use of zoning to protect residential suburbs also appealed to those interested in promoting the single-family residence. But its ultimate inclusion in the zoning resolution owed more to the imperatives of legal justification than social reform. As a proper constitutional use of the police power, the zoning resolution would have to be not only nondiscriminatory but based on, as the leading expert on the police power put it, "an informed and deliberate public opinion."[90] If zoning restrictions were applied to the Fifth Avenue and Wall Street districts alone, the zoning resolution might be declared a discriminatory and hence unconstitutional use of the police power. But "as part of a comprehensive plan for the control of building development throughout the entire city" it could be legally defended.[91] Between 1913 and 1916 a second commission, similar in composition to the first, was charged with the responsibility of making specific recommendations. Bassett and other members of the commission attended public meetings with homeowners in the fashionable districts of the city. As a result certain neighborhoods were zoned as exclusively residential districts, from which not only commercial and industrial enterprises but low-income and multifamily buildings were excluded. In conjunction with the campaign of the Fifth Avenue merchants, the public meetings constituted the informed and deliberate public opinion on which zoning's legality rested.

In the 1920s zoning became the lodestar of the profession and it spread across the country. Bassett understood that as "court approval of police power regulations depended to a large extent on the general use and application of that form of regulation, we ought to spread zoning throughout the country." During the next twenty years, Bassett did exactly that as counsel to the second zoning commission.[92] In 1921, at the behest of Commerce secretary Hoover, Bassett helped Nelson Lewis and Veiller draft the Standard State Zoning Enabling Act, which included provisions for "the creation of one-family residence districts."[93] Chicago enacted its zoning law in 1923; Cincinnati followed a year later. By the end of the decade nearly eight hundred cities, representing 60 percent of the nation's urban population, had adopted zoning resolutions.[94]

"THE LEGAL AGENT OF INTELLIGENT CITY PLANNING"

Notwithstanding its great popularity among professionals, zoning had relatively little to do with any broader conception of city planning. In the best of circumstances, Lewis Mumford argued in 1929, zoning represented "the legal agent of intelligent city planning." In establishing a "social concept of real property," zoning had "performed a salutary service to the commonwealth." But the host of cities that had adopted zoning legislation as a substitute for comprehensive planning, Mumford feared, revealed the widespread misconception that "zoning is an automatic relief for all the evils of unregulated or badly regulated city development."[95] Once divorced from a broader conception of city planning, zoning encouraged or at best regulated existing trends.

Although the zoning ideal superficially resembled Ebenezer Howard's garden city scheme, it actually owed more to metropolitan trends dating back to the late-nineteenth century. Howard argued that controlling the size of cities was the essential first step in planning, but zoning advocates accepted and even encouraged unlimited metropolitan growth.[96] New York's zoning resolution allowed for a residential population of 77 million and a working population of 344 million.[97] Chicago's resolution would have enabled Chicago to crowd the entire population of the United States as well as all the trade and industry of the Midwest within its borders.[98] Howard had not only urged that industrial areas be segregated from residential ones, but he had hoped to make industrial production compatible with a cooperative social order. Zoning merely extended the effort to segregate the disagreeable elements of industrial production, including industrial workers, from the consumer culture upon which the legitimacy of corporate capitalism increasingly rested.[99] The segregation of factories and low-income housing from exclusive residential and shopping districts represented the acme of the zoning ideal. At best it provided a legal framework for preventing gross disorder from disrupting the status quo, but at the same time zoning preempted the growth of alternative plans of development.[100]

In their infatuation with zoning, professionals abdicated the responsibility to plan. Instead they opted to manage existing trends in concert with the powerful. As they retreated from the challenge of imagining alternatives, professional planners embraced the comforting theory that the crucial factors of urban development were beyond their control. Certainly there was some truth in the statement of John Ihdler, one of the more reform-minded planners, that "there are forces beyond our control which determine the location and size of cities."[101] When George Ford urged planners to study the "laws" of urban growth, at least he argued that those laws could in some measure be "controlled or modified by intelligent planning."[102] More disturbing was Robert Whitten's response to the charge that zoning segregated residential districts along economic and racial lines and permitted dangerous congestion in lower-class districts. Such problems were inevitable, he argued, but perhaps zoning did "in a small measure . . . facilitate the natural trend."[103]

The professionals' insistence that their efforts were distinct from larger political conflicts underwrote such casuistry and disguised their subservience to vested interests. The Chicago Plan Commission's Walter Moody found "something paradoxical in the whole situation of labor versus capital." Rather than being "devised solely in the interest of a class," the Chicago plan was a rational plan "worked out by experts," he insisted, and would benefit all equally.[104] Such planning organizations as the Sage Foundation's Regional Plan Association, argued Thomas Adams, were "free from political influence."[105] City planning, according to Harland Bartholomew, concerned the "physical rather than the political development of cities."[106] Such statements obscured the role of political and economic power in both urban development and city planning.

Despite the planners' caveats the distribution of economic and political power influenced both planning and zoning. As Bassett frankly explained to a group of Chicago realtors, it was the "practical people," the property owners, who would determine the zoning regulations.[107] Acknowledging that under New York's zoning resolution "a very congested type of tenement can still be built," Bassett was sincerely "trying to bring about some amelioration to that, but the officials are not responding as readily as we might wish because they do not feel any popular demand."[108] The officials did not feel any public demand at least partly because Bassett and the other zoning commissioners had done little to organize such a demand. The "grass roots" campaign conducted by New York's zoning commission reached down only as far as middle-class home owners. The social groups generally found in the tenement districts had little to do with the zoning campaign.[109] Those planners who genuinely hoped to secure social reforms limited their own effectiveness by failing to enlist popular support.

The effects of zoning reflected the character of the political forces that supported it. While managing the conflicting rights of property owners and stabilizing realty values, zoning did little to improve conditions in the tenement districts and actually exacerbated the problem of residential segregation. The most important legal challenge to zoning, *Ambler Realty Co. v. Village of Euclid*, illustrated that point. Situated on Cleveland's eastern border, Euclid lay in the path of the larger city's industrial and commercial expansion. Euclid's zoning resolution would halt that expansion by establishing exclusive residential districts. The resolution was unconstitutional, federal judge David Westenhaver argued, because it restricted the property rights of the Ambler Realty Company, which held speculative real estate in the village. Westenhaver thus declared Euclid's zoning resolution invalid not because it was unfair to those in need of low-income housing, but because it interfered with free market forces. His decision did include, however, the gratuitous charge that zoning tended to "classify the population and segregate them according to their income or situation in life." No crusading reformer, Westenhaver nevertheless recognized that zoning played an important role in "furthering such class tendencies."[110]

When the case reached the Supreme Court, Ambler's attorney, Newton Baker, argued that the zoning resolution was an unconstitutional use of the police power because it was not supported by an informed public opinion. Zoning advocates, he argued, had made only a limited effort to develop "new conceptions of social needs" such as the "communal control of private property" which would "bring within the legislative power fields previously not occupied."[111] While Baker's arguments did not convince the Supreme Court, which overturned Westenhaver's decision and firmly established the constitutionality of zoning, the one-time reformer understood how widely zoning and social reform had diverged and how little of zoning's initial promise had been realized.

Of course tenement dwellers, labor leaders, and social reformers can be blamed for failing to shape the zoning resolution to their needs and ideals. In fact, some of New York's building trade unions did oppose zoning for the less than admirable reason that its restrictions threatened jobs.[112] Elsewhere labor leaders, as one planner explained, complained that zoning allowed the well-to-do to "live in protected . . . restricted home neighborhoods and let all the stables and public garages and other dirty businesses intrude into any block of workers' home neighborhoods."[113] But such isolated protests had little impact. Part of the problem was that the political strategy behind the zoning campaign had been conceived in such a way as to exclude the propertyless. New York's 1916 zoning resolution was the result of a series of compromises among realtors, merchants, industrialists, and, to a lesser extent, home owners. The propertyless were simply not part of the bargaining.

The legal principles behind zoning as well as the entire legal process surrounding it also held the rights of property predominant.[114] In 1917 when the Supreme Court invalidated a Louisville zoning ordinance that created racial districts, it did so not on the basis of social justice but on the right of sellers to choose their buyers. In 1924 when the Supreme Court upheld once and for all the legality of zoning in the *Euclid* case, it based its decision on the doctrine of *sic utere tuo. ut alienum non laedus* (use your own property in such a way as not to injure that of another).[115] Once established, zoning regulations could be challenged before a zoning appeals board, but only by property owners deprived of a fair return on their property.[116] Property owners loved zoning, George Ford reported; they "throng hearings to protect their rights as established by zoning."[117] Without legal standing, one critic noticed, the propertyless were left to resent the "invasion of their district by big public garages which house the motors of prosperous citizens."[118] Through zoning the management of conflicting property rights came to define the essence and the limits of professional city planning.

THE SCIENTIFIC MANAGEMENT OF URBAN SPACE

In the 1920s the Russell Sage Foundation's *Regional Plan of New York and its Environs* (RPNYE), the most ambitious planning project of the period, extended the close association of planners and property interests that had emerged during New York's zoning campaign. The inspiration of Charles Norton, a patron of the *Plan of Chicago*, the RPNYE completed its work while New York was tripling its office space with such massive projects as the Empire State Building, the Chrysler Building, and Rockefeller Center. Enlisting the efforts of New York's most talented and powerful leaders, the RPNYE's board of directors included representatives of such institutions as J. P. Morgan and Company, the Rockefeller Institute, and the First National Bank of New York, which were the architects of the real estate boom. The experiences of Bassett, Purdy, McAneny, and Lewis (all veterans of the zoning campaign) with what was rapidly becoming New York's dominant industry also shaped the work of the RPNYE.[119]

But the RPNYE did not simply do the bidding of the realty interests. Its greatest achievement was the development of a strategy that maximized opportunities for capital accumulation while si-

147

multaneously managing the conflicting needs of realty, financial, construction, and industrial interests.[120] That strategy, first outlined in New York's zoning resolution, might best be called the scientific management of urban space.

A central element in the scientific management of urban space was the long-time dream of real estate promoters, expressed by Henry Morgenthau at the First National Conference on City Planning, to devote all of Manhattan below Fifty-ninth Street to those financial and commercial uses that would maximize realty values. What had been called the "city beautiful" would give way to the "city rentable."[121] The mix of land uses south of Fifty-ninth Street occasioned an uncharacteristic sense of outrage in planners who had been hardened to the intractable problems of the tenement districts.

> Some of the poorest people live in conveniently located slums on high priced land. On patrician Fifth Avenue, Tiffany and Woolworth, cheek by jowl, offer jewels and jimcracks from substantially identical sites. Child's Restaurants thrive where Delmonico's withered and died. A stone's throw from the stock exchange the air is filled with the aroma of roasting coffee; a few hundred feet from Times Square, with the stench of slaughter houses. In the very heart of this "commercial" city on Manhattan Island south of 59th Street, the inspectors in 1922 found nearly 420,000 workers employed in factories. Such a situation outrages one's sense of order. Everything seems misplaced. One yearns to re-arrange the hodgepodge and to put things where they belong.

Certain activities, "managing and administering, buying and selling, financing and risk-bearing, investigating and advising," belonged in the central city. Others did not.[122]

Market forces generally provided for the dominance of the higher functions; but where they did not, as in the case of the garment industry, the scientific managers of urban space would step in to encourage a more rational, and profitable, use of space. That, the RPNYE explained, was the essence of city planning.

> One of the most stupendous dreams of the social control of civilization concerns the remaking of cities. It is proposed to decen-

148

tralize them deliberately. By removing obstacles or interposing deflecting factors, the decentralization which is actually going on may be guided, accelerated and focused. This is the meaning of city planning. In the process of deliberate decentralization, science is ultimately to decide what elements in the present city ought to remain and what ought to go.

The natural law at the core of that science was the maximization of realty values.[123]

Although the maximum realty values meant that most industrial production would be removed from Manhattan, the RPNYE planners were not insensitive to the needs of industry. The "American city must be planned," explained planning director Thomas Adams, as "a center of highly organized and standardized production." Professional planners had gained valuable experience since the zoning crusade that would guide the work of the RPNYE. During World War I, when planners offered their services to the Council on National Defense and built army cantonments, industrial plants, and workers' housing, the profession became acquainted with the high rate of labor turnover and other problems facing the industrial employer.[124] Professionals increasingly included the problems of industrial design in their understanding of planning. Zoning, Charles Cheney argued in 1919, would "guarantee a definite and safe place for industrial investment . . . and assure more contented labor conditions." Alfred Bettman suggested in 1923 that the city plan performs the same function for the city as a plan for an industrial plant. Planning, George Ford added in 1924, meant "merely doing for the city what every good business man or manufacturer does for his own plant."[125] Industrial efficiency and the promotion of a stable work force, planners had come to understand, were important elements in a comprehensive city plan.

The brief popularity of the Industrial Workers of the World and other radical groups and especially the postwar wave of strikes focused new attention on the tenement and the slum as factors in the labor problem. The ugliness and disorder of the industrial city, John Nolen argued in 1919, was "one of the main causes of unrest and strikes." Poor housing and living conditions, the veteran housing reformer Lawrence Veiller added in 1920, were key factors behind "industrial discontent and low productivity." In exploring that theme Veiller explained that the "slum is exactly like a cancer on the body social and the body politic." Conditions in the tenements drove workers to the IWW and other radical groups. "'Destroy all the skyscrapers and tenement houses of the present. Build hoses surrounded by garden and orchards,'" read Veiller from a radical manifesto distributed in the streets. "This may not be divine discontent," he argued, "but it is discontent that must be reckoned with." Thus Veiller seconded Ihdler's hope that the new "liberal attitude" of employers, even if inspired by "a fear of labor," would encourage them to attack the housing shortage and other community problems.[126]

Veiller broadened the discussion in 1922 in an article titled "Are Great Cities a Menace?" Recent strikes in New York, Veiller argued, had demonstrated "that a small group of men, controlling vast numbers of workers, held the city in the hollow of their hand, and by their ability to manipulate the transportation of the city and its food supplies could . . . bring New York to its knees." Quoting Lord Bryce, Veiller warned of the dangers of the great city:

> People live in crowds, under the ceaseless stimulus of always seeing one another in crowds, always moving to and fro in street cars and railroads and automobiles . . . at an increasing rate of speed. . . . The more men are crowded in great masses the more easily they become excited, the more they are swept away by words, and the more they form what might be called a revolutionary temper.

Such concerns drove Veiller to a consideration of the garden city idea, an idea he had long resisted. Having been assured by Ebenezer Howard that the public ownership of land was not an essential part of the garden city, Veiller recommended it to employers concerned with the "stabilizing of labor" through the "improvement of the living environment of the workers."[127]

Apparently employers heeded only part of Veiller's message. In 1924 George Ford argued that "industry and wholesale business must be legislated or pushed or encouraged to move out into the suburbs." While he found a "marked tendency" towards industrial decentralization, he lamented that the "majority of workers" were "still living in the heart of the city . . . spending much time and energy in commuting."[128] The pattern of industrial decentralization established at the turn of the century, a pattern that did not generally include improved housing for the laboring population, continued into the 1920s.

The RPNYE planners joined in the enthusiasm for industrial decentralization. Congestion and other diseconomies of scale had made Manhattan an inefficient place for manufacturing. Trade unions had created additional problems. The RPNYE planners heard "much complaint regarding the competitive disadvantage suffered because of the 'exactions' of trade unions." Cigar and silk manufacturers blamed difficulties with trade unions for their decision to leave the region. One clothing manufacturer bluntly revealed his "intention to move his plant from New York to some town where he could tell those damned Bolsheviks to go to hell." The "trade unions appeared to find it an easier task to organize workers in a large city," the planners reported.[129] The region included hundreds of new sites for industrial development free of Manhattan's drawbacks, however, of which the RPNYE compiled a careful inventory.

The regional planning of the RPNYE was far different from the regional planning simultaneously promoted by Mumford and his colleagues in the RPAA.[130] Essentially zoning writ large, the Regional Plan of New York and Its Environs was geared towards the needs of capital accumulation. "The metropolis," the RPNYE planners explained, "is essentially a piece of productive economic machinery competing with other metropolitan machines." The economic costs of congestion, which made the metropolitan machine less competitive, had long concerned planners. While helping to draft New York's zoning resolution George Ford had argued:

Counts should be taken with a view to determining the loss of time to pedestrians and to the various forms of traffic due to

151

congestion and blocks caused by the narrowness of the street. This loss of time multiplied by the money value of the time of the people involved and by the time interest on the capital tied up in vehicles and their loads, will give a definite figure.

The urban development of the past fifty years, the RPNYE argued in the same vein, had made the city "slower and less efficient."[131] The RPNYE was determined to speed the circulation and hence the accumulation of capital.

In addressing that task the RPNYE planners looked to the example of industrial production. The "area of New York and its environs may be likened to the floor space of a factory," the RPNYE planners explained. Transport systems and land uses would be arranged so as to minimize the frictions of space and eliminate unnecessary movement. The rearrangement of the region would not only bring the many superfluous rural inhabitants into the metropolitan circulation of "shirts, breakfast foods, radio, and warm radiators," but it would benefit manufacturers through the "lower cost of supplying consumption goods at convenient assembly points."[132] In its review of the completed regional plan, the *New York Times* marveled that people and goods would move throughout the region "with the precision of parts and materials through a modern automobile factory."[133] Indeed, the RPNYE planners had borrowed the strategy and the techniques of the scientific managers of wage labor, who had sought to maximize profits through the control of the labor process.

THE VELOCITY OF CAPITAL AND THE PROBLEM OF COMMUNITY

Henry Ford's River Rouge plant provided a model of such planning. The Rouge site, an undeveloped valley in suburban Detroit, "had been tamed, paved, and molded in steel and concrete into geometric forms of an industrial design," converting "land into machines." Inside the plant, its numerous assembly lines perfected the "flow of production." The elaborate technology allowed management to control both the pace and the character of work and to turn labor into a factor of production as passive as coal or steel. Machine processes dictated and circumscribed human organization. The simple act of walking across the floor of the Rouge plant was next to impossible. Philip Haglund, a Ford engineer, noted that the plant's "limited space and measured time . . . imposed a kind of physical isolation" upon the worker. The work force had to be "made over" to accept the new conditions. Greater efficiency justified the measures; outside experts agreed that what appeared to some as congestion was actually efficiency. But Haglund, responsible for the smooth operation of the plant, recalled that "everybody was on edge. They ran around in circles and didn't know what they were doing. Physically everybody was going like a steam engine but not so much mentally." [134] This picture of isolation amid constant motion and confusion amid furious activity suggests similar problems in the metropolis.

At the First National Conference on City Planning, Simkhovitch had complained of the effects of the constant scurry of metropolitan life.

> The industrial and the social pace go hand in hand, and there is something in the presence of huge numbers of people which makes people desire more and more excitement to satisfy the jaded senses. Congestion means the gradual substitution of sensationalism as opposed to reason, and that means social demoralization, ever ready to catch at the latest news, to float on the surface of the hour, never to think a thought through, but to go on rapidly from one sensation to another.

The "clang and honk and shriek" of traffic enveloped the city in the 1920s. "Are the finer lives of peace and depth," asked one citizen, "to give way to the . . . jaded thirst for 'getting somewhere in order to get somewhere else,' the endless trailing of moving multitudes that watch rather than think." [135] Their shared goal of maximizing the velocity of capital created similar problems for the scientific managers of wage labor and urban space. Difficulties of

153

adjustment, rapid labor turnover, and a lack of morale among workers who had become little more than machine tenders or automatons troubled the scientific managers of wage labor and gave rise to the discipline of industrial psychology.[136] The scientific managers of urban space faced the problem in a slightly different form, the problem of community.

Treating the city as a piece of economic machinery, planners had lost sight of its social and communal functions. An excessive concern with the circulation of commodities, including wage labor, tended to crowd out other human purposes. "From earliest times bridges have been meeting places," one city planner observed. "There did people stop to chat." But now, he cautioned, our bridges "accommodate itinerant mankind who must needs be in constant motion. . . . Nervous excitement" and the ubiquitous automobile created "such a tension that a few minutes delay" made people "desperate." A bridge plaza might enhance community life, this planner concluded, but efficient circulation demanded its elimination.[137] In 1927 Lewis Mumford lampooned the fixation on efficient circulation. He predicted the "spread of subways and . . . more efficient means of packing them," and the "disappearance of the dwelling house, partly due to the small amount of time left, after subway rides, to enjoy that ancient fixture."[138] But it was the automobile that had become the linchpin of metropolitan circulation. While planners built hundreds of "new major arteries exclusively for automobile use," complained one streetcar executive, they ignored the deterioration of public transportation.[139]

Throughout the 1920s planners widened streets at the expense of sidewalks and parks, sacrificing beauty to traffic.[140] Widening the thoroughfares and rounding the corners increased the usefulness of the street for economic purposes, but it made the city less sociable and more dangerous.[141] Once a vital element in the life of family and neighborhood, where children played and neighbors chatted with vendors and with one another, the newly paved and widened street became an increasingly dangerous place.[142] In 1925 New York State alone recorded forty-seven thousand accidents resulting in fifty-four thousand injuries. In 1934 thirty-six thousand fatalities nationwide attested to the automobile's intensification of the "bitter war . . . between drivers and pedestrians."[143] A foreign critic of the motorist quipped, "Speed permits me to avoid the look of those whom I offend. . . . I hardly have time to feel ashamed." The "automobile has not conquered space; it has spoiled it, ruined it," he concluded.[144] An excessive concern with efficient circulation proved detrimental to, if not incompatible with, the life of the community.

The scientific managers of wage labor and urban space also shared a common skepticism about the abilities of the average citizen. Just as the scientific managers of wage labor redesigned work for supposedly incompetent laborers, professional planners tended to minimize the role of the average citizen in the city planning process. RPNYE director Adams argued that the "incalculable force" of the modern city "lessened the value of past experience as a guide to the solution of present problems." But before "the public will accept the proposals in the Plan it must understand them," he conceded. "This means that much educational work must be undertaken." Working from a "scientific basis," Adams doubted he had much to learn from a confused public.[145] That skepticism was itself a major reason why both morale and community were so difficult to achieve.

In the same year as the publication of the first volume of the RPNYE survey, H. A. Overstreet read an address to the national conference on city planning that suggested the planners' recognition of the problem of community and the difficulty they had in resolving it. The neighborhood life of the nineteenth-century city, Overstreet argued, where people "knew each other . . . played together, worked together, bought and sold together" was gone forever and had been replaced by "a kind of futile atomicity." Proclaiming the collapse of "the older group formation of our social life," he described city dwellers as "simply human integers in spatial juxtaposition." Ignoring the planners' own role in the collapse of a sense of community, Overstreet suggested that the "revitalization of our community life" could be accomplished by "enlisting groups in vital community projects" like city planning.[146]

But in promoting community involvement, Overstreet cautioned, planners would have to recognize the fundamental difference between "the Leaders and the Led." The planners' primary appeal was to "the man who owns lots of property . . . the banker . . . the active controlling minds." Once the property interests had been lined up, public enthusiasm could be manufactured. Advocating the use of visual images that "instantly tell the story" and "arouse people's emotions," he noted "that mere repetition has an almost compelling effect. . . . Say a thing enough times and people will at last believe it." The public hearing was important if only to avoid the appearance of arrogant and dictatorial methods, he warned. But he assured professionals that such hearings would not jeopardize their expert decisions: "There will be no suggestions, for the simple reason that each suggestion will involve so many other changes that the task will at once appear too difficult for the ordinary citizen." An increasingly dominant element of the realistic tradition that city planners helped to shape, profound skepticism about the abilities of the average citizen undercut any useful discussion of the problem of community.[147]

Exhibiting great faith in economic efficiency, professional city planners, like their counterparts in the factory, had come to believe that advances in productivity would resolve social conflicts and preclude the need for political debate. Embracing the view of the city as a potentially smooth-running mechanism, they had obscured the impact of economic and political power on urban development, disguised their own subservience to powerful propertied interests, and championed the role of the expert. The professionals' strategy for the scientific management of urban space neglected the social functions of the city, minimized the role of the average citizen in city planning, and left both city and citizen bereft of a sense of community. But the logic of social efficiency that had done so much to shape the early planning debate still demanded attention to social problems and to the question of social harmony. The planners' own best instincts also led them back to a concern with the social aspects of the city. What professional planners needed was a social theory of the city that was consistent with their own assumptions about the city and its inhabitants and that pointed the way to a new sense of community or, at least, to social adjustment and social stability. In the 1920s they would find that theory in the new academic discipline of urban sociology.

5

An Urban Sociology:
Robert E. Park and the Realistic Tradition

Writing at the end of the 1920s, the University of Chicago sociologist Harvey Zorbaugh surveyed the last half century of urban reform from good-government and anti-vice campaigns through muckraking to the settlement houses. Those efforts, he argued, had been "the inevitable result of the conflict of urban and rural cultures." The typical reformer, burdened with the cultural baggage of rural America, had been a "fanatic who has waged an uncompromising war on reality. He has been a sentimentalist and romantic who has thought all things possible." While acknowledging the idealism and imagination of the romantics, Zorbaugh insisted that "their dreams are hopeless while they remain unrelated to the realities of life." Clinging to outmoded concepts and traditions, the romantics frustrated social progress. Their allegiance to the neighborhood and local community, even to democracy and republican government, stood in the way of an effective program of reform.[1]

In the concluding chapter to his study *The Gold Coast and the Slum* (1929), Zorbaugh welcomed the emergence of a new realistic tradition in urban reform in which city planning was central.

Lauding the work of zoning and planning commissions, Zor-baugh argued that the city planning profession, in alliance with realtors, public utility corporations, research foundations, and urban academics, had developed "a new city plan, a plan that is possible because it is based upon a recognition of the natural pro-cess of the city's growth, a plan that is the dream not of an ideal, but of a real, city." Their realistic strategy of "recognizing the trends of city growth and evolving new techniques to utilize them" offered the best hope for reform.[2] Zorbaugh recognized that city planners had abandoned not only idealism and imagina-tion but even the discussion of alternative paths of development, and he applauded them for it.

SOCIAL POLITICS AND SOCIAL PLANNING

City planning, however, did not represent a complete program of realistic reform. While city planning encompassed the manage-ment of urban space, the human and social problems of urban in-dustrialization remained unaddressed. Because of the incompe-tence of representative governments in the late-nineteenth century, Zorbaugh argued, "the host of social questions that came with the industrial society, and which were the real if imperfectly recog-nized issues of the day, were rarely acknowledged as political is-sues." But Zorbaugh traced the origins of a new program of "so-cial politics" (his awkward term for an emerging policy of expert social planning) to the late-nineteenth century. The muckrakers had first stepped into the political vacuum to expose the social problems of urban-industrial society. Despite their sentimental at-tachment to the values of rural America, the muckrakers "had cre-ated a faith in publicity, a realistic tradition, which was to play a leading role in the development of a new politics."[3] The social survey, typified by the Russell Sage Foundation's Pittsburgh sur-vey, supplanted muckraking and addressed the same social prob-lems with less sensationalism and a greater emphasis on the expert collection and publication of facts. The social survey initiated the

159

new social politics, a struggle for remedial legislation fought less in the legislature with the weapons of debate than in the arena of public opinion with the weapons of publicity.[4]

Unfortunately, the romantic effort to revive the neighborhood still distracted the social politicians. The decline of the neighborhood, Zorbaugh insisted, was an inevitable "result of the fundamental processes of the city's growth." Most of the problems social politicians addressed resulted from the inevitable dissolution of the neighborhood. Social politicians only slowly came to recognize that. Neither were they yet "fully aware of the potentialities of the public that has replaced" the local community. The techniques of publicity had been "left to the exploitation of the tabloid and the demagogue." But city planners, who had taken a leading role in the development of a realistic conception of city life, were also the first to alert the social politicians to the effective uses of publicity. The campaign for the *Plan of Chicago*, for example, including motion pictures and the use of the plan as a civics textbook in the city's schools, had given "the city a conception of itself—a self-awareness, a sense of its history and role, a vision of its future—in short, a personality." Social politicians, Zorbaugh argued, were finally learning to use mass forms of communication and the techniques of publicity to bring social problems to the attention of the public.[5]

The same alliance of professional experts and the metropolitan elite that had come to dominate the city planning movement would also direct the new social planning. Social politics, Zorbaugh warned, was "not democracy in the old sense. . . . Those who formulate the legislation and put it across are not members of the communities most affected. Moreover, social agencies tend more and more to a system of interlocking directorates, where a *small* number of experts control, to all intents and purposes, the policies of these agencies and of social legislation" [italics in original]. Along with such parallel movements as city planning, bureaus of municipal research, the commission and city manager forms of government, social politics served "to introduce into city government the standardization and scientific management already found in industry."[6]

The decay of local community life and the trend toward standardization and scientific management, Zorbaugh explained, also demanded a "re-evaluation of the city's human resources." While the "old democracy" cherished the political competence of every citizen, the "realistic attitude toward the city and its problems attaches a new importance to good will, vision, leadership, and wealth." Those resources were concentrated in the city's socioeconomic elite. Chicago's Gold Coast, he concluded, "is the only element in the city's life that sees the city as a whole, dreams dreams for it as a whole. . . . No other group of citizens is competent to do what the Gold Coast is doing for the life of the city."[7] Social politics complemented the city planning movement both in articulating a social theory of the city that exalted the political forces and assumptions behind city planning and in addressing the social problems that city planners often overlooked.

Zorbaugh's work reflected the self-confidence and ambition of the social scientists at the University of Chicago during the 1920s, where Zorbaugh earned his doctorate in sociology. An examination of the complex social mosaic of Chicago's near North Side, *The Gold Coast and the Slum* represented one of the more ambitious studies in the new urban sociology. In his introduction to Zorbaugh's work, the pioneer urban sociologist Robert E. Park argued that "we must base our program for the reorganization of our own political and collective life" on such studies.[8] Carried out under Park's direction, Zorbaugh's study, one of the first fruits of the Local Community Research Council (LCRC) which the University of Chicago political scientist Charles E. Merriam had organized, also suggested the growing interest in social science and realistic reform among metropolitan elites. The preeminent entrepreneur of social science research, Merriam had created both the LCRC and the Social Science Research Council (SSRC) in 1924–25 as vehicles for attracting foundation grants to the social sciences. In 1925 representatives of the Rockefeller, Spelman, Sage, Carnegie, and other foundations began meeting annually with the SSRC to discuss funding and research. By 1933 the SSRC had distributed more than four million dollars from the foundations.[9]

Merriam's career illustrated Zorbaugh's analysis of the emergence of the realistic tradition. Merriam served his apprenticeship as a scholar-in-politics with New York mayor Seth Low early in the Progressive Era. He continued to explore the potential of representative, parliamentary politics as a Chicago alderman and an unsuccessful candidate for mayor. In the wake of his defeat at the hands of the demagogic Thompson machine in 1915, Merriam joined the Committee on Public Information, a federal propaganda agency during World War I. In 1925, in a passage that suggested the impact of those experiences, Merriam argued that the modern "demagogue employs the arts of his classical predecessor, but with the added weapons of modern high-geared machinery and the scientifically manufactured poison gas of propaganda."[10] Like Zorbaugh he came to believe in a need for "a readjustment of the bases of the political order." As responsible agencies learned to use new techniques, politics would become less a matter of representative institutions and parliamentary debate than "the science of constructive intelligent control."[11] Civic organizations such as the Commercial Club and the Municipal Voters' League would work "more closely with the press" and replace the role of the national parties in "formulating and administering policies" and creating a "discriminating and informed public opinion."[12] Shedding his faith in representative government, Merriam embraced publicity and expert social planning.

Merriam also shared Zorbaugh's admiration for the city planning movement as a model for the new political order they imagined. A member of the Chicago Plan Commission, author of the city's zoning resolution, and a founder of the Regional Plan Commission, Merriam heralded the *Plan of Chicago* as "one of the miracles of recent urban progress." Before the creation of the Chicago Plan Commission, Merriam recalled, "real estate speculation, industrial expansion, street railway extension" and other private and conflicting forces had shaped the city in irrational ways. Burnham's plan had pointed to a way of managing those conflicting interests, and publicity had proved crucial in securing public acceptance of the plan. "Newspapers and commercial interests generally supported the plan, and helped override the objectors who were many," Merriam explained. "Illustrated lectures and newspaper publicity were incessant in their appeal."[13]

The successful formula of the city planning movement had wider applications. "Masses of facts are being compiled in zoning, planning, housing, and transportation studies," Merriam reported, but "much of the material is lost for local use even, to say nothing of more general utilization." Endorsing Walter Lippmann's proposal for intelligence bureaus at the federal level, Merriam called for a greater role for experts and social scientists in government. But that effort would have to be supplemented by "widely increasing education," Merriam added, for "only as insight and judgement are generously diffused will the suggestions of the savants be found to have any weight."[14] A public educated to endorse the wisdom of the expert would preserve the form if not the content of democracy.

Merriam's greatest contribution to the realistic tradition was in his ability to articulate what he called the "new aspects of politics," the union of social science with the private and public sources of power. From his organization of the SSRC and his co-chairmanship of President Hoover's Recent Social Trends Survey to his membership on FDR's National Resources Planning Board and his drafting of the Executive Reorganization Act, Merriam more than anyone served to institutionalize the expert practice of social planning. Although he had his own grandiose ideas on social engineering, Merriam concentrated his energies on creating the institutional apparatus of social planning.[15] It had been his colleague Robert Park who had created the new urban sociology and thus provided the intellectual groundwork for a realistic program of social planning.

THE APPRENTICESHIP OF AN URBAN REALIST

Robert Park was well prepared to develop a realistic sociology of the American city. Born in 1864 Park grew up with the new urban society. He came to know the metropolis intimately in the 1890s as a reporter in Minneapolis, Detroit, Denver, New York, and Chicago. As a police reporter he covered the violence and disorder of the city. Feature writing for the Sunday editions allowed him to indulge his fascination with the city's obscure corners. Although he was, in his own words, "one of the first and humbler of the muckrakers," Park became disillusioned with the moral bombast of that genre. His extensive fund of observations, taste for tramping through the city, and skepticism about the effectiveness of moral reform helped him to create the new discipline of urban sociology. He also brought to the discipline his iron determination to see things as they are, not as they might be. It is difficult to believe that Park knew nothing of the spate of urban utopias written around the turn of the century, or the reformist hopes attached to the single tax, rapid transit, and the garden city movement, or the example of German city planning that stirred so many of his contemporaries; but none of those factors figure prominently in Park's writing or his thought. It was the underlying reality of the city, not romantic dreams of its transformation, that fired his imagination.[16]

Park's education, with John Dewey at the University of Michigan and later with William James at Harvard, reinforced his pragmatic orientation and his conviction that knowledge came from experience. In 1892 Park, Dewey, and Franklin Ford (a financial reporter) launched a newspaper called *Thought News* based on their belief that experiential knowledge could be used to promote social progress. Ford conceived of the paper as "a union between the newspaper and the increasing knowledge of the university scholar."[17] Park recalled his hope that "with more accurate and adequate reporting of current events the historical process could be appreciably stepped up, and progress would go forward steadily, without the interruption and disorder of depression or violence, and at a rapid pace." Characteristically, Park believed that *Thought News* would not alter the direction of change; by removing obstacles it would simply speed the natural evolution of society.[18]

Added to his disillusionment with muckraking, the short-lived project convinced Park "that the reporter performed a more important function than the editorial writer in bringing about needed reforms, that facts were more important in the long run than opinions."[19] Skeptical of the power of reform-minded journalism but still fascinated by the role of news in shaping public opinion and social change, Park returned to academia in 1898. As other urban realists experimented with municipal reform, Park would complete his apprenticeship in a quest for a science of social change.

Although Park's graduate studies were formally pursued within the disciplines of psychology and philosophy, his dissertation, *The Crowd and the Public*, was essentially a contribution to the emerging discipline of sociology. After a year at Harvard that included James's courses in psychology, Park went to Germany where he completed his dissertation under the philosopher William Windelband at the University of Heidelberg. His study of the urban social order, with the elements that held it together and even more with how it changed, led him to the founders of sociology.

The early sociologists, particularly Auguste Comte, had inherited from the era of the French Revolution a concern with the stability of society. The development of commerce and industry, the spread of market relations and libertarian and individualistic ideologies, and the aggregation of strangers in cities all seemed to threaten social stability. Those concerns underlay Comte's embrace of an organic theory of society, his insistence that society was something greater than a mere collection of discrete individuals. Adopting that organic view of society, Park came to believe that there was a moral order, a set of commonly held beliefs and opinions, that held society together. Park also shared Comte's faith in sociology as a predictive and ameliorative science. Social progress, in that view, depended on the development of a science that would uncover the essential facts of society and the laws that governed its development. Efforts to reform society that did not recognize its underlying moral order, and therefore ran roughshod over it, were destined to fail.[20]

In Quest of a Science of Social Change

Comte's emphasis on the scientific discovery of the laws of social development and the importance of opinion and belief in the social order complemented Park's pragmatism and his interest in the newspaper and public opinion. But in certain matters he differed sharply with Comte, especially with Comte's emphasis on consensus as the basis of social order. The same liberalism, individualism, industrialism, and urbanism that Comte feared were undercutting the social order, Park accepted as fundamental elements of the social order. Like Spencer and Durkheim, Park believed that the functional interdependence characteristic of modern society added the weight of mutual utility to the consensual bonds of society. Denying the fundamental threat to the social order that Comte saw in modern urban society, Park was free to explore his interest in the sources of social change as opposed to social stability.[21]

But Park did not uncritically endorse the views of Spencer and Durkheim anymore than those of Comte. Whereas Spencer saw social progress as the result of the pursuit of individual, rational self-interest, Park's familiarity with both the volatile urban crowd and the malleability of public opinion led him to emphasize the role of group interaction, of sociability, in social change. Like Simmel, whose work he admired, Park would show how the forms of social interaction, as distinct from the interests of social actors, shaped individual and group action. The study of sociability would help to clarify the limits of the rational theory of individual action without totally abandoning it. An examination of the crowd and the public, specific and particularly dynamic forms of sociability, might even reveal the secrets of social change in the urban environment.[22]

Park began *The Crowd and the Public* with a review of the work of an Italian criminologist, Sighele, and challenged Sighele's view of the crowd as a purely lawless and destructive phenomenon. Park observed that people were subject to suggestion in every social situation; what made the crowd distinctive was simply that the attention of its members was focused on a single situation and its action aimed at a common goal.[23] Thus the crowd was only a special form of the social group. Factoring out its distinctive elements, the crowd could be studied as a guide to the dynamics of all social groups. On the basis of those initial observations, Park developed a scientific definition of society. The actual physical basis of the social group and of society itself, he asserted, was to be found "in the brain and the physiology of the nervous system." Thus sociology "necessarily becomes social psychology" and its basic units are "volitional attitudes . . . of individuals interacting in a group situation." A study of those attitudes and how they were formed would uncover the moral order that underlay society and the laws that governed social relations. It would reveal the secret of what Park would later call social control, the process whereby groups regulated the behavior of their members.[24]

Social control and moral order were not alien restraints imposed upon the individual or the social group; they were derived from a spontaneous "natural social instinct," Park argued. The instinct consisted of a capacity for sympathy and imitation whereby individuals placed themselves in the position of another and thus reproduced in themselves the other's feelings. Sympathy and imitation not only facilitated the transmission of tradition between generations, but they also facilitated social control within generations. Through sympathy, imitation, and mutual suggestion, Park concluded, "the group as a whole exerts coercion upon the individual."[25] Having identified the primary sources of social stability, Park shifted his attention to his main interest, the processes of social change.

THE CROWD AND THE PUBLIC AS AGENCIES OF CHANGE

From the sociological perspective the forces of social stability, especially tradition and social control, formed the general will.

The general will, the mentality of the social group, established a stable relationship among individual wills. It represented "what is morally valid for the collectivity." The forces for social change, on the other hand, were centered around what Park called collective attention, "a process in which the group acts upon itself; that is, the group takes a stand on something in its environment." Parliaments, courts of law, political parties, and sects directed collective attention to specific situations in order to change the disposition of their members or the other members of society. Such formal and established groups defined themselves in terms of the general will, in support of or in opposition to some element of it. But the crowd and the public were different, Park explained:

> They serve to bring individuals out of old ties and into new ones. . . . The historical element which plays such an important role for the other groups is partially or completely absent for the crowd as well as for the public. Instead, the crowd and the public reveal the processes through which new groups are formed, although they are not yet conscious of themselves as groups.

The crowd and the public, in which communication took a particularly open-ended and volatile form, were the most dynamic forces for social change.[26]

Through collective attention, which interrupted normal social activity and focused the group on some problem, the crowd and the public came into being. The crowd was a form of collective attention in which legal as well as traditional and customary limits might collapse. Great crowd movements played a double role: "they were the forces which dealt the final blow to old existing institutions, and they introduced the spirit of the new ones." A strike in the industrial city, where the old ties of master to journeyman had dissolved, provided just such conditions. The strike served "to draw the public's attention to a condition considered unjust and unbearable by the workers. It is an appeal to the judgement of the whole because no existing court had jurisdiction."[27] New institutions such as collective bargaining and the regulatory state, Park seemed to anticipate, would emerge from the wreckage of the old.

Notwithstanding its creative elements, the crowd had a tendency to degenerate into a mob. In a highly charged gathering of people whose attention was directed to the same object, such as a political meeting, emotions were contagious. Individuals unconsciously imitated the emotions of others in a circular process of extreme suggestibility. However, such behavior was not confined to strikes and political meetings. The various techniques of modern advertising, Park noted, were designed precisely to take advantage of the suggestibility and impulsiveness of the urban crowd.[28] Even what passed for public opinion was "generally nothing more than a naive collective impulse which can be manipulated by catchwords." Modern journalism, the former newsman warned, excelled in controlling the attention of urban crowds and encouraging simplistic and unreflective responses.[29]

In Park's definition, however, the public and public opinion differed sharply from the crowd and crowd behavior. In the crowd individual impulses were inhibited in favor of a collective drive; in the public individual impulses remained salient and developed through reciprocal interaction. Out of the competition between individuals within the public, Park concluded, came a rational public opinion similar to market prices.[30] Despite Park's caveat that his distinction between the crowd and the public was "purely logical and cannot be viewed as a value difference," there was no mistaking his preference for the public as a vehicle of social change. While "instincts dominated" the crowd, "reason prevailed" in the public. No norm other than the ability to feel and empathize governed the crowd; within the public "people are at least controlled by the norms of logic." Guided "by prudence and rational reflection," the public offered the high road to social change.[31] Park's public resembled what Zorbaugh later termed social politics, the realistic program of urban reform. *The Crowd and the Public* thus anticipated the contributions of the Chicago school and suggested some of its weaknesses.

Park's study of the crowd and the public illuminated the formal dynamics of social interaction and social change in the urban environment. But in his exclusive emphasis on the forms of social interaction, he neglected the content and the substance of those interactions. Whereas Simmel, whose work provided an important basis for Park's, had warned that the study of the forms of interaction must be supplemented by the study of economic and political interests and of power, Park developed a science of social change that focused exclusively on formal interaction. Although Park acknowledged that individual and group interests influenced social interaction, he did not make those interests a part of his analysis. He thus obscured the extent to which the exercise and unequal distribution of political and economic power influenced all social life and social change.[32] While Park's apparent preference for the public as a vehicle for social change is understandable, his analysis only hinted at the function of the crowd as a means for the relatively powerless to draw attention to their problems and to demand social change. Nor did Park's analysis suggest that the success of the public as a vehicle for social change might depend on the willingness of the powerful shapers of public opinion to orchestrate change from above.

REALISM AND RACE RELATIONS

When Park completed *The Crowd and the Public* in 1904 at the age of forty, he was already impatient with the limitations of the scholarly life and with his self-perceived failure to find a proper outlet for his energies and ambitions. During the next decade he developed sociological interests in the black American and the evolution of race relations. In association with Booker T. Washington and the Tuskegee Institute, Park enlisted in the cause of practical education for blacks as a means of adjustment to modern life. He saw Washington as a man "engaged in a fundamental task who has a sense of reality . . . who knows what should be done and how to do it."[33]

Checking Park's own genuine capacity for moral outrage at racist excesses, Washington encouraged him to see that "beneath the superficial pattern and external aspect of southern life was the working of a great historical process, a process which was slowly but inexorably changing . . . the traditional relations between the races." As more and more southern blacks flocked to northern industrial cities, Park, like Washington, came to see them as peasants unprepared for urban life. But unlike Washington, Park believed the urbanization of southern blacks to be inevitable, and he was fascinated by and concerned to alleviate the consequent problems of adjustment. In 1912 at Tuskegee's International Conference on the Negro, Park met William I. Thomas, a University of Chicago sociologist and student of the immigration of Polish peasants to the American city. The two quickly recognized common interests. It was Thomas who convinced Park to come to Chicago and arranged for him to teach a graduate course, "The Negro in Chicago," in the fall of 1913.[34]

The move to Chicago was a fortuitous one for Park. A city of more than two million when he arrived, Chicago was in the process of nearly doubling its population between 1900 and 1930. In Park's first six years in the city, its black population more than doubled to 110,000.[35] Park was able to witness firsthand the large-scale migration of southern blacks and to study the problem of adjustment. Moreover, Chicago boasted an active and civic-minded leadership, flush with the success of *The Plan of Chicago*, eager to advance the city's interests. The lavishly financed University of Chicago was becoming the center of a confident and scientific sociology. With the city as his laboratory, Park was able to explore his interest in the crowd and the public as vehicles for social change and in the problems of race relations and to extend his scientific search for the keys to social progress.

In 1916 Park published his most influential essay, "The City: Suggestions for the Investigation of Human Behavior in the Urban Environment," which outlined an ambitious program of research. The organizing theme of the wide-ranging essay was the concept of human ecology. Impersonal forces within the urban environment, Park explained, "tend to bring about an orderly and typical grouping of its population and institutions." Human ecology was the scientific study of those forces, of the natural areas (distinctive, unplanned districts) they produced, and of the forms of human interaction found within those natural areas.[36] The central focus of Park's essay was on that last issue and especially on the distinction between primary, face-to-face, and intimate as opposed to secondary, impersonal, and indirect relations.

In an urban environment secondary relations normally provided the basis for order. The ease of communication and transportation meant that most urbanites moved freely through a variety of natural areas. Thus the moral order of the city emerged less from primary relations in local communities than from a variety of secondary relations on a citywide and metropolitan basis. Similarly, the social order relied less on the intimate and personal forms of social control associated with the family, the church, and the neighborhood than on impersonal forms of social control provided by metropolitan agencies including the legal system, the schools, and social welfare agencies, as well as by publicity and advertising.[37]

The segregated residential area and the ghetto, however, represented important exceptions to the dominance of secondary relations in the urban environment. To a great extent those insulated neighborhoods preserved and even intensified the primary relationships, the moral order, and the forms of social control typical of simple societies. But they were also areas in which the social scientist could examine the inevitable breakdown, under the impact of the ecological processes of invasion, competition, and succession, of those simpler social forms and the creation of new forms of social control that facilitated the adjustment to urban life.[38] Thus the segregated ethnic neighborhoods and the black ghetto of Chicago's south side, where racial and ethnic tensions would erupt into racial violence in 1919, offered Park a laboratory for the study of human ecology and the problems of adjustment in an expanding metropolis. Park's analysis of those problems would focus on the forms of social interaction rather than its economic and political determinants.

THE SOCIOLOGY OF CHICAGO'S SOUTH SIDE

A generation before the great black migrations of the twentieth century, Chicago's south side neighborhoods housed thousands of working-class families who found employment in the nearby stockyards, steel mills, and agricultural processing plants. At least since the 1880s, ethnic tensions had exacerbated labor conflicts and created a bitterly competitive social order. Hundreds of southern and eastern European immigrants, who had been brought in to break the eight-hour-day movement in 1886, crowded into the contested neighborhoods surrounding the stockyards, driving the less recent German and Irish immigrants further south. Employers first used blacks as strikebreakers in the stockyards in 1894 when workers there struck in support of the Pullman strikers. In the first years of the twentieth century, Chicago steel manufacturers and the University of Chicago also employed black strikebreakers.[39] The use of black strikebreakers added racial antagonisms to an already volatile situation.

The racist attitudes of many white unionists, reinforced by the use of blacks as strikebreakers, extended the color line into organized labor. Blacks had their own reasons for resisting unionization, including the exclusionary principle of the whites-only unions, their experiences with Jim Crow unions that afforded no protection from dismissal, the unfamiliarity with union ideals of many rural migrants, and the legacy of paternalism many brought with them from the South. Regardless of the reasons, however, the resistance exacerbated the antagonism of white unionists.[40] But at least one union, the Amalgamated Meat Cutters and Butcher Workmen (AMCBW), endeavored to organize across racial lines and succeeded in enlisting many of the five hundred black workers employed in the stockyards in the early 1900s. For a time racial antagonism eased. In 1904 when negotiations with the packers broke down and the AMCBW called a strike, however, the packers imported trainloads of southern black strikebreakers. Muted

173

racial antagonisms quickly revived and racial violence erupted. In a 1905 teamsters strike, blacks were again used as strikebreakers and again found themselves the victims of racial violence.

During World War I, with European orders flooding in and immigrant sources of labor cut off, union leaders saw a unique opportunity to organize the stockyards. The various stockyard unions created the Stockyard Labor Council in 1917 and launched a concerted organization drive in September. A central goal of the council was to unionize the ten to twelve thousand black workers in the yards, about 25 percent of the total labor force. The appointment of a federal labor arbitrator, Judge Samual Alschuler, and his award of an eight-hour day and other benefits encouraged the effort. But the history of racial tensions within the work force contributed to a lag in black union membership even as the black percentage of the work force increased.[42] On the eve of the 1919 race riot, nine thousand of the twelve thousand black workers in the yards were still nonunion and racial tensions were high. On the Monday following the riot's outbreak (Sunday, July 27) several black workers were assaulted in and around the yards, three of whom died of their wounds. On Tuesday few blacks reported for work. When troops arrived in the city on Thursday, the violence subsided throughout much of the South Side, but not in the yards where the bloodshed continued. Yet on Saturday the packers announced plans to bring twelve to fifteen thousand blacks to work despite the bitter complaints of white workers and unionists. After rejecting the union's offer to take responsibility for peace under a closed shop agreement, the packers brought twelve thousand black workers, nine thousand of them nonunion, into the yards under armed guard, while ten thousand white unionists walked out in protest.[43]

Labor conflict was not the only arena of racial tension. As Chicago's black population increased during the early years of the century, the competition for housing contributed another dimension. In 1904 the packers had housed thousands of black strikebreakers in the lard houses, killing halls, and canning rooms of the stockyards in deplorable conditions. Once the strike was broken, most

174

blacks were discharged to make their way in the already crowded ghetto along nearby Wentworth Avenue.[44] During World War I, explained Sears, Roebuck president and philanthropist Julius Rosenwald, Chicago employers were forced "to seek another source of labor supply. This exists in the colored population."[45] The packers' "placarded warehouses, set close by the railroads, dotted every sizeable town of the South, calling for men," while Chicago railroads and the federal Department of Labor (until challenged by southern congressmen) facilitated the migration of an estimated fifty thousand blacks in an eighteen-month period between 1917 and 1918.[46] The migrants flocked to Chicago "because we have asked them to come," Rosenwald admitted, but no provision had been made for their housing. The "large employers . . . who lured my people to . . . Chicago have been derelict in providing housing," complained one black teacher. The black community, Carl Sandburg reported in 1919, faced the "biggest overcrowding problem" in Chicago.[47]

Despised by union men as scabs and their housing needs ignored by their employers, the migrants also found themselves hemmed in by organized white property owners, exploited by realtors, and shunned by bankers. The Hyde Park Property Owners Association typified the aggressive response of white property owners to the expansion of the ghetto. Hyde Park had been an unstable neighborhood long before blacks moved into it. As early as the World's Columbian Exposition in 1893, which stimulated the speculative construction of hotels and cheap apartments to accommodate visitors and construction workers, the character of fashionable Hyde Park had begun to change. In the early twentieth century, the proximity of the stockyards, the noise and filth of the lakefront railroads, and the invasion of the automobile industry along Michigan Avenue drove the wealthiest residents to the North Side or the suburbs. By 1916 the glut of apartments and the exodus of residents had left an estimated 25 percent of the buildings vacant, especially the older single-family residences.[48]

Hyde Park realty values were at best unstable as the black migrants' demand for housing began to intensify. Realtors and property owners consented to sell to the migrants, many of whom arrived in Chicago with the proceeds of the sale of their property in the South, in order to stabilize realty values. But by 1918 the wartime slump in housing construction and the announcement of plans for revitalizing the lakefront revived the demand for Hyde Park housing among affluent whites and prompted the organization of a Hyde Park Property Owners Association (HPPOA).[49] Fearful that prospective white residents would not wish to live near blacks and that the rise in property values would be reversed, the HPPOA pledged to use all lawful means to force blacks back into "their own neighborhoods."[50] The HPPOA's argument that an influx of black residents inevitably led to the decline of both neighborhoods and realty values proved to be a self-fulfilling prophecy. Exclusion and segregation forced migrants to pay inflated prices for large, deteriorating residences within the ghetto or on its edges and to overcrowd the buildings with lodgers to meet expenses. When black owners sought loans to maintain and rehabilitate the structures, they found that "most large real estate firms and loan companies decline to make loans on property owned or occupied by Negroes."[51]

Those developments led to great anxieties and bitter tensions in the neighborhoods surrounding the ghetto. What would later be called "non-adjusted" or "contested" neighborhoods and the ecological processes of "invasion" and "succession" were largely the results of a speculative market in real estate. "The colored man," one Hyde Park resident explained, "would have never been in this district had not our real estate men in their ambition to acquire wealth and commissions, which is perfectly legitimate, put them here, although this action on their part has been very shortsighted, as some of them now admit." Speculative realtors had made handsome profits, as the black leader Charles S. Duke complained, in the "business of commercializing racial antagonisms."[52] Realtors, Carl Sandburg reported, frightened white property owners into selling at a loss then resold the properties to blacks at an inflated price. It was a scam, Sandburg charged, based on the illogical premise that "the larger the number of colored persons ready to pay higher rentals, the lower the realty values slump."[53] When realtors saw the possibility of making even higher profits through the revival of the fashionable neighborhood and were threatened with reprisals from white property owners, however, they shifted their tactics. The HPPOA boasted that all but five or six realtors had pledged not to show, rent, or sell any property "within our locality that we claim jurisdiction of in the future to colored people."[54] The entire campaign, in both public meetings and the HPPOA's journal, was conducted in a spirit of severe racial animosity. The racial tensions exploded between 1917 and 1921 in a series of bombings of black-owned and -occupied buildings and the residences and offices of offending realtors and bankers.[55]

Blacks and whites clashed not only over jobs and housing, but also over the use of public space. The segregation of Chicago's vice trade in the ghetto cast a pall over the area. Overcrowding also took its toll. Migrants from the South felt "the town too large for much friendliness" and complained that "people do not visit each other."[56] Black children especially suffered from a lack of public facilities. Most public schools in the ghetto lacked playgrounds, gymnasiums, and assembly halls. Chicago's celebrated system of neighborhood parks provided little benefit to black youth because of intimidation and violence from white children and because park officials and reformers discouraged the integrated use of facilities. Black youth had few options but to loiter around the catchpenny amusements of the city; a study of "retarded" black students revealed their recreation to be centered around the commercial movie house. At the segregated black beach at Twenty-fifth Street, crowded between railroad tracks and a high embankment, "the atmosphere of wholesome, recreative outdoor life [was] entirely lacking."[57] It was around that beach, the one beach open to blacks, and the nearby whites-only beach at Twenty-ninth Street that the race riot of July 1919 began.

THE CROWD ...

The riot began on a hot Sunday afternoon, July 27, when a clash of black and white bathers resulted in the death of a young black

man. A small group of black men and women, frustrated with segregated and inferior facilities, had determined to use the whites-
only beach at Twenty-ninth Street. Driven away by curses, threats,
and rocks, they returned in greater numbers to force the whites
from the beach. When a larger group of whites assembled, a violent struggle ensued. Meanwhile a group of five young black men,
unaware of the events on the beach, had appeared offshore. A
white man began hurling rocks at the boys hitting one, Eugene
Williams, who subsequently drowned. The black crowd sum-
moned a black policeman from the Twenty-fifth Street beach,
pointed out the man they believed to be guilty, and demanded that
the white officer on duty arrest him. The white officer refused
to do so and also prevented the black officer from making the arrest. While the crowd swelled and wild rumors began to spread,
the white officer arrested a black man on the complaint of a
white man. An enraged black man fired into a group of white
policemen, wounding one. The black officer shot and killed
the assailant, and soon other shots were fired. Angry crowds began
to leave the beach to spread the news, touching off five days of
rioting.[58]

The beach incident ignited a race riot that had been waiting to
happen. The presence of thousands of immigrants and migrants,
the pressure of population on its neighborhoods, and the intensity
of labor conflict had all made the social order of Chicago's south
side both extremely competitive and unstable. Well before the
riot's outbreak, numerous groups had emerged which displayed
what could be called crowd behavior in an effort to call attention
to what they saw as intolerable conditions and to provide their
members with protection. Much of that crowd behavior, like the
angry meetings of the Hyde Park Association, exacerbated racial
tensions.

The youth gangs that blanketed the immigrant neighborhoods
typified the role of crowds in the riot. Located in the "broad
twilight zone of railroads and factories, of deteriorating neighborhoods and shifting populations" the gangs, as the Chicago sociologist Frederic Thrasher later explained, represented "the spon-

178

taneous effort of boys to create a society where none adequate to their needs exists." In the face of disorganized families, corrupt and indifferent politicians, poor housing and sanitation, and frequent unemployment, membership in a gang gave its members a sense of security. Its code focused on "the group rather than the welfare of its individual members." The gang often stole "for the family larder" and the "loyalty of the members to each other" increased "in times of unemployment."[59] But towards those outside the gang its behavior was predatory, and blacks were decidedly outside the gang.

The central role of crowds in both the events leading up to and during the riot revealed the concerted and purposeful action of social groups (as opposed to the criminality of the isolated individual) as the major cause of the riot. In an incident typical of many others during the riot, swarms of white children, as young as four and five, blocked a trolley while whites pulled blacks off the car and beat them. The social order of the South Side had not suddenly collapsed; the riot had illuminated in a particularly lurid way the bitterly competitive aspects of that order. On both sides there were many who believed their actions to have been justified. The white policeman who had refused to arrest the rock-thrower on the beach where the riot had started later said that it "wouldn't take much to start another riot, and most of the white people of this district are resolved to make a clean-up this time." A black veteran countered, "I done my part and I'm going to fight right here till Uncle Sam does his. I can shoot as good as the next one, and nobody better start anything."[60]

Not all of the crowd behavior on Chicago's south side was violent and destructive. There was at least one example of the positive and creative aspect of crowd behavior to which Park had alluded. Just weeks before the race riot a group of black and white stockyard workers paraded through the black ghetto to call attention to what they saw as the packers' cynical effort to exacerbate racial tensions. "The bosses think because we are of different colors and different nationalities that we should fight each other. We're going to fool them and fight for a common cause—a square deal for all,"

179

read one placard. "You notice there ain't no Jim Crow cars here today," a black organizer announcer. "That's what organization does."[61] Similar efforts were made among the milling crowds outside the stockyards, crowds that the packers endeavored to disperse.[62] The union-sponsored crowds reflected the assumption that the race problem, as one federal labor official suggested, was "at rock bottom a labor question" and served to lessen rather than to heighten racial tensions. "The one place in this town where I feel safest is over at the yard, with my union button on," explained another black organizer.[63] That was the creative element of crowd behavior, the ability to bring people out of old relationships and attitudes and into new ones.

Crowd behavior also suggested the role that political and economic interests played in shaping social interaction, the issue Park tended to ignore. During the riot the *New Majority*, organ of the Chicago Federation of Labor, called on union members to end the violence. "This responsibility rests particularly heavy upon the white men and women of organized labor," the paper editorialized, "not because they had anything to do with starting the present trouble, but because of their advantageous position to help end it."[64] Union organizers believed racial amity to be in their interest, and they used crowds to promote it. Recognizing the importance of their efforts, Herbert Seligmann wrote after the riot that "it will be largely on the job and in the labor union that the identity of interest of the colored worker and the white will be demonstrated."[65] Unfortunately, the interests of other groups, most notably anti-union employers, cynical realtors, and demagogic politicians, but also many ordinary, relatively powerless, and frightened citizens, seemed to demand greater racial tensions.

While the riot was still raging, a group of prominent Chicagoans, representing major industrial and social welfare institutions, called on Illinois governor Lowden to appoint a commission on race relations. Financed by the city's elite but possessing neither official authority nor a broadly representative character, the Illinois Commission on Race Relations (ICRR) was not in a position to manage or mediate racial conflicts. Rather, it chose to undertake a scholarly study of the causes of the riot and to make a series of policy recommendations, both of which were published in 1922 as *The Negro in Chicago*. [66]

An impressive interracial group of Chicago's leaders, the ICRR amassed an imposing array of facts in an effort to move public opinion toward greater amity in race relations. Adopting the National Urban League's program of industrial employment and social welfare programs as the route to black progress and racial justice, the ICRR represented Park's public in action. Indeed, his work in urban sociology and race relations and his presidency of the Chicago Urban League had placed Park in a position of considerable influence, and *The Negro in Chicago* bore his unmistakable imprint. [67]

In the ICRR's analysis of the race riots, crowds and the interests that motivated them were not an important factor. Examining crowds in only a four-page section of a nearly seven-hundred-page report, the ICRR discussed only the formal aspects of crowd behavior. In introducing the Crowds and Mobs section, the ICRR was careful to distinguish between the two: "It may be observed that a crowd is merely a gathering of people while a mob is a crowd with its attention so strongly fixed upon some lawless purpose that other purposes are inhibited." [68]

Crowds turned into mobs, the ICRR report explained, "when exciting rumors circulated and the suggestion of vengeance was made by leaders." Divided "in performance into a small active nucleus and a large proportion of spectators," the mob turned to violence "by having the direct suggestion put to them by one of the leaders." Yet the entire mob "must share the moral responsibility" for violence since without "the spectators mob violence would probably have stopped short of murder in many cases." [69] Mobs formed most easily at transfer corners on the trolley system, in parks, and at beaches and vice resorts; many of the deaths and the most serious injuries occurred at these points. In making its recommendations the ICRR urged the authorities to close vice resorts and to police transfer corners, parks, and beaches in greater numbers. "Precision and promptness of movement" had enabled the militia to prevent the formation of mobs. Thus the ICRR urged that "the police and militia work out, at the earliest possible date, a detailed plan for joint action in the control of race riots."[70] Laudable as such precautions were, they reflected the ICRR's overriding conviction that the average citizens who made up both crowds and mobs had little positive role to play in improving race relations.

. . . AND THE PUBLIC

As a vehicle for change the ICRR preferred the public. The 150-page section on public opinion was by far the largest part of the ICRR's report. It was also the basis for its most important policy recommendations. Even the ICRR's definition of the public reflected its elitist assumptions. In investigating the causes of the riot, the ICRR collected information from the public through a series of conferences. The character of those conferences, Arthur Waskow argues, "was a silent endorsement of the value of testimony from a number of different leadership groups rather than from randomly selected residents of Chicago, or from a representative sample of the entire population." The public opinion of the powerless carried relatively little weight with the ICRR.[71]

In investigating housing conditions, for example, the ICRR turned to builders and real estate managers. Although the housing conference did include interviews with some black families, the white families with whom they competed for housing were not consulted. In surveying employment conditions, the ICRR interviewed black workers but not the white workers with whom they so often and tragically clashed. The study of public opinion included a considerable number of statements taken from unexceptional white residents of the South Side, but even here greater emphasis was placed on the opinions of an exceptional group of well-educated business and professional men and women from both races. The ICRR's study of crime relied on the opinion of judges, police officials, and social workers rather than that of criminals or their victims.[72] The ICRR thus anticipated what Irving Horowitz has argued "was to become the dominant 'policy-making style,' i.e., an unconcern with politics, or at least a strict division between politics as a mass activity (with which the policy-making social scientists were unconcerned) and policy as an elite activity (with which they were intimately concerned)." It was to the development of a rational and progressive public opinion among Chicago's educated and powerful elite rather than to a direct assault upon the problems and the attitudes of the ordinary citizen that the ICRR looked for an improvement in race relations.[73]

The ICRR's recommendations faithfully reflected those elitist assumptions and were designed to implement that strategy. Although the commissioners had interviewed many black Chicagoans and undoubtedly sympathized with their plight, their recommendations implied that racial justice was something to be implemented from above rather than demanded from below.[74] Indeed the ICRR discouraged blacks from taking any aggressive action in their own behalf. Neither did the ICRR make any recommendations as to what active role the ordinary white citizens who had been responsible for so large a part of the violence could play in improving race relations. The ICRR did argue that whites too often judged blacks from contacts with "servants of families, or other Negroes whose general standing and training do not qualify them to be spokesmen of the group." It recommended that whites seek information on blacks from "responsible and representative Negroes," presumably not the ones with whom they competed for jobs and housing.[75] Those who had borne the brunt of racial injustice and precipitated the worst violence had, in the view of the ICRR, at best only a limited role in alleviating racial tensions.

With greater confidence the ICRR looked to elites for an improvement in the climate of racial opinion. The information collected on public opinion, the commissioners reported, could "be used to reduce, if not to prevent, racial unfriendliness and misunderstanding."[76] The "strict enforcement" of compulsory education would anchor an effort to impose a more enlightened public opinion. The ICRR urged elite organizations such as the Woman's City Club, the Union League Club, and the Urban League to extend their efforts to improve race relations and recommended that "the appropriate social agencies give needed attention to dealing extra-judicially with cases of Negroes." The ICRR called for the creation of a permanent race-relations body charged with the responsibility of "bringing sound public sentiment to bear upon the settlement of racial disputes, and with promoting the spirit of interracial tolerance and co-operation." The ICRR argued that the newspapers, as the linchpin of public opinion, were crucial to the effort. Having compiled considerable evidence to suggest that newspapers sensationalized racial incidents to boost circulation, the ICRR pleaded with them to prevent racial antagonisms by publishing "such matters as shall in their character tend to dispel prejudice and promote mutual respect and good will."[77]

Arguing that the city's powerful elite had an important part to play in improving race relations was justified. In the wake of riot, a number of commentators recognized that racial tensions were an integral part of the city's political structure and of the ways in which power was exercised. The race problem and the recent riots, Walter Lippmann argued, were "really a by-product of our planless, disordered, bedraggled, drifting democracy." Unless we "learn to house everybody, employ everybody at decent wages in a self-respecting status," he concluded, race relations would continue to deteriorate. "Insufficient and unsuitable housing . . . for the industrial classes," concurred the settlement leader Graham Taylor, lay behind the riot. Seligmann more pointedly blamed the "contest between organized labor and employer" and the "plotting and counter-plotting of factions in city government."[78] Although the ICRR's report lacked a critical analysis of the ways in which racial tensions shaped and reinforced the city's political structure, it contained considerable evidence to support such an analysis.[79]

The ICRR did make a series of recommendations aimed at the problems to which Lippmann, Taylor, Seligmann, and others had pointed. Condemning those who "arbitrarily advance rents merely because Negroes become tenants," the ICRR urged whites to "energetically discourage" all "methods tending toward forcible segregation or exclusion of Negroes." The commissioners disputed the equation of black occupancy with the depreciation of property values and urged lenders to treat blacks fairly. The ICRR asked unions and employers to treat workers of both races equally and, without encouraging blacks either to join or not to join unions, discouraged the creation of segregated unions. Citing "gross inequalities of [police] protection," discrimination in arrests and prosecution, and the inferior schools, playgrounds, and public utilities found in the ghetto, the ICRR called on municipal officials to end legal discrimination and to improve facilities for blacks.[80] All were laudable recommendations; yet they were ones which, by all accounts, had little positive effect on race relations. For at least another generation, the color line remained hard and fast in residential areas, skilled employment, union membership, civic affairs, and even in public opinion.[81]

The failure of the ICRR's recommendations to improve race relations suggested the weakness of the public as a vehicle for social change. What the ICRR had failed to explain was how industrial employers, real estate dealers, machine politicians, municipal officials, and others who benefited in one way or another from racial tensions could be made to change their behavior. Despite abundant evidence of the integral role of racial tensions in both the city's social and political order, the ICRR proposed no significant changes in that order. Instead, and paradoxically, the commissioners looked to elites with vested interests in the status quo for an improvement in race relations. The ICRR's strategy seemed to reflect a belief that racism was a purely irrational aberration that could be removed by an appeal to reason.

Or perhaps the ICRR believed, as Waskow suggests, that a "fear of future violence in the pattern of the 1919 race riot" alone would encourage elite Chicagoans to work toward improved race relations. But if this was the thinking of the commissioners, it conceded the preeminent role of crowd behavior in bringing about change. It was, after all, the violence that had brought the ICRR

185

into existence. In his foreword to *The Negro in Chicago*, Governor Lowden had argued that a key purpose of the commission was to prevent a reoccurrance of "the appalling tragedy which brought disgrace to Chicago in July of 1919." One of the ICRR's few recommendations that met with success, the creation of a permanent race-relations commission, was enacted only in the 1940s in response to a growing fear over the possibility of another riot. Whatever the thinking of the commissioners, both the origins of the ICRR and the fate of its recommendations pointed to pressure from below, and the crowd as one form of such pressure, as the most important engine of change.[82]

Of course pressure from below in any form was the last thing the ICRR was interested in promoting. Nor was it something in which Robert Park placed much faith. Skeptical of the ICRR's strategy, Mary White Ovington, chairman of the national NAACP, warned that "Robert Park . . . has never been aggressive . . . would dally and fail," was a "slow going conservative, the astute political kind."[83] Although that judgment may be too harsh, in the absence of a popular demand there was little incentive for elites to push for change and little possibility that race relations would improve. The critical problems on the South Side to which the rioting had called attention, the competition for employment, housing, and public facilities, and the cynical manipulation of racial tensions, demanded significant changes in Chicago's social and political order, changes that threatened powerful interests and could only be secured at the hands of an equally powerful political movement.

The ICRR had no intention and little chance of organizing a mass political movement and would have found the suggestion that it do so outrageous. However, the ICRR's claim to be developing a systematic and effective policy may have preempted other approaches. In any event unless the social, economic, and political problems that exacerbated racial tensions were addressed in some positive and effective manner, the ICRR could not even ensure that further violence would be avoided, much less that a new and enlightened period of race relations would ensue. Indeed, after roughly twenty years of relative quiet and continued racial injustice, racial tensions again erupted violently during and after World War II. Although a dramatic upheaval such as had occurred in 1919 was avoided, a decade of racial violence dashed the hopes and the best intentions of liberal public opinion. Racial prejudice and racial tension so distorted the emerging public policies of urban redevelopment and urban renewal that those ostensibly liberal policies played a major role in the making of Chicago's second, much enlarged if little improved, ghetto.[84] The realistic approach to race relations that Park promoted and that the ICRR embodied would prove unrealistic in its expectations of positive change.

A less charitable interpretation would suggest that the ICRR's desire for change was itself rather limited. In introducing the section of its report on public opinion, which the commissioners and their staff touted as the most important, the commissioners observed that "men are tormented by the opinions they have of things rather than by the things themselves." Focusing less on the role of interests than on the social psychology of race relations, the commission implied that racial tension was a problem of "moods and antagonisms expressed in words and shown in manners" rather than of overcrowding housing, job discrimination, and physical violence.[85] In that context "racial adjustment" becomes a paltry thing, an accommodation to the status quo.

In the area of residential integration, the ICRR's commitment to change was indeed limited. In January 1921 W. E. B. Dubois charged that the commissioners "under the guise of impartiality and good will are pushing insidiously but unswervingly a program of racial segregation."[86] As Thomas Philpott has shown, even the most sincere friends of the Negro on the ICRR supported a program of voluntary segregation and the rebuilding of the black ghetto. The ICRR's recommendations closely paralleled the plan announced in the riot's aftermath by the powerful interests within the Chicago Real Estate Board and the Association of Commerce, a plan that promised to transform the ghetto into "a housing section for colored people that cannot be equaled in any part of the country."[87] If realism meant, as Zorbaugh would later define it, "recognizing the trends of city growth and evolving new techniques to utilize them," this was certainly a realistic approach to race relations. But it was also one that left the city saddled with the worst aspects of racism, including a large and growing ghetto. From the perspective of the nascent profession of city planning, however, Park had outlined a realistic approach to social problems and a new urban sociology. Park shared the city planners' assumptions about the necessity of working with and through elites, the incompetence of the average citizen, and the inevitability of certain patterns of urban development. Moreover, human ecology offered a way to unravel the complex relationships between the physical environment and social behavior. A sociological theory that both explained social disorganization and offered solutions to it in terms of location and mobility could help city planners address the social implications of their work. In concert with urban sociologists in the 1920s, they would begin to work out new approaches to the problems of social disorganization and to seek a new metropolitan basis for the urban community. On the eve of the New Deal, after a decade of diverse investigation and experimentation, they had developed the foundations for an ambitious policy of urban planning that sought to rationalize not only the physical order of the metropolis but its social order as well.

6

The Alienation of Social Control: The Chicago Sociologists and the Origins of Urban Planning

Chicago in the 1920s was a city of striking contrasts, of the Gold Coast and the slum. Nowhere was the contrast more pronounced than at the lakefront where the astounding work of man abutted the majesty of nature. "Chicago comes howling to a standstill on the edge of eternity," observed a foreign visitor with a mixture of fascination and horror, as he watched a constant stream of automobiles along Lake Shore Drive pass before the endless blue of Lake Michigan.[1] Lake Shore Drive and the string of landfill parks through which it ran, parks created from the city's inexhaustible supply of garbage, represented one of city planning's greatest triumphs. For the University of Chicago social scientist Donald Slesinger, however, the city's headlong expansion into the lake suggested a desire to disown the uglier city to the west. The "stunning lake shore is a movie-set creating the illusion of a non-existent depth," he charged; its planning had been based on a "denial of the existence of the western slums." He concluded, "Chicago had flourished on a free, and therefore miserable, labor market, and a fancy showroom for its

189

customers."[2] The failure of city planners to challenge existing economic conditions, he implied, undermined even their best efforts.

The sociologist and pioneer of human ecology Robert Park, Slesinger's colleague at the University of Chicago, was well aware of both the triumphs and the limitations of city planning. He proposed to overcome those limitations through a wider application of the city planners' own methods. The city, he wrote in 1925, was "full of junk, much of it human, . . . men and women who, for some reason or other, have fallen out of line in the march of industrial progress and have been scrapped by the industrial organization of which they were once a part."[3] The ecologist's determination to recycle the human junk back into the economic order complemented the city planners' commitment to economic efficiency. The Illinois Commission on Race Relations (ICRR) had anticipated that approach in its determination to eliminate discrimination so that, in Arthur Waskow's words, "an indigestible mass of irrationally excluded persons would not clog the efficient processes of economic enterprise." In that view once discrimination was eliminated it was up to blacks to change whichever of their own values and behavior prevented them from fitting into the dominant society.[4] Park's faith in a rationalized, private-enterprise society, reflected in his association with the ICRR, underlay his work in the 1920s and particularly his association with professional city planners.[5] He helped shape a form of social planning that would facilitate individual and group adjustment to an unchallenged social reality.

The origins of urban planning are to be found, at least in part, in a series of exchanges between planners and urban sociologists in the 1920s and early 1930s. It was at the 1925 meeting of the American Sociological Society on "The City," which Park and his colleagues organized and planners from the Russell Sage Foundation's *Regional Plan of New York and Its Environs* attended, that those exchanges began. There the sociologists articulated a theory of urban life that helped planners unravel the social implications of physical planning. At the core of the theory, which had both shaped and been shaped by an ongoing series of practical reform efforts in which Park and his students had been involved, was a fascination with social control (the means by which groups regulated the behavior of their members). Adopting a strategy best described as the alienation of social control, Park and his students offered new and artificial forms of social control as the means to eliminate the wasteful aspects of metropolitan life that were out of step with the urban-industrial order. City planners thus found in the work of the Chicago sociologists not only a reassuring complement to their own realistic view of the city but what seemed a promising approach to the persistent social problems of the metropolis. Following the 1925 meeting planners and sociologists began to develop a program of urban planning, a program for rationalizing not only the physical and economic structure of the metropolis but its social order as well.

THE SCIENCE OF SOCIAL CONTROL

The period of Park's greatest influence began in 1916 when Ernest Burgess, the son of a minister eager to give social work a "scientific basis," joined him at the University of Chicago.[6] Park and Burgess first collaborated on the textbook *Introduction to the Science of Sociology* (1921), the "green bible" that profoundly influenced the American discipline of sociology.[7] Park and Burgess saw sociology as an ameliorative and pragmatic science designed "to give man control over himself."[8] They explored how social control worked, how "a mere collection of individuals succeed in acting in a corporate and consistent way." Earlier sociologists, Park and Burgess explained, had attributed all group activity to conformity, like-mindedness, or imitation.[9] But Park and Burgess understood the social group as something more than a mere collection of like-minded individuals. Through communication the social group took on a life and a purpose of its own. Public sentiments and opinions were derived from the "fermentation which association breeds." While those sentiments and opinions often reinforced the existing order, they were also "constantly recreating the old order, making new heroes, overthrowing old gods, creating new myths and imposing new ideals."[10] An understanding of that process would enable mankind to control social change more effectively.

The new science of social control had more immediate implications for practical reformers. Park and Burgess argued that "all social problems turn out finally to be problems of social control."[11] More specifically they suggested:

> Many, if not most, of our present social problems have their source and origin in the transition of great masses of population—the immigrants, for example—out of a society based on primary group relationships into the looser, freer, and less controlled existence of life in great cities. . . . All the problems of social life are thus problems of the individual; and all problems of the individual are at the same time problems of the group.

This was "not yet adequately recognized," they lamented, "in the technique of social case work."[12]

The early sociologists had provided an intellectual rationale for the efforts of those moral reformers who sought to remove the deviant individual from the group and subject him or her to uplifting influences within an institutional setting.[13] As early as the 1850s Charles Loring Brace had articulated an alternative strategy in his dispute with those reformers enamored of the institutional asylum. Critical of the "artificial and unnatural" methods of the asylum which treated the individual "as a little machine," Brace organized the Children's Aid Society, which placed wayward children in family settings. The voluntary kindness and "personal influence" of the family, Brace argued, would spontaneously bring out "the great natural impulses which train the character most vigorously."[14] By the 1920s, shorn of Brace's interest in spontaneity and wedded to a manipulative urge, the group approach had become dominant. The science of social control suggested the importance of understanding the group itself and of reshaping it as a means of controlling individual behavior. Park and Burgess joined a growing number of intellectuals interested not only in studying social groups but in discovering techniques for controlling them through the benevolent manipulation of their environment.[15]

THE SOCIOLOGY OF SMALL GROUPS

A number of sociological studies written under Park's direction in the 1920s reflected his interest in the small group as a convenient laboratory for the investigation of social control. Clarence Rainwater, who served as director of the Hamilton Park Recreation Center in Chicago's South Park system from 1910 to 1917, completed his dissertation, *The Play Movement in the United States*, in 1922. The play movement (the effort to use recreation as a vehicle for urban reform), Rainwater explained, had gone through a number of stages. Between 1912 and 1914 a variety of cities, under such reform mayors as Newton Baker in Cleveland and Carter Harrison in Chicago, had promoted municipal dances and other large-scale, citywide activities "open to promiscuous attendance, but inspected and chaperoned by public officials." The leaders of the play movement had abandoned such activities, however, because they were unable to control the atmosphere or the behavior of the patrons at those events.[16]

The play movement thus entered a new stage based on the conviction that "a reorganization of the method of administering the local recreation centers, instead of a city-wide attack upon the recreation problem independent of them, was necessary."[17] The small play groups commonly found in local neighborhood parks afforded a better opportunity for studying group behavior and developing the means to control it. Through the close supervision of neighborhood play groups and team sports, Rainwater argued, the play director could "harmonize personal ideals with social welfare, and thus bring to pass an automatic regulation of the behavior of the persons engaged in playground or recreation center activities." The intelligent development of small groups, "the 'little democracy,' the 'face to face' association small enough to permit personal acquaintance and full communication," Rainwater explained, was an important factor in "the perpetuity and efficiency of self-government." But as the ambitions of the play movement grew, the play group, which had once arisen spontaneously and had thus taught important lessons in self-government, became the artificial creation of the reformers.[18]

As the play movement made what Rainwater called the "transition from 'free' to 'directed' play" and moved "towards institutionalization," it increasingly imposed its agenda and values upon the play group. A group of delegates to the Playground Association of America's 1910 conference, for example, marveled at a model playground where "at the sound of the gong" the children began to play, the youngest ones fabricating identical and symmetrical sand pies in a manner reminiscent of the assembly line. Directed play, with its "efficiency tests," "correlated schedules, trained play leaders, and the classification of patrons," was well designed to prepare children for life in industrial society. But such exercises had little to do with self-government. They reflected a confusion of means and ends that beset many of the experiments with which the sociologists became involved.[19]

Frederic Thrasher's study of the gangs that proliferated in Chicago's slums similarly explored the process of social control within the small group. The gangs, Thrasher understood, were not simply the expression of the boys' anarchic and criminal instincts. In the harsh and competitive atmosphere of the slum, the gang represented "the spontaneous effort of boys to create a society where none adequate to their needs exists." Regulated by its own code of ethics which served as an internal means of social control, the gang was "capable of deliberation, planning, and co-operation in a highly complex undertaking."[20]

The gangs, Thrasher learned, reflected both the disorganization and the values of the larger society around them. Their absorption in "movement and change without much purpose or direction" reflected the city's own disorganization and its citizens' "flight from monotony and the pursuit of a thrill." The gang's in-group morality faithfully recreated the larger society's "failure to recognize obligations to other groups." Like the corrupt politicians, greedy industrialists, racists, and imperialists of the larger society, the gang's credo was "they are all Greeks and the barbarians must suffer."[21] For both Thrasher and Park the relationship to the larger society was the key not only to understanding the gang but to reforming it. The gangs sprang up "spontaneously, but only under favoring conditions and in a definite milieu," Park wrote in his introduction to Thrasher's study; "it is this that assures us that they are not incorrigible and that they can be controlled."[22] Either the gang's larger environment could be transformed or its response to that environment could be redirected. What was needed were "leaders who could organize the play of the boys," redirect their energies, and to lead each boy "to see the meaning of what society wants him to do and its relation to some rational scheme of life."[23] Thrasher pointed to the success of the Union League's Boys' Club which was based on "the notion of making the boys, many of whom were at that time wasted economic material, [into] valuable workers." Notwithstanding his own view of the inadequacies and rapacious ethics of the larger society out of which the gangs arose, Thrasher would channel the boys' energies and their loyalties back into that same society. It was through such efforts, Thrasher explained, that "order is established and habits are formed that are wholesome, or at least, harmless."[24]

The work of another of Park's students, E. T. Hiller's *The Strike*, revealed more directly the political implications of treating urban conflicts as problems of social control. Hiller's work clarifies what was involved in the alienation of social control. As a form of social interaction, the strike resembled the sort of crowd movements that were endemic to the urban environment and that had long fascinated Park. Through an examination of "the behavior characteristic of the striking group and the techniques used to direct and control it," wrote Hiller in explaining the purpose of his study, "reliable policies of social control" could be formulated.[25]

The strike, Hiller understood, was the result of the "emergence of a social group which is capable of collective action."[26] It was the "divergence of interests between employer and employees," he wrote, which gave rise to "self-conscious, or even mutually exclusive and hostile, classes." Corporate forms of organization and intrusive managerial control created a feeling among workers that they were "'working under someone' rather than that they are participating in a joint enterprise."[27] With the centralized control of production and an increase in the size of firms, he explained, personal interaction between employer and employee had decreased and the old ties of mutualism had eroded. Physical segregation in "places of residence and in institutional life" and the anonymity of metropolitan life exacerbated the impersonality of the workplace, which made it more difficult to amiably resolve disputes.[28]

Each new conflict widened the gap between employer and employee and solidified class lines. Encouraging workers to act in concert, the trade union further undermined the personal relations between employer and employee. By capturing the imagination of workers and forcing them to choose sides, the trade union forged new and stronger bonds. The result was "class-consciousness," which Hiller believed to be irrational.[29] Class-conscious workers harbored "a deferred goal, in a social change which will put an end to 'labor as a slave function, and establish in place of the wage or capitalist system an industrial commonwealth of co-operatives,'" Hiller wrote. He could see the desire for a different political order only as an irrational and hopeless dream.[30] The hope for a general strike and the creation of a dictatorship of the proletariat was similarly irrational. "Such a strike has never occurred, and moreover is impossible of achievement," Hiller insisted, primarily because of workers' dependence on employers and their fears of social chaos. Without sufficient numbers workers could never overcome governmental power and the opposition of the other classes that "exercise the decisive influence in the control of political decisions and economic functions." Disastrous failure was the "inevitable outcome" of the general strike. "Forcible methods," Hiller concluded, "when brought to bear against strikes, have always proved decisive."[31] Standing the logic of the revolutionary vanguard on its head, Hiller decried the false consciousness of the militant

196

worker and went on to suggest ways of supplanting that false consciousness with a new consciousness and a new system of social control. What Hiller had unwittingly made clear was that the strength of class consciousness, the contemporary factors that encouraged its development, and the techniques used to reinforce it meant that the new consciousness would have to be imposed from outside the work group as an alienated force of social control.

THE ALIENATION OF SOCIAL CONTROL

Consequently, it was to groups outside the workplace that Hiller looked first for the rational solution to the social problems of an industrial civilization. Key among those groups was the enlightened public. The public represented the "social medium in which the economic pursuits and conflicts of the disputants function," Hiller wrote. In a variety of ways employers and employees appealed to the public for support. Social disruption, the arousal of sympathy and pity, and appeals to patriotism were all methods of involving the public in the dispute. The public intervened in the strike either as a neutral arbiter, usually in the form of expert negotiators, or as a partisan force for one side or the other. "It appears, therefore, that the public, whether in the capacity of neutral or partisan, may be the decisive factor in the industrial warfare," Hiller concluded.[32]

In his introduction to Hiller's work, Park had also noted the importance of the public in determining the outcome of strikes. But in relation to industrial disputes, he cautioned, public opinion had not yet reached a high level of sophistication. The "public has been, on the whole, in the position of an innocent bystander," he argued, "uncertain of its own interest and divided in its sentiments."[33] Park's interest in these questions of consciousness and social control in the industrial setting and his concern that the public develop a more sophisticated approach to the problem of industrial conflict explain his interest in the Hawthorne experiments at the Western Electric plant in Cicero south of Chicago. The Western Electric Corporation, with assistance from the academic leaders of an enlightened public, was exploring similar questions of consciousness and social control and opening up the new field of industrial psychology. The techniques of industrial psychology would promote the development of what Hiller described as "shop loyalty" or "factory solidarity" and what Park would call "industrial folkways."[34]

The purpose of shop loyalty was to close the rift between employer and employee upon which class consciousness and the strike were built. As "long as attention is centered upon their joint output," Hiller wrote, employer and employee "constitute a social unit." A consistent emphasis on the "fact that both live from the joint product of their specialized and co-operating functions may compel adjustments of differences," Hiller argued. "When these common interests regulate behavior, 'factory solidarity,' as opposed to 'class solidarity,' exists." Combined with a lingering "personal attachment, traditional leanings, practical advantages, or controls manipulated by the employer," an emphasis on the joint product promoted shop loyalty. That strategy must be supplemented, he added, "by a favorable social situation, such as personal contacts between superiors and employees, or participation by the workmen in the regulation of the working conditions."[35] With the significant exception of labor's participation in the regulation of working conditions and with a decided emphasis on "controls manipulated by the employer," Western Electric's Hawthorne experiments employed that strategy.[36]

Elton Mayo, a professor of industrial research at Harvard University, began to study the experiments at the Hawthorne plant in 1928. Mayo had first become interested in experiments on industrial fatigue begun during World War I. He learned that fatigue was less a disease than a symptom of monotony and poor morale. Impressed with studies on delinquency and suicide by two of Park's students, studies which pointed to community disorganization as a source of individual maladjustment, Mayo argued that the "obsessive response" of workers in an industrial setting was "a symptom, in the individual, of disequilibrium in the group." Work groups suffered from low morale because the factory lacked "a non-logical social code, which regulates relations between persons and their attitudes to one another," Mayo wrote. The rise of scientific management and a "merely economic logic of production" had interfered "with the development of a [non-logical] code and consequently gives rise in the group to a sense of human defeat."[37] What Mayo confronted in his study of industrial morale was the problem of alienated labor, a problem exacerbated by scientific management.

In the late nineteenth century, industrial work groups had developed their own quite logical production codes as a means of regulating the behavior of their members and resisting the dictates of management. Establishing stints or quotas and adhering to an ethic of manliness (which demanded an unselfishness towards one's fellow workers and a dignified if not defiant bearing towards the boss), skilled workers maintained a high degree of autonomy even within the factory setting. In an effort to wrest control of production from workers, scientific management controlled the decisions made in the labor process and thereby determined the pace and character of work. As management appropriated the knowledge of production and imposed it upon labor in the form of an elaborate technology and routinized drudgery, workers lost the sense of a common purpose on which morale was based.[38]

It is "the essential nature of the human," Mayo understood, "that, with all the will to co-operate, he finds it difficult to persist in action for an end he can but dimly see." The logic of scientific management, which Mayo had no intention of challenging, was a major source of this problem. Instead Mayo prescribed the development of a "non-logical" code for industry, one which would not interfere with the scientific manager's "merely economic logic of production," as a means of raising the morale and the productivity of the work group. Without changing the structure of industry or the nature of the work itself, industrial psychologists would create and manipulate work groups, encouraging competition among them, in an effort to control the social order of the factory. On an individual basis the logic of industrial psychology, in which personnel counselors were instructed to deal (as one recalled), "with attitudes towards problems, not the problems themselves," allowed management to vent workers' frustration in ways that reinforced the status quo. Thus workers' complaints about the Hawthorne plant's intrusive supervision were channeled through personal interviews with industrial psychologists that, in effect, intensified that supervision. In short the Hawthorne experiments substituted an alienated form of social control, a body of mores and a morale imposed from above, for the spontaneous code of the work group itself which had encouraged resistance to the dictates of management.[39]

In his review of Mayo's *The Human Problems of an Industrial Civilization*, Park discounted the political dimension of those issues. The experiments had not convinced Mayo, Park reported, of "the necessity for any species of political remedy." Park endorsed both Mayo's expressed conviction that "as ever in human affairs, we are struggling against our own ignorance and not against the machinations of a political adversary" and his assertion that the most pressing needs in industrial society were "better methods for the discovery of an administrative elite [and] better methods of maintaining working morale." For his own part Park concluded that the experiments demonstrated that the "ills from which an industrial civilization is suffering are not fundamentally political; they are cultural."[40]

Characteristically, Park looked to the development of new forms of social control for solutions. The factory lacked "a body of industrial folkways," he argued, "a body of mores, and a code which represent at once the consensus and common understanding as well as the accumulated wisdom and common sense of the group." At the end of his review Park vented his frustration with reformers who "formulate and impose upon the community legislation which cannot be enforced because it is not understood, accepted, and adequately embodied in the mores of the community." The most effective form of social control, he understood, was that which spontaneously arose from the group itself. But

Park did not recognize or would not acknowledge that the peculiar organization of work within modern industry and especially the principles of scientific management had been specifically designed to prevent the spontaneous emergence of folkways, codes, or mores among the workers. At best the Hawthorne experiments had sought, as Park put it, "some sort of consensus between those who direct operations and those who work under this direction." At worst industrial psychologists had imposed an alien set of controls on the work group.[41]

SOCIAL PLANNING AND THE NEW MEANS OF SOCIAL CONTROL

Park saw that in many respects the Hawthorne experiments paralleled the work he and his associates had been engaged in for more than a decade. "The problems that arise in industry are in the last analysis identical with the problems of industrial civilization generally," Park wrote in his review. Mayo's work had immediate practical application to urban problems. "If any group, such as a clan or an in-group, has to fight opposition, it tends to build up solidarity and moral discipline. . . . If in America . . . we can keep up the rivalries between groups instead of Americanizing and demoralizing our immigrants, we can hope for morale. This is the problem to which Mr. Elton Mayo . . . has called attention," Park wrote. The problem of establishing effective mechanisms of social control and combating the social disorganization of the modern metropolis had been a central theme of the famous collection of essays, *The City*, which Park and his colleagues had published in 1925.[42] In those essays they outlined an urban sociology that would help planners use the science of social control.

The size, heterogeneity, and density of urban populations, the Chicago sociologists argued, made human behavior fundamentally different in the great city as compared to the village or small town. The diverse stimulations of urban life, Park wrote, allowed the individual to "bring his innate dispositions to full and free expression." While that freedom gave city life its attractiveness and creativity, Park explained, its reverse side was instability. "Strikes and minor revolutionary movements are endemic in the urban environment," he wrote. Cities were in "unstable equilibrium"; the "vast casual and mobile" urban populations were subject to "perpetual agitation"; the community was "in a chronic condition of crisis." The "easy means of communication and of transportation, which enable individuals to distribute their attention and to live at the same time in different social worlds, tend to destroy the permanency and intimacy of the neighborhood." Both the freedom and the instability of urban life, Park concluded, resulted from the relative ineffectiveness of traditional agencies of social control: the neighborhood, the family, and the church.[43]

The problem of social control in a large city, Park explained, was a function of the difference between primary and secondary relationships. A small, stable community created lifelong, intimate, and face-to-face relationships, what Park and others called primary relationships. Under such conditions, Park explained, social control was based upon spatial proximity and local association and arose "for the most part spontaneously, in direct response to personal influences and public sentiment." But in a large city relationships tended to be more transitory, less intimate, and indirect or secondary. The "intimate relationships of the primary group are weakened and the moral order which rested upon them gradually dissolved." As a result the "control that was formerly based on mores was replaced by control based on positive law," such as laws governing prostitution and liquor. A variety of organizations based on secondary relationships, such as bureaus of municipal research, social surveys, and foundations of various sorts, had begun to agitate for and secure public acceptance of remedial legislation. Thus "publicity" or "social advertising" was becoming "a recognized form of social control" that worked in concert with legislation. In that form social control arose not from spatial proximity but from a community of interest established through mental life and communication.[44]

Although legislation and an orchestrated public opinion became crucial instruments of social control, those relatively artificial forms of social control, Park warned, had to be based upon some "sort of instinctive and spontaneous control . . . in order to be effective." A system of social control might be orchestrated from above and through secondary relationships. "The practical methods which practical men like the political boss, the labor agitator, the stock-exchange speculator, and others have worked out for the control and manipulation of the public and the crowd," Park understood, demonstrated as much. But such large-scale manipulators still depended on their mastery of face-to-face primary relationships. The dynamics of collective behavior at the level of the small group remained the crucial factor.[45]

Drawing on the work of his students, Park suggested how social planning agencies might use the primary relationships of the small group in establishing social control. A bevy of new agencies, Park explained, including juvenile courts, the Boy Scouts, and playground associations "have taken over to some extent the work which neither the home, the neighborhood, nor the older communal institutions were able to carry out adequately." Those experiments illustrated that any "effort to re-educate and reform the delinquent individual will consist very largely in finding him an environment, a group in which he can live." Thrasher's work on the youth gang, for example, had suggested ways of rehabilitating the delinquent. Rainwater's study of the playground movement had illustrated the possibilities of preventing delinquency in the first place. The playground, Park argued, "should be a place where children form permanent associations." If associated with other "character-forming agencies like the school, the church, and other local institutions," the supervised playground could become an important and positive factor "in the defining of the wishes and the forming of the character of the average individual." Moreover such experiments would help develop "a rational technique for dealing with social problems, based not on sentiment and tradition, but on science."[46] A science of social control that combined the primary relationships of the small group with the secondary

203

relationships of a reform-minded public, Park suggested, formed the basis for an effective policy of social planning.

Soon after the publication of *The City*, planners from the Russell Sage Foundation's Regional Plan of New York and Its Environs (RPNYE) attended the December 1925 meeting of the American Sociological Society, on "The City," organized by the Chicago sociologists. The sociological director of the RPNYE, Shelby Harrison, explained the planners' interest in urban sociology. "While city planning, viewed broadly, has always been aimed at the creation of an environment which would not only exert a corrective, but also a preventive, influence in dealing with the causes of social wrong and social maladjustment," the time had come for "special study from that angle," he argued.[47] Pioneer planners and especially the proponents of the city beautiful had hoped to create a unifying civic ideal that would overawe the individual and, as Paul Boyer argues, help to "mold a morally cohesive, homogeneous urban populace." But Harrison recognized that the Chicago sociologists had shifted the terms of the debate. The Chicago sociologists took the heterogeneity of urban life as a given and argued that social control efforts should be directed not at individuals but at the multifarious groups that populated the urban environment.[48] Accepting urban diversity as an essential and even beneficial element in the social order, the Chicago sociologists suggested the restructuring of social and physical environments as a means to managing urban diversity.

THE SPATIAL PATTERN AND NATURAL ORDER
OF THE URBAN COMMUNITY

In his presidential address to the 1925 conference, "The Urban Community as a Spatial Pattern and a Moral Order," Park suggested that space was a common concern of city planners and urban sociologists. "Human relations can always be reckoned, with more or less accuracy, in terms of distance," Park argued. Such

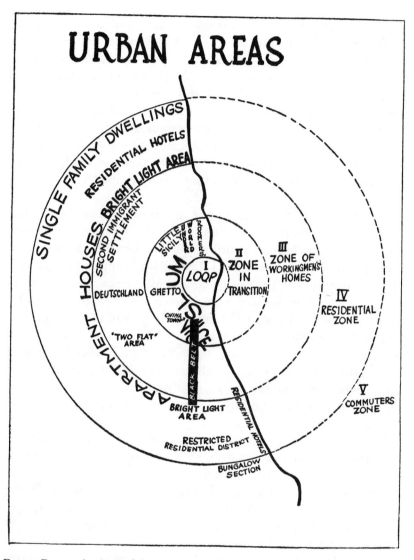

URBAN AREAS

Ernest Burgess's view of the new metropolitan form. The Chicago sociologist encouraged city planners to think about the connections between the social and physical environment and between social and physical planning. From Robert E. Park, Ernest W. Burgess, and Roderick D. McKenzie, *The City*, 1925. Courtesy of the University of Chicago Press.

elements of city planning as transportation and congestion, the heights of buildings, and the costs of real estate all had specific social implications. The speculative ring of real estate outside the central business district, for example, gave rise to peculiar social environments: "These neglected and sometimes abandoned regions become the points of first settlement of immigrants. Here are located our ghettos, and sometimes our bohemias, our Greenwich Villages, where artists and radicals seek refuge." Thus Park underscored "the importance of location, position, and mobility as indexes for measuring, describing, and eventually explaining, social phenomena."[49]

Park cautioned, however, against any simplistic equations. "Reduce all social relations to relations of space and it would be possible to apply to human relations the fundamental logic of the physical sciences," he speculated. But such a "happy solution" was probably impossible, Park warned, because unlike the elements of physical science humans were subject to change. Self-consciousness and personality complicated social planning. Still the physical and social order were closely intertwined, Park concluded, "because social relations are so frequently and so inevitably correlated with spatial relations; because physical distances, so frequently are, or seem to be, the indexes of social distances."[50] The successful urban planner would have to be alert to the subtleties of those interconnections.

While encouraging city planners to think about the connections between the social and physical environment and between social and physical planning, the Chicago sociologists also warned them that the city possessed a natural order that set strict limits on the possibilities of planning. In his address to the convention on "The Natural Areas of the City," Zorbaugh argued that the city was less a product of human design than was generally recognized. Zorbaugh employed Park's concept of natural areas, resistant to conscious human intervention, in his analysis of urban structure. The physical structure of the city, "the framework of transportation, business organization and industry, park and boulevard systems,

206

and topographical features," divided the city into small units. Sociologists termed those units "natural areas, in that they are the unplanned, natural product of the city's growth," Zorbaugh explained. Such areas were the result of competition among the city's inhabitants for position and therefore "each natural area of the city tends to collect the particular individuals predestined to it." The ghettos and Chinatowns, the rooming-house districts and the Gold Coasts were "the 'atoms' of city growth, the units we try to control in administering and planning for the city."[51]

Urban institutions neglected the existence of natural areas at their peril. The ward system of municipal government, Zorbaugh argued, ignored "the existence of distinct areas within the city, each with an individuality, and unequally adapted to function politically under our present system." Chicago's transient rooming-house district, for example, had few competent voters and was "administered by the social agencies and the police. . . . Such an area should be disfranchised and administered from the city hall." Community organizers too had ignored the existence of natural areas and had attempted to recreate the village order in neighborhoods composed of incompatible natural areas. A more promising approach, Zorbaugh suggested, would require "political recognition" of natural areas and a "geographical pluralism in city government."[52]

Planners, Zorbaugh continued, also needed to be aware of natural areas. Ghettos and slums, rooming-house districts, and Gold Coasts were all the inevitable results of urban growth. Even in a metropolis such as Berlin, which had grown from a small city according to a carefully directed plan, natural areas emerged. Those natural areas and the processes of speculation, competition, segregation, and succession that created them "are facts that must be taken into account by those who would control the city's growth as well as by those who would administer the city's government," Zorbaugh explained. Chicago's zoning ordinance was a case in point. "Where use districts cut across natural areas of the city," Zorbaugh reported, "there is a constant pressure upon the board of appeals, which invariably necessitates revision." The zoning ordinance, like other planning and administrative devices, "can neither control this organization of the city nor the inevitable succession of the city. It can, however, taking this organization and succession into account, stabilize the processes of city growth and prevent the waste involved in scattering and uncontrolled speculation." Social planners would face similar problems and might achieve similar results. The biggest obstacle to the development of effective social planning, Zorbaugh concluded, was the failure to compile social statistics on the basis of natural areas. Only when social statistics reflected the real divisions within the city would it be "possible to apply numerical measurement to that collective human behavior in the urban environment which is the growth of the city."[53] Within the limits established by the spatial pattern and natural order of the city, physical and social planners could eliminate the irrational and wasteful aspects of urban development.

THE ORIGINS OF URBAN PLANNING

Those arguments complemented the RPNYE planners' approach to social planning. In his address to the 1925 convention, Harrison suggested that regional, metropolitan, and local agencies should cooperate in creating a plan that "far from setting up barriers and difficulties for the various neighborhood entities, should conserve and promote such groupings."[54] By the time the RPNYE issued its volume *Neighborhood and Community Planning* (1929), Harrison clarified his position in a way that revealed the influence of the Chicago sociologists. Urban neighborhoods emerged "due to continual shiftings and relocations of individuals and groups in response to economic, cultural or racial considerations," Harrison explained. "Like seeks like," he added, and therefore each neighborhood acquired "a more or less distinct group consciousness." Yet neighborhoods generally lacked "any real community life." Rapid urban growth and new technologies of communication and transportation created disruptions whereby "old social relation-ships are destroyed."[55]

City planners had begun to recognize the impact of their own actions on community life. City planning, Harrison explained, could prevent "the destruction of neighborhood values already es-tablished" and encourage "the creation and the conservation of these neighborhood interests." The purpose of the RPNYE's study of community planning, he added, was "to discover the physical basis for that kind of face-to-face association which characterized the old village community and which the large city finds it so difficult to re-create."[56] While the Chicago sociologists might have questioned the wisdom of trying to recreate the village commu-nity in the large city, they would have agreed with (and recog-nized) Harrison's analysis of the problem. The most important re-sult of the cross-fertilization between the RPNYE planners and the Chicago sociologists was Clarence Perry's "neighborhood unit" plan.[57]

Clarence Perry, a social planner hired by the RPNYE to deter-mine the most desirable distribution of playgrounds throughout the region, also attended the 1925 conference. In the course of his study, he had recognized, as he explained to the conferees, that the proper distribution of playgrounds involved much more than an analysis of population densities and the proper mathematical equa-tions. It involved traffic and safety as well as a recognition that "a certain degree of racial and social homogeneity must be assured among playground patrons or healthy play-life will not occur." Consequently, he had enlarged his inquiry to include the question of "what arrangement of streets, open spaces, and public sites would best serve and promote a normal neighborhood life." He had already settled on a neighborhood unit of five thousand people covering one-half square mile bounded by arterial streets; only local traffic would be permitted within the unit. A civic center with a school and a central commons would provide a "physical stimulus for a definite local community consciousness." Impressed with "current real estate tendencies," Perry optimistically predicted that "commercial effort . . . will of itself bring about the development" of such units with minimal help from municipal planning agencies.[58]

The conference had reinforced Perry's conviction and served as a stimulus for the further development of his plan. In 1929 the RPNYE published Perry's description and defense of the neighborhood unit, replete with supporting evidence gleaned from the latest research in urban sociology. The residential neighborhood was essential to urban life, Perry explained, because families "wish to live away from the noise of trains, and out of sight of the smoke and ugliness of industrial plants." But contemporary neighborhoods lacked both cohesiveness and community spirit because of the disruptive effect of heavily traveled streets and because they "usually have no visible boundaries." Citing Burgess's contribution to *The City*, "Can Neighborhood Work Have a Scientific Basis," Perry argued that arterial streets divided urban areas up into natural areas. In the hands of an intelligent planner, the arterial street could be an important factor in promoting neighborhood consciousness instead of disrupting community life. Moreover, if residential areas were carefully planned and constructed as part of large-scale developments that took into account the relationship between the physical environment and the creation of natural areas, then stable and cohesive neighborhoods could be created.[59]

A variety of factors including the growing popularity of city planning, the development of mass production, and the desire among American consumers for luxury items boded well for the success of large-scale developments using the neighborhood unit plan, Perry argued. On the eve of the Great Depression, the unsuspecting planner wrote, "The United States is today so wealthy that most of her citizens have stopped worrying about mere food or shelter." They were willing to pay a higher price for something fine, and planners were eager to give it to them. The problem had been, Perry argued in a sharp attack on the contemporary use of zoning, "the lack of positive residential standards." Without such standards the zoning resolution satisfied business priorities first and polluted residential districts with unnecessary commercial streets. The neighborhood unit plan and especially its segregation

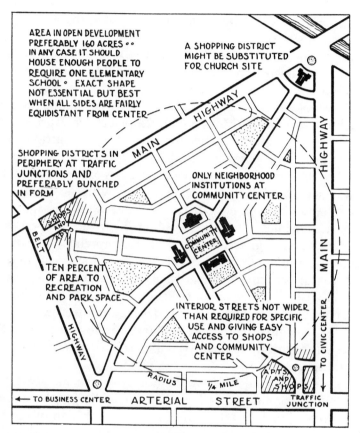

The most important result of the collaboration between the Chicago sociologists and city planners was Clarence Perry's neighborhood plan. Instead of disrupting community life, the arterial street would define the boundaries of the cohesive neighborhood. From the *Regional Survey of New York and Its Environs, Vol. 7, Neighborhood and Community Planning*, 1929. Courtesy of the New York Regional Plan Association.

of commerce on the unit's boundaries provided the missing positive standards.[60]

Still, certain obstacles to the widespread adoption of the neighborhood unit plan remained. "Since only large subdividers and
strong corporations will be able to plan and construct complete
neighborhood units," Perry conceded, "it is evident that the spread
of such developments through unaided private enterprise will be
slow." Public support was needed. Rejecting an outright public
housing program, Perry discussed a number of options that foreshadowed the urban redevelopment strategies of the New Deal and
postwar periods. Referring to experiments with the use of excess
condemnation in slum clearance, Perry urged the passage of legislation that would allow the "pooling of private properties and
their development in accordance with a comprehensive plan promoting the public welfare." He also endorsed state aid to developers meeting specified standards. Such legislation, he acknowledged in a passage that suggests Park's influence, "must have the
sanction of public opinion and the backing of powerful social motives."[61] Consequently, the rest of Perry's monograph consisted of
a series of arguments in favor of public support for the neighborhood unit plan.

The neighborhood unit would not only enhance safety, improve living conditions, and promote neighborhood consciousness, Perry argued, but it would improve the health of the body
politic. He suggested that the decay of civic virtue and political
responsibility was the result of "sections where widely different
classes and races live side by side and yet never touch each other
in informal neighborly relations." The "vertical cleavages which
notably characterize the social life of great cities," he added, discouraged the development of social movements; those that did develop were stigmatized as "labor" or "capitalist" or "silk-stocking"
and quickly died for want of a broader appeal. The problem was
that "if the people who have a common interest in a specific section are not in face-to-face contact with each other, the natural
method of protecting or improving that interest through spontaneous concerted effort is not available." In a passage that combined

212

the realistic language of urban sociology with a concern for the decay of the republic, Perry argued:

> [The city] is a vast accretion of business, industry and dwellings around the original civic nucleus which has become diseased through the effort of functioning in the midst of a mass of politically inert tissue. What urban growth has needed is a process whereby the village civic cell would be repeated at a rate corresponding with the expansion of the population.

While the key to the village community was a juxtaposition of work and residence that was no longer possible, the neighborhood unit would recreate village conditions in the modern city by bringing a homogeneous group of people together and uniting them around a set of neighborhood services. Those cohesive neighborhoods would then breathe new life into the moribund civic life of the city.[62]

Reviving civic virtue and political responsibility in the stable middle class, the neighborhood unit plan also had a role to play in promoting moral values among the less stable classes. Quoting Park on the proliferation of crime and other forms of deviance when group organizations decayed, Perry noted that the "healthy life of a society always depends more on the spontaneous organization of its members than on formal legal and political regulations." That was particularly a problem among the poor and the young. "The gang may be properly regarded as one symptom of the type of community disorganization found in our cities," Perry quoted Thrasher in a passage intended to highlight the danger of the slum to respectable society. Yet the cost of housing in Perry's neighborhood unit would place it out of the reach of the poor. The business creed, which dictated that housing could be provided only at market prices and which Perry was hesitant to challenge, continued to hold firm. Thus the "chief claim for public support" of the neighborhood unit, Perry concluded, was not that it would eliminate the problems of the slums but "that it will improve the environment of the great mass who can afford better residential conditions" and thus "prevent the increase of the classes that are beyond the reach of housing reform because of either social or economic reasons."[63] Perry's plan would not only reinvigorate the city's politics, but it would also slow the growth of the property-less and demoralized poor who posed a threat to the republic.

GEMEINSCHAFT ENDS AND *GESELLSCHAFT* MEANS

In 1932, in the midst of the Great Depression, Perry took his neighborhood unit idea to President Hoover's Conference on Home Building and Home Ownership, where he served on the Committee on Housing and the Community. Citing the work of Park's students, Perry's committee reiterated the connection between the slum and crime as well as between the slum and the political machine. Slum residents lacked "respect for government or belief in its beneficent functions" because in their neighborhoods "ignorance flourishes and civic vision is crushed by virtue of the hard circumstances of daily life." Current economic conditions had closed all avenues out of the slum and not only threatened to "create a permanent slum population but a slum-minded population as well." The lack of proper community amenities in the city's poorer neighborhoods thus was more pressing than ever and dangerous to ignore. It was now imperative, the committee argued, that the principles of the neighborhood unit plan be extended to low-income housing, even to apartment and tenement housing.[64]

In promoting that idea Perry had to overcome a widespread attachment to single-family housing and the ritual invocations of American individualism with which it was associated. In his address to the conference, President Hoover waxed sentimentally on the "individual abode, alive with the tender associations of childhood, the family life at the fireside, the free out of doors, the independence, the security, and the pride in possession of the family's own home. . . . To own one's own home is a physical expression of individualism, of enterprise, of independence." But Perry's committee insisted that there was nothing sacred about the single-

214

family house "if it is too small, ugly in design, and in an area where there is no community teamplay—where neighbors are not neighbors." Abandoning the commitment to the single-family house would allow planners to overcome the economic obstacles to extending the benefits of urban planning to the lower classes.[65]

The key to building stable low-income neighborhoods was not so much improved housing, Perry's committee explained, but the creation of the sort of face-to-face, village relationships that one occasionally glimpsed even in the most congested districts. Housing reform "is no longer concerned with the home alone but with the home in its neighborhood setting." Under the influence of wholesome, primary relationships "delinquency is lessened, character is strengthened, individual skills are whetted by friendly rivalry" and neighbors were encouraged "voluntarily to work together to promote their own interests and realize their individual capacities." The neighborhood unit plan, with its distinct boundaries, its commons, and its homogeneous population, Perry argued, would promote that sort of local community life and community consciousness even among the multi-story, dense residential arrangements of the poor.[66]

Other committees at the president's conference made similar arguments. Warning that the "traditional organization of the neighborhood is weakening under the conditions of modern life," the Committee on House Design urged planners to make greater efforts to reverse the trend. The "true unit of design is the group," the committee reported, because the "most natural, the most stable and the strongest position for the individual in this complex world is to become a member of a strong, successful residence group." Home ownership gave "the individual a sense of security that is a liberating influence." Sharing the enthusiasm for housing developments created by large-scale corporations in partnership with professional planners and government bureaucracies, the Committee on Housing and Citizenship added that "comprehensive real estate developments alone are able to develop a rich community environment."[67] One private developer told the Committee on Large-Scale Operations that speculative builders "can

215

develop out of this social order something just as fine in the end as the skyscraper or the industrial development." He suggested that the "same business brains" that built skyscrapers and industrial satellites (and saddled American cities with scores of blighted areas of speculatively built housing for the lower-middle class) would now solve the housing problems of the nation's fifty million wage earners.[68]

Carrying that logic to its illogical end, one might conclude that the same metropolitan agencies (including large-scale corporations, speculative building, professional planning, and government bureaucracy) that had undermined the integrity of the local community in the first place could now somehow restore that integrity. Nevertheless, the arguments had a considerable impact on the planning profession. Addressing the national conference on city planning in 1933, Frederic Delano acknowledged that the urban sociologists had "been most useful for their advice on housing and community life." The "recognition of the influence of environment on human behavior," the sociologist Edwin Burdell added at the same conference, "is at the bottom of the movement for slum eradication."[69] But at least a few planners doubted that their colleagues really understood the complexity of the problem, especially as it related to low-income groups, and they questioned the efficacy of the proposed solutions.

Speaking on the "housing program from the community point of view" at the 1932 national conference on city planning, John Ihdler rehearsed the arguments he had heard expressed at the president's conference and urged his fellow planners to recognize the necessity of a public housing program. "For the sake of their children and because sub-standard living is a community menace," Ihdler insisted, the poor "must be provided with decent housing." In light of recent discussions of the social dimensions of planning, however, Ihdler expressed a certain uneasiness about the direction urban planning was taking. He feared that his fellow planners. only "dimly recognized" that the "inhabitants of the slums are a very real concern in slum reconditioning." He urged his colleagues to consider more carefully "the social and human problems of dealing with these people and aiding them or developing

216

or habilitating them at the same time that we construct and reconstruct the areas in which they live."[70] Considerable confusion existed about exactly what role the former inhabitants of slums were supposed to play in the new developments. Should public housing be placed under "strict supervision," Ihdler wondered. Burdell recommended the provision of "a suitable resident family whose ostensible function may be to collect rent and supervise the building, but who are really there to act in the capacity of friend and counsellor to the families in the unit." Ideally, the family would provide "suitable examples of clean and intelligent living, worthy of emulation" and "immeasurably hasten the process of acculturation."[71] Such discussions raised the larger question of whether closely knit, organic communities really could be mass-produced in the form of prefabricated large-scale developments that combined the efforts of professional planners, urban sociologists, government bureaucracies, and private corporations.

Fredrick Bigger doubted the effectiveness of centralized planning in community building. The slum, he argued, suffered from the disappearance of "local leaders whom everyone knew" and who "had knowledge of their community problems." Since the explosion of government bureaucracy and professional planning had played a role in the "complete loss of identity," Bigger doubted whether similar methods could now restore it. Burdell pointed to an equally important problem when he argued that "no amount of paternalism, however skillfully administered, can take the place of self-sufficiency and economic independence on the part of the worker." Ihdler too saw that an "effective distribution of wealth" was a key factor in the elimination of slums.[72] Perhaps because of the tremendous impact of the depression, some planners had begun to recognize that the slum problem was not so much a social as an economic and political problem.

Thus a few dissenters within the profession began to recognize the limitations and the confusion of means and ends inherent in the emerging discipline of urban planning. Without challenging the existing economic order, planners could do relatively little to ameliorate the living conditions of the poor. The subsequent strategy of manipulating social forms was the logical residue of

THE ALIENATION OF SOCIAL CONTROL

the planners' and the sociologists' common decision to treat existing economic conditions as part of the unalterable natural order of
the city. But in their effort to create stable and cohesive neighborhood communities through a partnership of large corporations
and centralized public planning, planners sought *Gemeinschaft* ends
with *Gesellschaft* means, that is, to recreate a face-to-face organic
community through the efforts of impersonal bureaucratic agencies.[73] The official tenant codebook for Cincinnati's Laurel Homes,
a neighborhood unit project, reflected the problem. Full of detailed prescriptions for the creation of a spontaneous, organic
community ("make friends with your neighbor, avoid gossip or
acts that may cause people to gossip"), the codebook betrayed a
bureaucratic and mechanical logic in urging tenants to "cooperate
with the management and you will help keep the wheels of this
community turning smoothly."[74] To be sure the early experiments
in urban planning were crude and confused translations of the
work of the Chicago sociologists. Despite the sociologists' repeated calls for a realistic approach that recognized and utilized
urban trends, planners were still transfixed by the moral homogeneity and face-to-face relations of an idealized village community. But the confusion, which paralleled the effort to replace
spontaneous forms of social control with alienated forms, could
be found in the work of the sociologists themselves, in a lingering
attachment to the local community that clashed with a growing
reliance on metropolitan and supermetropolitan agencies. Like
city planners, urban sociologists struggled to find a new basis for
the urban community.

THE PROBLEM OF COMMUNITY REVISITED

Despite his own fascination with the mobility and fluidity of
the urban environment, Park recognized the difficulty it presented
for the development of a sense of community. In a brief but in-
triguing essay, "The Mind of the Hobo," Park argued that the

hobo exemplified metropolitan man's difficulty in "carrying on an associated existence." Pursuing "locomotion for its own sake," the hobo found it impossible to develop lasting relationships or even to maintain communication with others. The restless hobo suffered through "so many dull days" because all "forms of association among human beings rest finally upon locality and local association." If there was to "be permanence and progress in society, the individuals who composed it must be located." The tragedy of the hobo was that he "sacrificed the human need of association and organization to a romantic passion for individual freedom."[75] That "romantic temper," a restlessness and inordinate desire for physical mobility, Park argued elsewhere, afflicted urbanites generally and was "but the reflection of a corresponding mental instability."[76]

Those concerns underlay Park's interest in the small group and in agencies that might replace the disintegrating family and neighborhood of the deracinated urbanite. Yet he knew that no agency had been found that "has thus far succeeded in providing a wholly satisfactory substitute for the home."[77] Although Park's focus was generally on the disorganized family and neighborhood and the associated tangle of social pathology, the more stable families and neighborhoods of certain immigrant groups, the Japanese for example, also attracted his attention. It was precisely those communities, Park argued, which had "maintained in this country their simple village religions and mutual aid organizations who have been most able to withstand the shock of the new environment." Park went on to argue that such immigrant neighborhoods "may be regarded as models for our own."[78]

Neighborhood organization or disorganization did not only affect individual behavior; it was also central to the health of the body politic. "If the local community is organized, knows its own local interests, and has a mind of its own, democracy prospers," Park explained. Unfortunately, we no longer lived in a society where "public life was the vocation of every citizen." As a leisure-time activity, politics suffered from competition with "livelier forms of recreation." The busy urbanite lost sight of the local community and fled the "dull routine of life at home" in search of excitement and adventure. The problem "is to encourage men to seek God in their own village and to see the social problem in their own neighborhood."[79] Both republican concerns and the idealized village community survived in certain elements of Park's thought despite his quest for a realistic approach.

Yet Park wavered in his view of the proper basis for the urban community. Simultaneously, and sometimes within the same arguments, Park was developing a critique of the concept of neighborhood community and of the political system based on it. In introducing his discussion of the "romantic temper," Park noted that it was only "the incompetent people," women, children, ward heelers, and political hacks, who maintained "an interest that could be called lively in the local communities of our great cities." The competent, especially the urban professionals, treated their local neighborhoods simply as dormitories; only their work and citywide associations engaged their full interest. If "we could organize our politics, as the Russians have sought to organize theirs, on the basis of occupation, that is, in soviets, it might be possible to awaken in our intelligentsia a more than dilettante and sporting interest in local politics and the problems of the local community," wrote the always unpredictable Park. However, our "political system is founded on the presumption that the local community is the local political unit." On the basis of his criticism of the romantic temper, developed in the same essay, one might have been tempted to conclude that he saw this as right and proper. But elsewhere Park made clear his objections to the existing urban political system.[80]

The disposition to extend the power of the executive at the expense of the legislative branch, Park wrote, was based on a recognition "that the form of government which had its origin in the town meeting and was well suited to the needs of a small community based on primary relations is not suitable to the government of the changing and heterogeneous populations of cities of three or four millions." Highly critical of the incompetence of machine politicians and their inability to deal with metropolitan problems, Park saw the machine as an unfortunate "attempt to maintain, inside the formal administrative organization of the city, the control of a primary group." Much more promising were those groups engaged in social politics, including taxpayers' associations, good-government organizations, bureaus of municipal research, and agencies such as the Russell Sage Foundation, which were based on secondary relationships and used the techniques of publicity to educate the voter. Fortunately, the politics of "social advertising" employed by a "profession with an elaborate technique supported by a special body of knowledge," Park concluded, was replacing the old-style machine politics based on the neighborhood and the political party.[81]

THE METROPOLITAN COMMUNITY

The tension in Park's work between a neighborhood and a metropolitan basis of community would not prevent the younger generation of sociologists from seizing the opportunities that federal planning on a metropolitan basis offered. Those developments were foreshadowed in the work of Park's colleague, Roderick McKenzie. The most obvious symbol of the collapse of the traditional neighborhood community, Park had argued, was automobility. By increasing the mobility of the individual, the automobile had "multiplied the difficulties of maintaining a stable social order" and had undermined the "primary source of control, namely, the vigilance of neighbors and the desire of every individual to retain the respect and esteem of his local community."[82] In *The Metropolitan Community*, a monograph prepared for President Hoover's survey, *Recent Social Trends*, McKenzie offered a more optimistic appraisal of the effects of automobility. The metropolitan community, he explained, was "essentially an expanded pattern of local community life based upon motor transportation."[83] More completely than Park, McKenzie translated the sociologists' concern with community from a neighborhood to a metropolitan basis.

Physical proximity, McKenzie argued, no longer played a significant role in the metropolitan community. Unlike the traditional city, the metropolitan community "obtains its unity through territorial differentiation of specialized functions rather than through mass participation in centrally located institutions." Neither did neighborliness and daily contact on city streets have much to do with community. The automobile and the modern means of communication meant that spatial distance no longer correlated with social distance. "Physically adjacent population groups may be interrelated in an economic or symbiotic manner and yet live in vastly different social worlds," he explained. Rather than destroying community, however, the "increased mobility of products and people," McKenzie argued, had created "a more closely knit community structure." Speeding automobiles, the telephone call, and, most important, the metropolitan agencies of communication, finance, distribution, and management, McKenzie suggested, provided the basis for the new community.[84]

A recognition of the many problems that beset the metropolitan community tempered McKenzie's optimism. Among the problems was a vigorous competition among metropolitan centers for regional dominance. Since superior size invariably won out, he reported, "the will to grow, to increase in population, wealth, and prestige, dominated the psychology of most American cities." As the metropolis grew, its problems of traffic and congestion, sanitation and public health, policing and crime, taxation and financing became not only more complex, but they transcended existing political boundaries and outstripped the ability of established governments to deal with them. The peculiar distribution of population within the metropolitan area further exacerbated the problem:

It is a matter of common observation that the inner and older sections of a city, particularly those lying close to the main business center, are usually inhabited by the weaker and less stable

222

elements of the population, while the outer zones and the suburbs tend to have higher proportions of the more substantial members of the community.

Annexation had solved the problems of both administration and personnel for some time, but it was no longer practical in light of suburban opposition and the extended geographic scope of metropolitan activities.[85]

The rise of the metropolitan region and the many problems of the metropolitan community demanded new political arrangements. The rise of "the new supercity points, therefore, to the need of some sort of supermetropolitan government," McKenzie explained. In extending metropolitan influence to surrounding communities through various public authorities and in calling for official status for the master plan and a suspensive veto for the planning commission, city planners had pioneered in the creation of metropolitan government. Regional planning, such as that undertaken by the Sage Foundation, promised greater rewards; but such efforts were still "thwarted by the large number of politically independent communities with which planning bodies have to deal." That problem, the political scientist Thomas Reed suggested in a chapter on "Metropolitan Government" in McKenzie's *The Metropolitan Community*, demanded the creation of new political "units of metropolitan scope possessing sufficient powers to deal with those matters which affect the metropolis as a whole." Reed's discussion of recent experiments in metropolitan governance concluded with his and McKenzie's call for "supermetropolitan government."[86]

McKenzie's study culminated in a brief for the perpetuation and extension of expert, professional planning. Although the economic depression had revived efforts "to revert to a simpler order" and a greater reliance on the family and the neighborhood, McKenzie warned that "our metropolitan society is too complex a mechanism to be adjusted by such expedients." The interest in planning would not only survive the current economic crisis, he concluded, but it would be extended to "an increasing range of economic and social activities." Pointing to the interdependence of metropolitan areas and their creation by "economic and cultural forces that are world-wide in scope," McKenzie's analysis provided a rationale for the sort of federal planning on a metropolitan basis that began to emerge during the New Deal.[87] In alliance with metropolitan elites and government officials, McKenzie suggested, physical and social planners would play an increasingly important role in shaping and maintaining the metropolitan order.

After a decade of intellectual exchange and practical experimentation the union of urban sociologists and city planners seemed on the verge of realization. Without rejecting the city planners' view of the city as primarily a piece of economic machinery, and while reinforcing their strategy of working with elites, their skepticism about the political competence of the masses, and their realistic assumptions about the limits of significant change, the urban sociologists had alerted city planners to the social implications of their work. Exploring the connections between physical environment and social behavior, the sociologists had helped city planners think in new ways about social problems and to devise plans that appeared to promote social adjustment and social stability. While both sociologists and planners remained perplexed about the proper basis for community in the modern city, they had begun to develop a theory of a metropolitan community that complemented both their practical policies and their underlying assumptions. What they had failed to do was to analyze critically the economic and political forces that had made the ideal of community problematic in the first place.

7

Urbanism as a Way of Life:
The Paradox of Professional Planning

For more than a quarter of a century, the ambitions of social scientists and professional planners had been steadily expanding. Combining academic social science, professional planning, and federal authority, President Hoover's Committee on Recent Social Trends seemed to herald the realization of those ambitions. The purpose of the *Recent Social Trends* survey, as President Hoover had originally conceived it, was to investigate the "elements of instability rather than stability in our social structure" and to discover the means of managing them. Columbia University economist and chair of the committee Wesley Mitchell explained that the survey would provide "a basis for the formulation of large national policies."[1] But before the survey could be completed, indeed before it was well started, the Great Depression shook the prestige and the confidence of social scientists and professional planners.

Ironically, that same economic disaster and the federal response to it in the New Deal would afford social scientists and professional planners significant new opportunities to shape public policy.

While a full examination of urban reform and urban thought during the New Deal is beyond the scope of this work, this concluding chapter examines two interrelated texts, the National Resources Planning Board's study of *Our Cities: Their Role in the National Economy* (1937) and the Chicago sociologist Louis Wirth's famous article "Urbanism as a Way of Life" (1938). Those texts, both of which came from the work of the Urbanism Committee of the National Resources Planning Board, carry the issues, themes, and events examined in previous chapters into the 1930s. They illustrate both the persistence of republican ideals and the powerful influence of realistic assumptions. An analysis of the texts will explicate the paradox of professional planning, a paradox that was implicit in and central to the development of the realistic tradition.

A Crisis of Confidence

The expanded governmental role for social scientists and professional planners, anticipated in the Hoover administration, would become more complex and controversial in the context of the economic crisis. A former engineer, Hoover had viewed planning as the wider application of the principles of scientific management; the idea for the *Recent Social Trends* survey originated in Hoover's own 1921 report on "waste in industry," which he had undertaken while serving as the secretary of commerce. The same sort of planning that had been successful in industry, Hoover believed, could also rationalize social organization.[2] Even in the best of times, however, the logic of social planning would never be as obvious as the industrial analogy was meant to suggest. Moreover, Hoover had conceived of the survey as a rational blueprint for social management in a period of unprecedented prosperity; but it was published amidst a profound economic crisis that had paralyzed conservative leadership and brought into question the efficacy of the industrial model upon which the prestige of social science and social management was based.

226

A debate on the role that social scientists should play in formulating and implementing public policy, which had begun within the president's committee, became public with the survey's publication in 1933. In his review of *Recent Social Trends*, Charles Beard predicted a "coming crisis in the empirical method" of American social science. President Hoover, Beard explained, had assumed "that when once the 'data' have been assembled important conclusions will flow from observing them" just as in "physics or mathematics." Yet even Hoover had recognized, Beard added in quoting him, that the social scientists had set "forth matters of opinion as well as strict scientific determination." Many social scientists themselves worried about what would become known as the "problem of objectivity," that is, the tendency of their own subjective values and prejudices to undermine their claim to a disinterested and objective expertise. Echoing the concerns of some of the members of the president's committee, Beard argued that if policy-making was to remain democratic in an era of expert planning, then the public would have to take a more prominent role in questioning the social scientists' values and deciding upon their appropriateness.[3] Meanwhile, the Great Depression had also shaken the planning profession.

As the economic boom of the 1920s began to collapse in the year before the stock market crash, dissenting voices were already surfacing at the national conference on city planning. By May 1929 Harold Buttenheim, editor of *The American City* and long-time planning enthusiast, had come to agree with those "radical" critics of the profession who argued that zoning resolutions "are devised with tender solicitude for upper economic groups," while the poor suffered from congestion "to the financial gain of a few." Buttenheim saw much truth in Charles Beard's contention that "apart from decorative work, such as boulevards making it easy for the Rotary boys to go from their offices to their country clubs, or civic plazas—that is, putting diamond crowns upon leprous brows—there has been very little achievement in the field of city planning." At the same conference Lawrence Veiller bemoaned the lack of progress in tenement reform. He described a "benighted" city, full of darkness and disease, and argued that zoning laws made "inadequate provision for light." The regional plan of New York's standard of "one-half hour's sunshine in each room or its equivalent," he insisted, was wholly inadequate.[4] This professional introspection and self-criticism would intensify in the coming years.

In 1931 Harland Bartholomew, then serving as president of the national conference, blamed the planning profession for failing to control speculation in real estate and metropolitan aggrandizement. While countless blighted areas infected American cities, he charged, planners had continued to promote metropolitan expansion under the guise of a false regionalism. Amending the profession's earlier fascination with efficient and orderly movement, Bartholomew declaimed: "There is beauty in crowds massed in order. Rows upon rows of people in a vast arena, or marching in rhythm, are impressive. But when the rhythm is broken, and the crowd become a mob, terror seizes us." Economic disaster and social disorder had forced a reconsideration of the profession's assumptions. In the following year Bartholomew extended his critique. He compared the planners' vision of metropolitan grandeur to the mistaken "prophecies of some new order" that had collapsed with the stock market. The crucial task now, he insisted, was to save the "decaying" urban core from the "speculative debauchery in real estate."[5] As the Roosevelt administration took office in 1933, self-doubt and internal dissent had reached the highest levels of the planning profession.

THE PRESERVATION OF THE PROFESSIONS

Harold Ickes, head of a vast new public works program, represented the Roosevelt administration at the 1933 national conference on city planning in October. His appearance helped the planning profession recover its confidence. Lauding the work of the Chicago Plan Commission and the regional plan of New York,

Ickes supported the conference's resolution describing planning as "an essential public work" and urging that planning agencies be made "eligible to receive grants and loans" from Ickes's Public Works Administration. He also announced the immediate alloca- tion of $400 million to "join arterial highways."[6] Alfred Bettman, the current president of the national conference, spoke on the role of city and regional planning in the recovery program and noted "that the arm and hands of the federal government reach down into the localities to an extent which belies or repudiates many a boasted principle of local self-government." The "field of federal legislation and federal activity," he added with satisfaction, gave planners "greater sources of encouragement" than local govern- ments ever had. The National Recovery Act, he explained, called for national planning and required that local projects be consistent with federally "coordinated planning." He rejoiced, "Members of the planning profession have been given important positions in the Public Works Administration" and on the newly created National Resources Planning Board.[7]

Social scientists, facing their own professional difficulties which included a dearth of employment, also found important new allies in the Roosevelt administration. Adolf Berle, Wesley Mitchell's colleague at Columbia who had just joined the Roosevelt admin- istration, outlined a new and ambitious governmental role for so- cial scientists in his review of *Recent Social Trends*. Like Beard, Berle understood that Hoover's "impartial analysis of the facts" was a chimera. What was worse, Berle added, was that the social scientists themselves had been paralyzed by the unrealizable dream. Social scientists should overcome their self-doubts and take on a more aggressive role in the current crisis, Berle wrote. He urged them to accept a responsibility to "interpret the data" for the policymakers and to suggest ways in which recent trends were "susceptible of guidance towards real civilization." Berle agreed with the vice-chairman of the Committee on Recent Social Trends, Charles Merriam, who argued "that central control over social and industrial forces is . . . almost inevitable." Given that inevitability, who better to control the central machinery than the social scientist, Berle asked. The Roosevelt administration and its celebrated brains trust, Berle concluded, was taking over the "formless and chaotic machinery devised during the brilliant decade" and preparing to give it "a directive purpose."[8] While President Roosevelt ignored Hoover's *Recent Social Trends*, he extended even greater authority to its union of social scientists and professional planners.

Charged with the responsibility of coordinating physical and social planning, Roosevelt's National Resources Planning Board gave urban planning its first institutional base in the federal government. Uniting key figures in the development of city and social planning, the three-member National Resources Planning Board was composed of Mitchell, Frederic Delano (former chair of the American Planning and Civic Association and the National Capital Park and Planning Commission) and Merriam (the University of Chicago's entrepreneur of research). Charles W. Eliot, a landscape architect and city planner, served as executive officer of the new agency. Delano, Merriam, and Eliot remained the most influential figures throughout the history of the board.[9] Merriam and his Chicago colleagues played an especially important role in bringing social scientists, professional planners, and the urban planning perspective into the federal bureaucracies created during the New Deal.[10]

Under the prodding of Merriam, the National Resources Planning Board undertook a study of the role of the city in the national economy. Merriam believed that the massive economic problems that beset the country provided an opportunity for the development of the sort of federal planning on a metropolitan basis that he had long advocated. Assembling a research committee on urbanism headquartered in Cincinnati, which included city managers, urban planners, and the Chicago sociologist Louis Wirth, the National Resources Planning Board published its report, *Our Cities: Their Role in the National Economy* in 1937. *Our Cities* made an impressive and convincing case for a nationwide assault on urban problems. As the composition of its research committee might suggest, the report reflected in part the realistic approach that had matured in the past decade. Forswearing any utopian scheme of remaking the city or creating garden cities, the report argued that "the realistic answer to the question of a desirable urban environment lies not in wholesale dispersion, but in the judicious reshaping of the urban community and region by systematic development in accordance with forward looking and intelligent plans." In particular the success of what the report called "urban planning" depended upon taking advantage of such "natural trends" as industrial decentralization and residential suburbanization to create "a moderately decentralized and yet integrated urban structure." Calling for "planned and supervised recreational projects, slum eradication, and programs of better housing for the low-income groups, particularly in areas with high delinquency and crime rates," the report also endorsed the urban planners' policy of social control.[11]

THE ROAD NOT TAKEN

Yet despite the prominent role played by Merriam and Wirth, the urbanism committee went far beyond the orthodoxy of the realistic tradition to project a radical alternative to realistic urban planning. Explanations for the committee's boldness vary, including the dire economic conditions that seemed to demand more radical solutions, the political and labor turmoil that beset the nation's cities in the mid-thirties (the report described the metropolis as "the dusty and sometimes smoldering and reddened arena of industrial conflict" and the "great battleground of the Nation"), the more progressive orientation of the national administration (reflected in Berle's challenge to guide the nation toward real civilization), and the profession's own recent self-examination. For all those reasons, and perhaps for others that remain unclear, the urbanism committee drew upon the surviving body of republican criticism of the city to outline a far more ambitious program of urban reform than had ever been considered.[12]

The work of the urbanism committee signaled the recognition among at least a small group of federal planners that America's future depended on the creation of an urban civilization worthy of the name. "There is democracy in the scattered few," the report asserted, "but there is also democracy in the thick crowd with its vital impulse and its insistent demand for a just participation in the gains of our civilization." Arguing that the spread of sharecropping and tenantry threatened to create a propertyless rural proletariat just as the factory had stripped urban artisans of their independence, the report also reflected the abandonment of a nostalgia for a rural order, which if it had ever existed certainly no longer did. Calling for the "harmonious adjustment and happy interrelation" of the city and the country, the report recommended the "equalization between country and city of as many material and cultural opportunities as possible." The most remarkable aspect of the report, what set it apart most clearly from the realistic tradition, was its sharp criticism of the economic organization of American life, which it blamed for the host of problems that beset American cities.[13]

The economic insecurity of the urban worker, the committee charged, was one of the greater obstacles to social progress. Low wages meant that "a large proportion of the urban population . . . is barred from any of the advantages which urban life can offer." The federal government should "formulate the requisites of an acceptable minimum standard of living" and ensure that industries that "are not paying the cost of their existence in terms of the human energies they consume" abide by the standard. A federal industrial policy was also needed to "combat the present tendency of industry to move from urban regions to otherwise often uneconomic areas in order to exploit labor and escape undue taxation." A "unified taxation policy and a uniform labor policy" would further "combat exploitation of labor and inequitable taxation." Such policies would help create "a better balance between the cost to the community of services to its industries and the income of the community from its industries."[14] Economic planning, *Our Cities* suggested, was an essential prerequisite to successful urban reform.

Our Cities outlined urban taxation, land use, and public works policies, which also owed a great deal to the republican critique of the American city. State and local authorities, the report suggested, should "consider the reduction of the rate of taxation on buildings and the corresponding increase of such rates on land." A study of a tax on speculative realty values, it added, should be undertaken to determine if it "would make possible the financing of public improvements more nearly through tax revenue derived from the increased values which these improvements create, and whether such a tax would aid in combatting speculation in land." The committee also called for a more "liberal" policy of municipal land acquisition, a "wider interpretation" of the term "public use," and a thorough reconsideration of all constitutional and statutory limitations on the general property tax.[15]

Such radical changes in fiscal policy, the report continued, would facilitate the development of a "Nation-wide, coordinated, long-range program of planned public works" involving all levels of government with federal assistance. The program would not only serve "as one of the means of minimizing the impact of business cycles," but would facilitate an attack on the slum, that most "visible evidence of our failure in city building." A major focus of the public works program would be "the widest program of demolition possible," guided by a policy "of not compensating the owners of buildings unfit for human use." A commitment to the "satisfactory rehousing of displaced families" and a constructive national housing policy "for rehousing the low-income groups at acceptable minimum standards" would complement the policy of slum clearance.[16]

Both metropolitan aggrandizement and the belief in the unity of private and public interests, two elements of the realistic tradition, also came under the urbanism committee's scrutiny. A key element in an effective urban policy, the report argued, was the "substitution in place of the philosophy and aspiration of bigness the philosophy and aspiration of quality" and a reexamination of the "expectation of continuous and unlimited growth."[17] The report also took issue with the "widely held belief that the special interests of groups and individuals are identical with the public

233

interest" and called for "a form of economic organization better attuned to the public interest," especially in the provision of public utilities. Government regulation of privately owned utilities, it charged, had "perpetuated and, in some cases, accentuated the pattern of economic activity and of urbanization which competitive private enterprise developed with little or no consideration for the public interest and under policies and practices which, with each advance in the technology, successively supported and stimulated the then prevailing economic and urban pattern." In language that the republican proponents of rapid transit would have recognized, the committee urged city planners to develop a transportation policy directed toward an "economically effective and socially more desirable distribution of economic activities and urban pattern."[18] A sharper riposte to the realistic tradition, especially in its insistence that planning include the transformation of the economic and well as the physical and social environment, is difficult to imagine.

Although at least one commentator greeted the report by inexplicably blasting its timidity, the urbanism committee had offered an analysis of urban problems that owed much more to the republican critics of urban America than to the realistic tradition. It outlined a reform program that could have led to dramatic improvements in urban life. Far more than the urban planners' policy of prefabricating stable and homogeneous neighborhoods, the recommendations in *Our Cities* had a chance of creating "a social and political coherence which can arouse and hold community loyalty and participation, [and] inspire responsible civic loyalty." The problem with *Our Cities* was not, as an editorial in *The Nation* had it, that it remained "well within the safety zone of more and more facts, more and more education, more and more cooperation with agencies, public and private, hopelessly prevented from taking any drastic, long-range action."[19] The problem was that *Our Cities* lacked an effective mass constituency committed to its implementation. Just as the aggressive antitrust policy of the later New Deal had died for lack of a mass constituency (even within organized labor), so too did the urbanism committee's program of urban reform.[20]

The failure to support and implement the program outlined in *Our Cities* cannot be blamed entirely on the urban experts who compiled the report. Just as the labor movement had come to accept the inevitability of corporate capitalism and to moderate its goals (exemplified in its lack of enthusiasm for antitrust legislation), the urban citizenry had come to doubt its ability to effect significant change and had embraced realistic assumptions, thus "coming to terms" with the metropolitan order. But in the face of a profound crisis, the urban citizenry now desperately needed innovative and practical proposals for change; and those who had such proposals likewise needed a powerful constituency to implement them. Urban reformers who worked within the republican tradition had seen the mobilization of a democratic movement as an essential part of their task. In contrast social scientists and professional planners worked within the realistic tradition, which doubted the political competence of the people and saw little to be gained in a dialogue with popular movements. Thus, even as the urbanism committee overcame some of the limitations of the realistic tradition and critically examined the role of economic and political power in city building, the longer term legacy of the realistic tradition vitiated their efforts. In their failure to cultivate a mass constituency, social scientists and professional planners had contributed to the atrophy of democratic politics; in their isolation from the potential sources of such a constituency, they had left themselves powerless to challenge the status quo even when their own analysis demanded it.

URBANISM AS A WAY OF THOUGHT

Nineteen-thirty-seven was the year of Roosevelt's searing indictment of one-third of a nation ill-housed, ill-clad, and ill-nourished and his call for new initiatives to attack those problems. The proposals contained in *Our Cities* would have fit well into such a program. Yet for want of an effective constituency, a more radical New Deal was never legislated. Soon a revived conservative and rural opposition to the New Deal as well as Roosevelt's own tendency to pander at least occasionally to the antiurban bias of parts of his constituency ("Today many people are beginning to realize that there is inherent weakness in cities which become too large for their times," he said barely a week after *Our Cities* appeared) combined to bury the report's recommendations.[21] The urban sociologists who had done so much to shape the emergence of urban planning, however, still had at least one important constituency in other sociologists. It was among that constituency that the experience of the urbanism committee would have its greatest influence.

Louis Wirth's classic essay, "Urbanism as a Way of Life," published a year after *Our Cities* and more widely read, was the fruit of his participation on the committee and helped to inspire the work of the coming generation of urban sociologists. Wirth, of course, had a long and distinguished career that bracketed his work with the urbanism committee. Moreover, he was generally a more subtle and generous thinker than "Urbanism as a Way of Life" might suggest. That particular essay, however, illustrates the powerful and deleterious influence of realistic assumptions on urban thought. Unfortunately, in "Urbanism as a Way of Life," Wirth's most famous and influential essay, the recognition of the role of economic and political interests in urban development that characterized *Our Cities* gave way to the sociological emphasis on natural and impersonal urban processes and the forms of social interaction.

In "Urbanism as a Way of Life," Wirth offered a sociological definition of city life. His emphasis thus was on "the peculiar characteristics of the city as a particular form of human association" and as "a distinctive mode of human group life." He argued that a combination of three overlapping factors (size, density, and heterogeneity) gave urban populations their distinctive character. Indeed, Wirth warned against confusing urbanism with any specific historical influences and in particular with capitalism or industrialism. Having removed industrial capitalism as a factor in his analysis, Wirth went on to describe with remarkable equanimity

236

the exploitation, competitiveness, and anomie which, along with individual freedom, characterized life in the modern American city.[22]

It was the sheer number of people in the city, Wirth explained, that had given rise to "segmental relations." Since urbanites were both more dependent on people in general and less dependent on individual persons, the multiplication of contacts prevented them from having a thorough knowledge of or acquaintance with one another. As a result urbanites tended to regard others principally "as a means for the achievement of our own ends." In combination with the "pecuniary nexus," such an attitude gave rise to "predatory relationships." The corporation had proved so adaptable to urban conditions, Wirth observed, precisely because it had "no soul." There were, of course, compensating factors. The "superficiality, the anonymity, and the transitory character of urban-social relations" gave the urbanite greater individual freedom, Wirth explained, even as it robbed him or her of "the spontaneous self-expression, the morale, and the sense of participation that comes with living in an integrated society."[23]

The density and heterogeneity of population reinforced those characteristics of urban life. Population density gave rise to a competition for space that resulted in segregation and the creation of "a mosaic of social worlds." The "close living together and working together of individuals who have no sentimental and emotional ties fosters a spirit of competition, aggrandizement, and mutual exploitation" and created a need for a variety of formal controls. The heterogeneity of urban life, its incessant physical and social mobility, Wirth argued, also undermined neighborliness and created a situation where the "task of holding organizations together and maintaining and promoting intimate and lasting acquaintanceship between the members is difficult." Heterogeneity gave rise to a complex division of labor and eventually to modern mass production; as a result the "pecuniary nexus which implies the purchaseability of services and things has displaced personal relations as the basis of association." In the great city, Wirth added, "there is virtually no human need which has remained unexploited by commercialism."²⁴ Wirth thus described urbanism in terms similar to those the harshest critics of the American city might have used. But whereas the radical might have traced such a culture to industrial capitalism, land speculation, or the exploitation of public utilities and the conservative might have traced it to the anarchic excesses of democracy and unrestrained individualism or the collapse of traditional forms of authority, Wirth treated it as an inevitable result of the size, density, and heterogeneity of urban population.

Although Wirth discussed the pathological aspects of urban life with what might be described as an excess of detachment, he was certainly not content with the status quo. He had just completed an intensive study of urban problems and helped to author a blueprint for radical change in urban policy. In some ways that experience still shaped his approach to the study of urbanism. For even in the guise of the dispassionate sociologist Wirth placed much less emphasis on the factors that compensated for the exploitation, competitiveness, and anomie of urban life (the freedom, diversity, and liberality of urban life, the critical and sophisticated outlook) than did Simmel in his classic essay "The Metropolis and Mental Life," on which Wirth's was based.²⁵ But in other ways Wirth's sociological approach to urbanism differed sharply from that found in *Our Cities*.

In the final pages of his essay, Wirth looked to the probable future of urbanism as a way of life. In the city, Wirth argued, the isolated individual was "reduced to a stage of virtual impotence" and it was "only through the organizations to which men belong that their interests and resources can be enlisted for a collective cause." It was to the "emerging trends in the communication system and to the production and distribution technology that has come into existence with modern civilization that we must look for the symptoms which will indicate the probable future development of urbanism as a mode of social life." He warned that those social organizations were often "subject to manipulation by symbols and stereotypes managed by individuals working from afar or operating invisibly behind the scenes through their control of the instruments of communication." Wirth was not entirely comfortable with pinning the future development of the urban community to modern technology and to the "soulless" corporations that controlled it (as Wirth well knew) for private rather than public ends.[26] But it was the only logical conclusion to which his analysis could lead.

Based on the factors of size, density, and heterogeneity, Wirth's definition and analysis of urbanism ensured that the problems of urban life, at least from a sociological perspective, would be defined in terms of the forms of social interaction rather than the political and economic interests that shaped social interaction. Notwithstanding the often bleak picture of urban life that he offered, Wirth still insisted that social progress depended less on changes within the economic, political, and physical structure of the city, or on any mass political movement, than on the evolution of the forms of social interaction. The forms of social interaction, Wirth argued, followed their own natural evolutionary course independent of the political aspirations of the average citizen or the best intentions of the urban planner. Thus in Wirth's thought the two most salient elements of the realistic tradition, a skepticism about the role that the urban citizenry could play in shaping urban development and the assertion of a set of natural factors that set strict limits on the discretion of professional planners, reinforced one another.

In complementary ways *Our Cities* and "Urbanism as a Way of Life" serve to remind us that the new metropolitan form (or any urban form) involves something more than mere landscapes and streetscapes. *Our Cities* argued that underlying the new metropolitan form was a specific configuration and exercise of economic and political power and that a redistribution or redirection of that power would produce a different urban form. "Urbanism as a Way of Life" illustrates the role of thought in the creation and development of an urban form, for even a body of thought that minimized the role of choice and of power in urban development had its impact on urban form, if only to discourage innovation and popular participation and to reinforce the status quo. As an alternative to social theories that made the distribution of political and economic power primary, the concept of urbanism reinforced realistic assumptions.[27]

Epilogue

Since 1937 the realistic tradition has become enmeshed and codified in the terms *urban* and *urbanism*. In warning against the "danger of confusing urbanism with industrialism and modern capitalism," the Chicago sociologist Louis Wirth urged urban experts to avoid "identifying urbanism as a way of life with any specific locally or historically cultural influences which . . . are not the essential determinants of its character as a city."[1] Wirth's admonition influenced not only planners and social scientists, but even historians who should have been most interested in "specific locally or historically cultural influences."

In an oft-quoted call for a "new urban history" in 1961, Eric Lampard wrote:

> If the urban historian is to be more than a historian who happens to do his research and writing on the subject of cities, it will be necessary to show that the term "urban" explains something in history that cannot be better explained by recourse to other frames of reference. In short, "urban" must signify not subject matter alone but a scheme of conceptualization in much the same manner as "economic" or "cultural" history.

241

In searching for impersonal urban processes, the new urban historians have added to our understanding of urban life; but they have often done so at the cost of obscuring the politically conscious agents of urbanization.[2] That task has even been slighted by the most talented historians on the left. Sam Bass Warner, Jr., for example, has argued that from "a particular technological climate, a particular configuration of transportation . . . the form of our cities . . . inevitably takes shape."[3] Ironically, just as the realists' growing enthusiasm for public planning had been linked to a skepticism about the potential for change, so too as Americans have come to understand more fully the character of their urban society, they have despaired of shaping it to their own ideals.

THE INTELLECTUAL AS SOCIAL TYPE

That irony is in part the result of the changing position of the intellectual in American society. The development of social theory has often been enriched by and in turn has enriched political activity. When conscious social groups, guided at least in part by the practical implications of social theory, confront new problems and search for new solutions they, in turn, force theorists to reinterpret the meaning and reexamine the context of social conflicts. In that way a body of social criticism and a tradition of political action are developed upon which future theorists and reformers can build.[4] In the Gilded Age, for example, Henry George, Henry Demarest Lloyd, Edward Bellamy, and other members of what John L. Thomas has called the adversary tradition, tested their social theories in the political arena.[5] If they did not always learn as much from their failures as they might have, they at least provided lessons for other theorists and other activists. By the 1920s, however, American intellectuals carried on their work in almost complete isolation from mass political activity. With little or no connection to a mass political constituency, social critics cultivated their alienation from society in the form of idiosyncratic theories while realistic urban reformers managed existing trends even when their own analyses demanded fundamental change.[6]

The isolation of the intellectual in the twentieth century was associated with the political and social transformation that occurred during the sixty years examined here. The collapse of such mass political movements as the Knights of Labor and the Populist party and the decline of the ideal of a republic of self-reliant, independent citizens weakened the American faith in and commitment to democracy. By the 1920s the democratic impulse that had inspired the Populist movement had given way to the interest-group politics of the Farm Bureau Federation that excluded sharecroppers, tenants, and migratory workers. Similarly, the Knights of Labor gave way to the American Federation of Labor, whose strategy was to organize the "aristocracy" of skilled labor and eschew political struggle in favor of more immediate economic goals. Black leaders turned away from the militant demand for equality and towards accommodation in the South and promotion of the "talented tenth" in the North. Even the Socialist party, which had championed the cause of democratic change through the 1920s, succumbed to the sectarian infighting initiated by its would-be Leninist vanguard.[7] By the 1920s critics of American society could not engage in a dialogue with a mass movement even if they had so desired.

The atrophy of American democracy and the political isolation of the intellectuals it engendered was linked to the changing social structure of urban-industrial America. The growing rift between the new middle class of managers and professional servants of the corporate order, on the one hand, and the industrial working class, on the other, discouraged popular coalitions and hampered the rise of democratic movements. The prohibition movement, for example, which in the late-nineteenth century had united both marginal and aspiring small producers across class lines in opposition to the liquor trade and the growth of monopoly, had become by the twentieth century a movement of middle-class professionals and business leaders committed to transforming the "pathological" culture of the working class.[8]

Many intellectuals of George's generation had been part of or aspired to the traditional middle class of small producers and shared its concern over the rise of the new industrial elite and the corporate order. Adopting an adversarial position, they forged links with those elements of the working class that shared their attachment to the values of republican and free labor America. In contrast intellectuals of Park's generation were more often associated with the new middle class of managers and professionals who provided a variety of services to the corporate order. Even when they criticized the corporate order, as did those reformers whom Christopher Lasch has described as "the new radicals," they generally shared such corporate values as efficiency and treated politics as a problem of social control. In the name of progress, they embraced the material promise of the corporate order and rejected the cultural conservatism of the working-class opponents of corporate development.[9] While maintaining a rhetorical allegiance to democracy, they spoke *for* rather than *to* or *with* the average citizen and thus preempted a democratic critique of corporate capitalism.

During the same period many members of the working class abandoned as utopian their own hopes for fundamental change and pursued more immediate and realistic goals. Like the new radicals the new organizations of the labor movement adopted the realistic perspective of the corporate order. "The trade unions," AF of L leader Samuel Gompers explained, "are the business organizations of the wage-earners, to attend to the business of the wage-earners." Looking back, Gompers recalled "the danger of entangling alliances with intellectuals. . . . I saw that the betterment of workingmen must come primarily through workingmen."[10] In such a movement there was no room for intellectuals or their theories. Of course the labor movement and the intellectuals achieved a rapprochement of sorts in the 1930s, in the marriage of the Congress of Industrial Organizations (CIO) and the New Deal and the establishment of the National Labor Relations Board (NLRB). But by then realistic assumptions dominated both partners. Labor leaders and New Deal intellectuals each saw the

CIO and the NLRB as components in a scientifically managed, mass-consumption economy overseen by a national welfare state.[11] The long period of political and social isolation contributed to the intellectuals' growing consciousness of themselves as a peculiar social type. While some intellectuals may have cynically calculated their interests and decided to serve the corporate order, the origins and the logic of the social thought of the reform-minded intellectuals are to be found in their group consciousness. Living through a period of intense social change and political conflict, intellectuals felt the precariousness of their position. Lacking both economic power and the power of numbers, they had everything to lose and nothing to gain from political strife. Simultaneously, their academic disciplines convinced them that new forms of social control, from education to eugenics, could replace the role of physical force in stabilizing the social order.[12] The concept of social control moved to the center of the reform agenda and political ambitions of the intellectuals. In 1901 the sociologist and theorist of social control Edward Ross put it this way: "As the enlightenment of the public wanes relatively to the superior enlightenment of the learned castes and professions, the mandarinate will infallibly draw to itself a greater and greater share of social power."[13] If a new science of social control was to replace traditional political conflict over the distribution of resources, however, intellectuals would have to increase their power relative to both the short-sighted corporate elite and the ignorant masses.

THE LEGACY OF PROGRESSIVE REFORM

Historians have argued endlessly over the character of the Progressive Era and particularly over whether any specific social group or class dominated the progressive movement. It now seems clear that no monolithic progressive movement ever existed and that a variety of social groups and political philosophies were active in the Progressive Era. There is little point in rehearsing or reopening the debate.[14] But the story told here suggests that the growing confidence, ambition, and class consciousness of the intellectuals was one of the more important legacies of the period of progressive reform. At the center of that legacy was the science of social control.

As Ross and other theorists first articulated the concept of social control it signified, Morris Janowitz explains, a "spontaneously emergent and spontaneously accepted consensus." Indeed, as a means of controlling the actions of both groups and the individuals that composed them, social control had traditionally arisen spontaneously from within the group. Industrial work groups, for example, established stints or quotas and developed an ethic of manliness to regulate their members and as a way to control the process of production. The pattern of "soldiering" (the practice of skilled craftsmen who collectively refused to work at the pace demanded by management), which so maddened the scientific manager Frederick Taylor, was actually a spontaneous form of social control. For the craftsmen soldiering was part of an ethic of manliness through which they sought to control production and resist the dictates of management. In that form social control was, as Janowitz argues in reference to the ideals of the early sociologists, an important part of the "efforts of men to realize their collective goals."[15] But as intellectuals lost faith in the competence of the public, they looked to new techniques, from scientific management to publicity, in order to impose a new form of social control from above.

"The passiveness of the average mind will make it safe to weave into . . . moral instruction certain convenient illusions and fallacies which it is nobody's interest to denounce," Ross explained. That this was a process fraught with the danger of totalitarian manipulation even Ross recognized. He wrote:

> The coalescence of physical and spiritual forces in the modern state may well inspire certain misgivings. When we note the enormous resources and high centralization of a first-class edu-

cational system; when we consider that it takes forcible possession of the child for half the time during its best years, and sub-
mits the little creature to a curriculum devised more and more
with reference to its own aims . . . we may well be apprehensive
of future developments.

Yet Ross went on to urge society, working through an "ethical
elite" with high-minded motives, to "impose upon the individual
its own valuations of life's activities and experiences." In that alienated form social control had much less to do with the realization
of collective goals than with the adjustment of the individual to an
unchallenged social reality.[16]
Many of the reforms of the Progressive Era, notwithstanding
the democratic rhetoric that pervaded the era, owed a great deal
to the view of politics as essentially a process of social control.
With the growing sophistication of the rational approach to social
problems, the sociologists W. I. Thomas and Florian Znaniecki
explained at the end of the Progressive Era, "We are less and less
ready to let any social processes go on without our active interference and we feel more and more dissatisfied with any active interference based upon the mere whim of an individual or a social
body; or upon preconceived philosophical, religious, or moral gen-
eralization." The pace of change, the complexity of urban life, and
its recurrent crises, they added, meant that the "substitution of a
conscious technique for a half-conscious routine has become . . .
a social necessity."[17] Many Progressive Era reformers had already
embraced that logic. But it was the American experience in World
War I and its immediate aftermath that brought not only the science of social control but the realistic tradition to maturity.
The wartime propaganda campaigns in which many intellectuals participated seemed to confirm the political incompetence of
the general public. Walter Lippmann, who served as a propagandist in the Military Intelligence Branch, argued in 1922 that modern society had become too complex for the average citizen to
understand. Propagandists succeeded in duping the public by of-
fering an oversimplified and distorted picture of society. Traditional democratic principles were no longer appropriate to a soci-

ety, Lippmann argued, that was composed of so many people "whose experience has comprehended no factor of the problem under discussion." Instead, Lippmann recommended the establishment of an intelligence bureau, "managed only by a specialized class whose personal interests reach beyond the locality," that would define and pursue the public interest.[18] Such attitudes contributed to the development of a political culture that placed greater emphasis on scientific knowledge, technical expertise, and managerial skill than on virtue, individual competence, and democratic debate.

In the 1920s, the decade of the Hawthorne experiments in industrial psychology, President Hoover's survey, *Recent Social Trends*, the Russell Sage Foundation's *Regional Plan of New York and Its Environs*, and a generally expanded role for the intellectual in public affairs, the realistic tradition and the science of social control dominated the reform agenda. In his 1925 study, *The New Aspects of Politics*, the political scientist Charles Merriam unwittingly revealed the antidemocratic and even totalitarian attitudes that sometimes underlay the science of social control and the realistic tradition:

[Social scientists possess] two great mechanisms of control that have never before existed in the same form or with the same possibilities of effective use. These are education and eugenics, which are likely to play a greater role in the government of mankind than have force and tradition in the past. . . . We are very rapidly approaching a time when it may be necessary and possible to decide not merely what types of law we wish to enact, but what types of person we wish to develop.

Merriam went on to argue that although education and eugenics were rapidly approaching the point "where by scientific process we can breed and train what types of men we would, it does not seem that we should breed and train 3 per cent of genius and 97 per cent of morons. We should probably contrive a more balanced society . . . leaving the mass of human beings on something like a democratic basis." Social engineering might "cause restlessness" or "revolution" among those designed for "toil," Merriam admitted, "but that is a part of the chance that the governing group would have to take in such a world."[19]

Few were as forthright as Merriam in taking the logic of scientific social control to its stark conclusion, and his grandiose vision of social engineering was unusual among realists. But his argument serves as a reminder of how different the political assumptions and attitudes of the realists were from the republicans. Although republican attitudes and democratic aspirations never completely disappeared, it was the realists' skeptical view of popular abilities, their embrace of the values of the corporate order, and their quest for a science of social control that most profoundly shaped urban life and the urban landscape in the twentieth century.

Notes

Introduction

1. National Resources Committee, Research Committee on Urbanism, *Our Cities: Their Role in the National Economy* (Washington, D.C., 1937). See also George Mowry and Blaine A. Brownell, *An Urban Nation, 1920–1980* (New York, 1981); Mark I. Gelfand, *A Nation of Cities: The Federal Government and Urban America, 1933–1965* (New York, 1975); and Roderick McKenzie, *The Metropolitan Community* (New York, 1933), which was prepared as a volume in President Hoover's *Recent Social Trends* survey.

2. On the growth of American cities in population and in number, see Paul Boyer, *Urban Masses and Moral Order in America, 1820–1920* (Cambridge, Mass., 1978), 123–24. On annexation and the physical expansion of American cities, see Jon C. Teaford, *City and Suburb: The Political Fragmentation of Metropolitan America, 1880–1970* (Baltimore, 1979) and Kenneth T. Jackson, *Crabgrass Frontier: The Suburbanization of the United States* (New York, 1985), especially chap. 8. An excellent description of the walking city is found in Jackson, *Crabgrass Frontier*, 14–20. On the walking city also see Raymond Mohl, *The New City: Urban America in the Industrial Age, 1860–1920* (Arlington Heights, Ill., 1985), 28–29 and Zane L. Miller and Patricia M. Melvin, *The Urbanization of Modern America: A Brief History* (New York, 1987), 48.

3. The classic description of the new metropolitan form is Ernest W.

251

Burgess, "The Growth of the City; An Introduction to a Research Project," in Robert E. Park, Ernest S. Burgess, and Roderick D. McKenzie, *The City* (Chicago, 1925), 47–62. See also the work of Chicago sociologist McKenzie, *The Metropolitan Community*. An important statistical study of metropolitan development is Adna Weber, *The Growth of Cities in the Nineteenth Century* (New York, 1899).

4. "An intricate symbol of mystery, the great city proved a source of mystification, the very place where incorporation, pervading the spheres of everyday life, disguised itself. . . . To anxious reformers and their constituents, the causes of growth, of greatness, remained baffling, beyond control." Alan Trachtenberg, *The Incorporation of America* (New York, 1982), 112–21, quoted passage on 112. Trachtenberg's attempt to unravel "the mysteries of the great city" has influenced this study in many ways. Other recent historians who have examined the emergence of the new metropolitan form include Mohl, *The New City*, and John R. Stilgoe, *Metropolitan Corridor: Railroads and the American Scene* (New Haven, 1983). Stilgoe's work is an especially fascinating analysis of the built environment of the new metropolitan form. "Trains, right-of-way, and adjacent built form had become part environment, part experience," Stilgoe argues, "a combination perhaps best called metropolitan" (ix). Also useful is John Zukowsky, ed., *Chicago Architecture, 1872–1922: Birth of a Metropolis* (Chicago, 1988). See my review of that volume in *Planning Perspectives* (September 1990), 335–36. John H. Mollenkopf, *The Contested City* (Princeton, 1983) dates the emergence of the new metropolitan form to a somewhat later period and traces its evolution in the fifty years after 1932.

5. Alan Trachtenberg, *The Incorporation of America*, 117; Charles Beard, "Some Aspects of Regional Planning," *American Political Science Review* 20 (May 1926), 273–83.

6. For discussion of the role of the private pursuit of wealth in urban development, see Sam Bass Warner, Jr., *The Private City: Philadelphia in Three Periods of Its Growth* (Philadelphia, 1968).

7. For discussion of the origins and early development of the republican tradition and especially Olmsted's role in it, see Thomas Bender, *Toward an Urban Vision* (Lexington, Ky., 1975). Mark A. Lause, "Progress Impoverished: Origin of Henry George's Single Tax," *The Historian* 53 (May 1990), 394–410, similarly traces the origins of George's single-tax to the labor politics of the 1840s. Although I read Bender's work only after completing the first draft of this manuscript, his effort to describe a lost historical tradition and a developing pattern of thought offers a precedent for the task I have undertaken here. Although my work takes into greater account such "external considerations as personal or institutional connections or geographic proximity" its unity is, like Bender's, based on "thematic links." Bender, *Toward an Urban Vision*, ix–x.

8. For a useful explication of the notion of balancing the city with the country, or more properly urban values with rural values, see Bender, *Toward an Urban Vision*, 189–94.

9. On the strength of the laissez-faire and social Darwinist view and the challenge to it launched by George and others, see Sidney Fine, *Laissez-Faire and the General-Welfare State: A Study of Conflict in American Thought, 1865–1901* (Ann Arbor, 1956); on George, see 289–95. While Bender argues that little of Olmsted's thought survived the Progressive Era (at least until Lewis Mumford resurrected his reputation in the 1930s), John L. Thomas offers a more positive account of George's legacy. Bender, *Toward an Urban Vision*, 185; John L. Thomas, *Alternative America: Henry George, Edward Bellamy, Henry Demarest Lloyd and the Adversary Tradition* (Cambridge, Mass., 1983), 354–66.

10. An excellent study of economic developments during the 1870s and the dramatic rise and fall of a republican challenge to urban industrialization in the context of one metropolis is Steven J. Ross, *Workers on the Edge: Work, Politics, and Leisure in Industrializing Cincinnati, 1788–1890* (New York, 1985), especially pt. 3. For an account of national developments, see Eric Foner, *Reconstruction: America's Unfinished Revolution* (New York, 1988), chap. 11. On the impact of mechanization and the conflict between capital and labor on American culture, see Trachtenberg, *The Incorporation of America*, chaps. 2–3.

11. Spokesmen for the new realistic tradition tended to describe their republican counterparts as antiurban romantics and celebrated their own tough-minded pragmatism. While I have avoided the term *romantic* in describing their opponents in favor of the term *republican*, which I believe more accurately describes their position, I will use the term *realist* to describe this second tradition without, however, endorsing its polemical implications. I have eschewed the term *progressive* because, although the realists fervently embraced the idea of progress and helped to shape the Progressive Era, I do not want to obscure the fact that both the republicans and realists were active within the multifarious progressive movement. For a very different view of American urban thought, which emphasizes antiurban attitudes, see Morton and Lucia White, *The Intellectual Versus the City* (New York, 1962).

12. In an earlier version of the city building argument, I employed the subtitle "from city building to urban planning." I am indebted to Christopher Lasch for his observation that the story told here is not really a "from . . . to" story. The republican tradition and what might be called the city building perspective continued to influence urban thought and reform through 1937 and beyond (as the work of Lewis Mumford, Paul and Percival Goodman, and Jane Jacobs among others would suggest). I have preserved the term *city building* because it suggests both certain assumptions implicit in the republican tradition and in the subject matter of this study. In the largest sense I mean city building to refer to a broader

and more comprehensive understanding of the urban development process than that which informs the discipline of urban planning. Thus this study focuses less on the largely two-dimensional and legal process of urban planning than on the three-dimensional process of city building, which includes political, economic, social, and intellectual forces and conflicts.

While that perspective is not what I call the city building debate per se, it is a view of urban development that was implicit in the republican tradition. Olmsted's ideal, for example, was to redirect the social, economic, and technological forces that had created the modern city and that heretofore had been geared toward selfish economic interests. Bender writes: "Olmsted insisted that in the future these city-building forces must be directed, on a metropolitan scale, toward social, even psychological, needs, instead of purely economic ones." Bender, *Toward an Urban Vision*, 171.

13. On the obstacles to change posed by the built environment, see Christine Meisner Rosen, *The Limits of Power: Great Fires and the Process of City Growth in America* (Cambridge, 1986).

14. "More than urban areas, the corridor spoke of the power of the new, expert builder, the engineer, the architect, the landscape architect. Democracy ruled little building in the corridor. . . ." Stilgoe, *Metropolitan Corridor*, 13.

15. *John Swinton's Paper*, October 24, 1886; quoted in Steven J. Ross, "The Culture of Political Economy: Henry George and the American Working Class," *Southern California Quarterly* 65 (Summer 1983), 145–66, quoted passage on 154.

16. Robert E. Park, "The City: Suggestions for the Investigation of Human Behavior in the Urban Environment," in Park, Burgess, and McKenzie, *The City* (Chicago, 1925), 1–4.

17. Robert E. Park, "The City As Social Laboratory," in T. V. Smith and Leonard D. White, *Chicago: An Experiment in Social Science Research* (Chicago, 1929), 9.

18. Park, "The City," 45.

19. Harvey Zorbaugh, "The Natural Areas of Cities," in Ernest W. Burgess, ed., *The Urban Community* (Chicago, 1926), 221. The first passage quoted is in Zorbaugh's own words. Beginning with "It is not" Zorbaugh is quoting Elihu Root's address to the Russell Sage Foundation's Regional Plan Association of New York.

20. Beard, "Some Aspects of Regional Planning," 273–83.

21. Robert E. Park, "The Urban Community as a Spatial Pattern and a Moral Order," in Burgess, ed., *The Urban Community*, 3–18.

22. Zane L. Miller, *Boss Cox's Cincinnati: Urban Politics in the Progressive Era* (Chicago, 1968); Steven J. Ross, *Workers on the Edge: Work, Politics, and Leisure in Industrializing Cincinnati, 1788–1890* (New York, 1985), quoted passage on 62.

23. Robert Fishman, "The Anti-planners: The Contemporary Revolt against

Planning and Its Significance for Planning History," in Gordon E. Cherry, ed., *Shaping an Urban World* (New York, 1980), 243–52, quoted passages on 251.
24. Henry George, *Social Problems* (New York, 1883), 3.

Chapter 1

1. On industrial development in antebellum America, see Douglass C. North, *The Economic Growth of the United States, 1790–1860* (New York, 1961) and Stuart Bruchey, *The Roots of American Economic Growth, 1607–1861* (New York, 1965). For a discussion of the urban component of antebellum industrial development, see Allan R. Pred, *The Spatial Dynamics of U.S. Urban-Industrial Growth, 1800–1914* (Cambridge, 1966), chap. 4. Of a total population of more than 23 million in 1850, only 3 1/2 million lived in towns of more than 2,500. Outside of New York fewer than 1 million Americans lived in towns of more than 50,000. *Historical Statistics of the United States; Colonial Times to 1957* (Washington, D.C., 1960), 14. David Montgomery has argued that as late as 1870 a great deal of American manufacturing still took place in rural areas. David Montgomery, *Beyond Equality: Labor and the Radical Republicans, 1862–1872* (Chicago, 1981), 26–27.

2. Eric Foner, *Free Soil, Free Labor, Free Men: The Ideology of the Republican Party Before the Civil War* (New York, 1970). Both Sean Wilentz, *Chants Democratic: New York City and the Rise of the American Working Class, 1788–1850* (New York, 1984), especially chap. 2, and Steven J. Ross, *Workers on the Edge: Work, Leisure, and Politics in Industrializing Cincinnati, 1788–1890* (New York, 1985), especially chap. 1, 7–8, discuss the role of artisan republicans in shaping the free labor ideology. The Frenchman Michael Chevalier, who visited the United States in the 1830s, was particularly impressed with its political culture. The average American, he wrote, "is more fit to take a part in public affairs" than the average European. Chevalier quoted in Christopher Lasch, *The Culture of Narcissism* (New York, 1979), 231–32.

3. Foner, *Free Soil, Free Labor, Free Men*, 36–38.

4. Allan Pred, *The Spatial Dynamics of U.S. Urban-Industrial Growth*, chaps. 1–3; for an analysis on the import-replacing function, see Jane Jacobs, *The Economy of Cities* (New York, 1969) and Jane Jacobs, *Cities and the Wealth of Nations* (New York, 1984).

5. John R. Stilgoe, *Metropolitan Corridor: Railroads and the American Scene* (New Haven, 1983); Alan Trachtenberg, *The Incorporation of America: Culture and Society in the Gilded Age* (New York, 1982), especially chap. 4; Edward C. Kirkland, *Industry Comes of Age: Business, Labor, and Public Policy 1860–1897* (New York, 1961); Alfred D. Chandler, Jr., *The Visible Hand: The Managerial Revolution in American Business* (Cambridge, 1977).

6. Phillips quoted in Richard Hofstadter, *The American Political Tradition* (New York, 1973), 205–6.

7. On the early Republican response to industrialization, the increasing importance of the labor vote, and the conservative critique of labor agitation and demagoguery, see Montgomery, *Beyond Equality*.

8. On the "revolution in values," see Robert H. Wiebe, *The Search for Order, 1877–1920* (New York, 1967), chap. 6.

9. For a similar discussion focusing on the response of American labor to industrialization, see Herbert Gutman, *Work, Culture, and Society*, especially the introduction and part 1.

10. Henry George, *Social Problems* (New York, 1883), 234; for other evidence of George's interest in the landscape, see 124–26. For a selection of Olmsted's writings on landscape, see Albert Fein, ed., *Landscape into Cityscape* (Ithaca, 1968).

11. In a similar argument Herbert Gutman has suggested that Gilded Age radicals anticipated and shaped the development of the social welfare state. See Herbert Gutman, *Work, Culture, and Society* (New York, 1977), 260–92. On the late-nineteenth-century debate on the future of America's urban civilization, see M. Christine Boyer, *Dreaming the Rational City: The Myth of American City Planning* (Cambridge, 1983), part 1.

12. An excellent biography of Olmsted is Laura Roper, *FLO: A Biography of Frederick Law Olmsted* (Baltimore, 1973). See also the editor's introduction to S. B. Sutton, ed., *Civilizing America's Cities* (Cambridge, 1971).

13. On Olmsted's Protestant outlook see Roper, *FLO*, 247, 249, 151–52 and Trachtenberg, *The Incorporation of America*, 107–112. On Olmsted's free labor and republican commitments, see Thomas Bender, *Toward an Urban Vision*, (Lexington, KY.), especially 167–69; on his view of the Cavalier critique see Olmsted's letter to his friend Charles Loring Brace (December 1, 1853), quoted in Bender, *Toward an Urban Vision*, 169. On the Cavalier-Yankee debate before the Civil War, see William R. Taylor, *Cavalier and Yankee: The Old South and American National Character* (Cambridge, Mass., 1961).

14. Downing quoted in William H. Wilson, *The City Beautiful Movement* (Baltimore, 1989), 14.

15. Frederick Law Olmsted, "Public Parks and the Enlargement of Towns," (New York, 1970; reprint of 1870 edition), 11, 18, 22.

16. An excellent account of Olmsted's view of cities is Bender, *Toward an Urban Vision*, chap. 7. See also Wilson, *The City Beautiful Movement*, chap. 1. He would, as Alan Trachtenberg has argued, teach the "metropolis about itself." Trachtenberg, *The Incorporation of America*, 108.

17. Olmsted, Vaux and Co., "Observations on the Progress of Improvements in Street Plans, with Special Reference to the Parkway Proposed to be Laid Out in Brooklyn" (1868), reprinted as "The Structure of Cities; An Historical View" in Sutton, ed., *Civilizing America's Cities*, 35.

18. Frederick Law Olmsted and James R. Croes, "Preliminary Report of the Landscape Architect and the Civil and Topographical Engineer, upon the Laying Out of the Twenty-third and Twenty-fourth Wards" (1877) reprinted as "The Misfortunes of New York" in Sutton, ed., *Civilizing America's Cities*, 45.

19. "The Misfortunes of New York" in Sutton, ed., *Civilizing America's Cities*, 45–49.

20. Olmsted, "The Structure of Cities," 36–39.

21. Olmsted, "The Structure of Cities," 40.

22. Olmsted, "Public Parks," 20–21; Olmsted's views of suburban design are quoted in Bender, *Toward an Urban Vision*, 183–84.

23. Henry George, *Progress and Poverty*, (New York, 1887), Christ's lessons, 473; instinctual capacities, 412; "city of God," 496; "the decrees of the Creator," 301. George's book was first published in 1879. I have used the fourth edition, which appeared when George's political influence was at its height.

24. George, *Progress and Poverty*, 5.

25. Jacob Oser, *Henry George* (New York, 1974), 68.

26. John L. Thomas, *Alternative America* (Cambridge, Mass., 1983), chap. 5.

27. Henry George to Jennie T. George, September 15, 1861, in Charles A. Barker, *Henry George* (New York, 1955), 50. The argument developed in Leo Marx, *The Machine in the Garden: Technology and the Pastoral Image* (New York, 1964) helps place the pastoral element of George's thought in the larger context of nineteenth century American culture.

28. George, *Progress and Poverty*, 350–51.

29. Steven Ross, *Workers on the Edge*, 294–325, especially 301.

30. George, *Progress and Poverty*, on Jefferson, 471–77, "prevent the tendency," 477, "Nature acknowledges," 301–2, "inequalities," 407.

31. George, *Progress and Poverty*, on cities and progress, 455–73, "the secret" 389, "diffuse population," 405. John L. Thomas, *Alternative America* (Cambridge, Mass., 1983), 123.

32. Olmsted quoted in Bender, *Toward an Urban Vision*, 169.

33. Trachtenberg's observation that the "logic of market relations eluded those liberal reformers who called for a restored Jeffersonian estate of responsible citizenship on the part of the property owners, many of whom held only precariously to their status in a fluctuating economy" suggests something of Olmsted's difficulties. Trachtenberg, *The Incorporation of America*, 122. Consider also Bender's argument that Olmsted's ideal "lost its relevance for a generation of urban leaders who relied upon machine metaphors to define the good society and who declared an end to the distinction between city and country." Bender, *Toward an Urban Vision*, 185.

34. Olmsted quoted in Bender, *Toward an Urban Vision*, 179.

35. Olmsted, "Public Parks," 10.

36. Olmsted, "Public Parks," 34. See also Trachtenberg, *The Incorporation of America*, 108.

37. George Fredrickson, *The Inner Civil War* (New York, 1965), 101–8. Boyer, *Dreaming the Rational City*, 18–20; Bender, *Toward an Urban Vision*, 191.

38. Trachtenberg, *Incorporation* 111–12; Boyer, *Urban Masses and Moral Order*, 237–38.

39. Olmsted, "Public Parks," 25–26.

40. Olmsted, "Public Parks," 23–30.

41. On Olmsted as an early environmental reformer, see Albert Fein, *Frederick Law Olmsted and the American Environmental Tradition* (New York, 1972) and Paul Boyer, *Urban Masses and Moral Order* (Cambridge, 1978), 236–39.

42. Olmsted, "Public Parks," 10.

43. Olmsted, "Public Parks," 12. Boyer, *Urban Masses and Moral Order*, especially chap. 15.

44. George, *Progress and Poverty*, 489–90.

45. George, *Progress and Poverty*, "proletarians," 270–72; simplicity in government, 408–9.

46. George, *Progress and Poverty*, on the causes of poverty and its remedies, 237–96, opportunities for the small producer, 392–94.

47. George, *Progress and Poverty*, 425–96; fate of a child, 446; "obstacles," 439.

48. George, *Social Problems*, 1–9.

49. For a fuller description of the contradiction between means and ends in George's thought, see Thomas, *Alternative America*, 119–20.

50. George, *Progress and Poverty*, 409–15, quoted passage on 415. See Thomas, *Alternative America*, 174, 320–22.

51. George, *Progress and Poverty*, 477–84, quoted passage on 477–78.

52. Henry George to Charles Nordhoff, December 21, 1880; quoted in Thomas, *Alternative America*, 174. As late as 1883 George was still appealing to a middle-class audience. "I do not wish to call upon those my voice may reach to demand their own rights," he wrote, "so much as to call upon them to secure the rights of others more helpless." George, *Social Problems*, 88.

53. On George's legacy among middle-class reformers, see Thomas, *Alternative America*, chap. 15. See also Daniel Aaron, *Men of Good Hope: A Story of American Progressives* (New York, 1951), 79–80, 113–14 and Barker, *Henry George*, 511ff.

54. George, *Progress and Poverty*, 281.

55. Samuel Gompers, *Seventy Years of Life and Labor* (Ithaca, 1984), 100.

56. George speaking to the anti-Tammany Irving Hall Democrats, quoted in Peter Alexander Speek, *The Singletax and the Labor Movement* (Madison, Wis., 1917), 80.

57. John R. Commons, David J. Saposs, Helen L. Sumner, E. B. Mittelman, H. E. Hoagland, John D. Andrews, and Selig Perlman, *A History of Labor in the United States*, vol. 2 (New York, 1918), 441–54; see also the accounts in David

Hammack, *Power and Society* (New York, 1982) and Trachtenberg, *The Incorporation of America*, 166–68.

58. Louis F. Post and Fred C. Leubuscher, *Henry George's 1886 Campaign* (reprint of 1887 edition, Westport, Conn., 1976), 153–54.

59. Lewis Mumford, *The Culture of Cities* (New York, 1938), 156–57. Mumford actually argued that George failed to recognize that only the community as a whole could enact the single tax. If seen only as a criticism of his later retreat to the Democratic party, that judgment seems fair.

60. Henry George to Edward K. Taylor, September 10, 1886; quoted in Thomas, *Alternative America*, 223.

61. Henry George, *Social Problems* (New York, 1883), 20–25.

62. As Ross explains, single taxers saw themselves as virtuous "citizens fighting to save the republic from corruption and dissipation." Steven J. Ross, "The Culture of Political Economy," *Southern California Quarterly* 65 (Summer 1983), 145–66, quoted passage in 157. See Leon Fink, *Workingmen's Democracy: The Knights of Labor and American Politics* (Urbana, 1983), 13, passim.

63. "Natural opportunities," part of George's proclamation of principles in the 1886 campaign, quoted in Louis F. Post, *The Prophet of San Francisco* (New York, 1930), 71. "Democrats," George's remarks recorded in *John Swinton's Paper* (October 24, 1886), quoted in Ross, "The Culture of Political Economy," 157.

64. Post and Leubuscher, *George's 1886 Campaign*, 27.

65. Steven J. Ross, *Workers on the Edge*, 294–325. See also Fink, *Workingmen's Democracy*.

66. Post and Leubuscher, *George's 1886 Campaign*, 48.

67. George, *Social Problems*, 128, 137.

68. George, *Social Problems*, 142. On the limits of George's understanding of changes in industrial production, see Ross, "The Culture of Political Economy," especially 152–53 and Commons et al., *History of Labour*, vol. 2, 446–47. On George's encounter with agrarianism and land reform, see Mark A. Lause "Progress Impoverished: Origin of Henry George's Single Tax," *The Historian* 53 (May 1990), 394–410.

69. George in the *Leader* August 17, 1887, quoted in Speek, *The Singletax and the Labor Movement*, 97. Speek, *The Singletax and the Labor Movement*, 90–100.

70. For George's recognition of the impact of corporate ownership and machine industry on the artisan ideal, see George, *Social Problems* (New York, 1883), especially chap. 14.

71. Passages from Camillo Sitte translated and quoted in Carl Schorske, *Fin-De-Siecle Vienna: Politics and Culture* (New York, 1980), 62–72.

72. George, *Progress and Poverty*, 399, 419, 428. Speek, *The Single Tax and the Labor Movement*, includes a list of the various trade union components of George's constituency.

73. George, *Progress and Poverty*, 388–93. In his years on the Pacific Coast, where balloon-frame construction contributed to rapid urban development, George must have seen many examples of owner-built housing. Sigfried Giedion, *Space, Time and Architecture* (Cambridge, 1941), 273.

74. Olivier Zunz, *The Changing Face of Inequality* (Chicago, 1982), pt. 2; James Barrett, *Work and Community in the Jungle; Chicago's Packinghouse Workers, 1894–1922* (Urbana, 1987); Kenneth Jackson, *Crabgrass Frontier* (New York, 1985), 126.

75. "Preamble to the Constitution of the Knights of Labor" (1878), reprinted in Paul F. Boller, Jr., and Ronald Story, *A More Perfect Union; Documents in U.S. History*, vol. 2 (Boston, 1984), 75. For an interesting discussion of who actually developed the balloon-frame, see Giedion, *Space, Time and Architecture*, 273–77.

76. Clarence Cook quoted in Gwendolyn Wright, *Building the Dream* (New York, 1981), 102–3.

77. Chicago workers often built their own frame houses and moved them from lot to lot as realty values and consequently their rents soared. The single tax was designed to alleviate such pressures. Christine Meisner Rosen, *The Limits of Power: Great Fires and the Process of City Growth in America* (New York, 1986), 97–101.

78. Ross, *Workers on the Edge*, chap. 12.

79. See Gerald Grob, *Workers and Utopia: A Study of Ideological Conflict in the Labor Movement, 1865–1900* (Evanston, 1961), especially 164–65 on Gompers's response to the defeat of the ULP; James R. Green, *The World of the Worker: Labor in Twentieth-Century America* (New York, 1980), especially chap. 2; Foner, *Reconstruction*, 514–15.

80. Both socialists and trade unionists, Thomas argues, "hoped to convert George to a more realistic view of the industrial problem." Thomas, *Alternative America*, 228.

81. I am indebted to Lause, "Progress Impoverished: Origin of Henry George's Single Tax" for the arguments about George's single tax claims.

82. The moderates feared, Ross writes, that the single tax "would undermine the most basic of all working-class family goals: homeownership." They questioned "whether a family would be forced to leave its home if a manufacturer offered to pay the city a higher tax for the use of the land than the family could afford." Steven Ross, *Workers on the Edge*, 320–22.

83. Socialists argued, Ross writes, that the "greatest need for the mass of workers lay less in guaranteeing access to homeownership than in providing adequate housing for the thousands of families forced to live in unhealthy and decrepit tenements." Steven Ross, *Workers on the Edge*, 322.

84. For discussions of the negative impact of home ownership on class consciousness, see David Montgomery, *The Fall of the House of Labor* (New York, 1987), 283, 286 and David Harvey, *Consciousness and the Urban Experience* (Baltimore, 1983), 42–43.

85. Post and Leubuscher, *George's 1886 Campaign*, 9.
86. Post and Leubuscher, *George's 1886 Campaign*, 14, 27. In 1886 Chicago socialists joined with single-taxers behind a platform that included a provision to tax "all lands held for speculative purposes . . . equally with cultivated lands." *Proceedings* of the Convention (manuscript), September 27, 1886; quoted in Edward B. Mittelman, "Chicago Labor in Politics," *Journal of Political Economy* 28 (May 1920), 407–27, quoted passage on 420.
87. George, *Social Problems*, 201.
88. George, *Social Problems*, 176.
89. The following spring socialists, trade unionists, members of the Knights of Labor, and others joined together in Chicago, Cincinnati, and other cities under the banner of the United Labor party and added such labor issues as compulsory arbitration of strikes and the abolition of convict labor to George's proposals. Post and Leubuscher, *George's 1886 Campaign*, 13–14; Ross, *Workers on the Edge*, chap. 12; Edward B. Mittelman, "Chicago Labor in Politics."
90. George, *Social Problems*, 17.
91. George, *Social Problems*, 316.
92. George, *Social Problems*, 235–42, quoted passages on 239, 242.
93. George, *Progress and Poverty*, 410; "natural distribution," in George, *Social Problems*, 321.
94. Post and Leubuscher, *George's 1886 Campaign*, 7–8.
95. Melvin Holli has argued that Pingree rather than George inspired Johnson and apparently found no evidence that George had influenced Pingree. But Johnson himself pointed to George's influence, and Pingree had flirted with the single tax. In any event Pingree's version of urban reform certainly resembled George's. Melvin Holli, *Reform in Detroit* (New York, 1969). See also John Buenker, *Urban Liberalism and Progressive Reform* (New York, 1973). For a fuller discussion of those developments, see chapter 3 in this volume.
96. The exposition, Trachtenberg argues, was the work of a new "corporate alliance of business, culture, and the state." Trachtenberg, *The Incorporation of America*, 217.
97. Henry Adams quoted in Trachtenberg, *The Incorporation of America*, 220.
98. Olmsted, "Public Parks," 11–15, 22; "corruption and irritation," 14–15, "contrast," 22. Bellamy quoted in Trachtenberg, *The Incorporation of America*, 215.
99. Fredrick Law Olmsted, "A Report Upon the Landscape Architecture of the Columbian Exposition to the American Institute of Architects," reprinted as "Chicago: Taming the Waterfront," in Sutton, ed., *Civilizing America's Cities*, 180–83. The emphases in that report are even more striking in comparison with his earlier "Report Accompanying Plan for Laying Out the South Park" (1871), which stressed domestic tranquility and public health in the development of Jackson Park. See Sutton, ed., *Civilizing America's Cities*, 156–81. Laura Roper has suggested that the international aspect of the exposition appealed to Olmsted's interest in "communitiveness." Laura Roper, *FLO*, 425.

100. Olmsted, "Chicago: Taming the Waterfront," 184.

101. Olmsted, "Chicago: Taming the Waterfront," 190–93.

102. Olmsted's letter to Burnham quoted in Bender, *Toward an Urban Vision*, 186.

103. William T. Stead, *If Christ Came to Chicago* (London, 1894), 110.

104. William S. Rainsford, *The Story of a Varied Life* (Garden City, N.Y., 1922; reissued, Freeport, N.Y., 1980); John J. Engalls, "Lessons of the Fair," *Cosmopolitan* 16 (December 1893), 141–49, both passages quoted in Boyer, *Urban Masses and Moral Order*, 183.

105. Daniel Burnham, "The City of the Future Under a Democratic Government," quoted in John Reps, *The Making of Urban America* (Princeton, 1965), 497.

106. David Schuyler, *The New Urban Landscape* (Baltimore, 1986), 182–90, quoted passage is on 185.

107. Raymond Williams, *The Country and the City* (London, 1973), 120–41, especially 121.

108. The exposition placed the new urban order, as Trachtenberg argues, "above reproach, beyond criticism." Trachtenberg, *The Incorporation of America*, Van Brunt, 216; Lloyd, 218; "reproach," 217.

109. "Lloyd was attacking the same chaotic and wasteful community-building that Henry George denounced in *Progress and Poverty*." Thomas, *Alternative America*, 217.

110. Henry Demarest Lloyd, "The New Independence," in *Men, the Workers*, eds. Anne Withingham and Caroline Stallbohm (New York, 1909), 151–52, quoted in Thomas, *Alternative America*, 281.

111. Henry Demarest Lloyd, "No Mean City," Lloyd, *Mazzini and Other Essays* (New York, 1910), 201–10.

112. Lloyd, "No Mean City," 212–20.

113. Lloyd, "No Mean City," 221–30.

114. Lloyd, "No Mean City," 220.

Chapter 2

1. George E. Mowry and Blaine A. Brownell, *The Urban Nation: 1920–1980* (1981). The 1920 census showed a majority of Americans living in cities and towns for the first time in U.S. history. The change that Mowry and Brownell describe is more profound, however, than merely a demographic one. Their opening chapter focuses on the "Rise of the Urban Mass Mind."

2. Adna Ferrin Weber, *The Growth of Cities in the Nineteenth Century* (New York, 1899), 469.

3. Richard M. Hurd, "The Structure of Cities," *Municipal Affairs* 6 (March 1902), 35–42, quoted passage is on 35.

4. Kenneth T. Jackson, *Crabgrass Frontier: The Suburbanization of the United States* (New York, 1985), especially chap. 3.

5. Paul S. Boyer, *Urban Masses and Moral Order in America: 1820–1920* (Cambridge, 1978), 123–31.

6. Hurd, "The Structure of Cities," functional segregation, 38; residence districts, 42.

7. Hurd, "The Structure of Cities," 41.

8. Weber, *The Growth of Cities*, 458–62. Weber found a growth of inner-city population in absolute numbers in New York and Boston, although not in Philadelphia.

9. On the economic consequences of the depression, see Eric Foner, *Reconstruction: America's Unfinished Revolution, 1863–1877* (New York, 1988), 512–13; for a discussion of its impact in Cincinnati, see Steven Ross, *Workers on the Edge: Work, Leisure, and Politics in Industrializing Cincinnati* (New York, 1985), 219–32. See also David Montgomery's discussion of an American society poised between the era of iron and the era of steel in *Beyond Equality: Labor and the Radical Republicans, 1862–1872* (Urbana, 1981), 3–44. On the rise of the new factory system, see Daniel Nelson, *Managers and Workers: Origins of the New Factory System in the United States, 1880–1920* (Madison, Wis., 1975). On the managerial revolution see Alfred D. Chandler, Jr., *The Visible Hand: The Managerial Revolution in American Business* (Cambridge, 1977). On the systematic application of science and technology to industrial production, see David F. Noble, *America by Design: Science, Technology, and the Rise of Corporate Capitalism* (New York, 1977). On the rise of the new middle class, see Robert H. Wiebe, *The Search For Order, 1877–1920* (New York, 1967), especially chap. 5.

10. Paul Boyer argues, "Urban disorder was familiar enough from the antebellum period, but in the Gilded Age it took on a more menacing aura as a direct expression of labor unrest." Paul Boyer, *Urban Masses and Moral Order*, 125. See also Foner, *Reconstruction*, 512–24; Herbert Gutman, *Work, Culture and Society* (New York, 1976), pt. 4; Herbert Gutman, "The Thompkins Square Riot in New York City on January 13, 1874," *Labor History* 6 (Winter 1965), 44–70; Alan Trachtenberg, *The Incorporation of America: Culture and Society in the Gilded Age* (New York, 1982), chap. 3.

11. Quoted in Wayne Andrews, *The Battle for Chicago* (New York, 1946), 105–7. For similar editorial opinion see Boyer, *Urban Masses and Moral Order*, 125–26.

12. Tom Scott, "The Recent Strikes," *North American Review* 125 (September 1877) 351–62, "possible power," 361; "riot," 352.

13. Pearson quoted in John Mahon, *History of the Militia and National Guard* (New York, 1983), 112. On the behavior of other militias see Jeremy Brecher, *Strike!* (Boston, 1972), chap. 1. On the industrialist as threatening outsider see Gutman, *Work, Culture and Society*, chap. 5–5a and Herbert Gutman, "The

Workers' Search for Power," in H. Wayne Morgan, *The Gilded Age: A Reappraisal* (Syracuse, 1970).

14. Quoted in Andrews, *Battle for Chicago*, 105–7.

15. "The Rioter and the Regular Army," *The Nation* 25 (August 9, 1877), 85.

16. "National Guard Gossip," *New York Times*, August 20, 1892. On the development of the new National Guard, its alliance with business, and its role in industrial disputes, see Mahon, *History of the Militia and National Guard*, chap. 8. On developments in Chicago see Andrews, *Battle for Chicago*, 109, 142. See also Jeremy Brecher, *Strike!*, chap. 1.

17. "The Seventh Regiment Armory," *Harper's Weekly* 21 (October 21, 1877) 801–2. "National Guard Gossip," *New York Times*, August 20, 1892. On the other armories see I. N. Phelps Stokes, *The Iconography of Manhattan Island*, vols. 3 and 4 (New York, 1918 and 1922).

18. John R. Stilgoe, *Metropolitan Corridor: Railroads and the American Scene* (New Haven, 1983), 82–88.

19. Weber, *The Growth of Cities*, 473. The phrase "municipal fiefdom" is from Jon C. Teaford, *City and Suburb: The Political Fragmentation of Metropolitan America, 1880–1970* (Baltimore, 1979), 14–17. On Munhall, Teaford quoted Margaret Byington, *Homestead: The Households of a Mill Town* (New York, 1910), 20–21. On Dearborn see Keith Sward, *The Legend of Henry Ford* (New York, 1975), chap. 17–18, 22–28.

20. Weber, *The Growth of Cities*, 473.

21. Stanley Buder, *Pullman: An Experiment in Industrial Order and Community Planning, 1880–1930* (New York, 1967), passim. On the McCormick plant see Bessie Louise Pierce, *A History of Chicago*, vol. 3 (New York, 1957), 52–53.

22. David Brody, *Steelworkers in America: The Non-Union Era* (Cambridge, 1960), 87–89.

23. Andrew J. Thomas, *Industrial Housing* (Bayonne, 1925), 13.

24. David Harvey argues that it "was no accident that some of the fiercest strikes and confrontations . . . occurred in company towns." Conflicts in living space where "capitalist values and habits are inculcated and the compensations for alienated labor are packaged," he argues, are an important element of the conflict between labor and capital. David Harvey, *Consciousness and the Urban Experience: Studies in the History and Theory of Capitalist Urbanization* (Baltimore, 1985), 48–58.

25. On patterns of urban politics, see Ira Katznelson, *City Trenches* (New York, 1981), Richard Oestreicher, "Urban Working-Class Political Behavior and Theories of American Electoral Politics, 1870–1940," *Journal of American History* 74 (May 1988), and John D. Fairfield, "Cincinnati's Search for Order, *Queen City Heritage* 48 (Summer 1990), 15–26. On local politics in Pullman, see Buder, *Pullman*, 110–13. On Pullman's socialist alderman, see Graham R. Taylor, *Satellite Cities; A Study of Industrial Suburbs* (New York, 1915), 63–64. Taylor discounts

the significance of the alderman's election, but he also points out that the 1894 strike had led to a strong socialist sentiment in Pullman.

26. Brecher, *Strike!*, 55–56.

27. Adna Weber, "The Significance of Recent City Growth; The Era of Small Industrial Centers," *Annals of the American Academy of Political and Social Sciences* 23 (March 1904), 223–36, quoted passage on 231.

28. Taylor, *Satellite Cities*, passim; Teaford, *City and Suburb*, 16. See also L. W. Schimdt, "Hunting for a Factory Location," *Industrial Management* 55 (June 1918), 461–64, John A. Piquet, "Is the Big City Doomed as an Industrial Center," *Industrial Management* 68 (September 1924), 139–44, and the discussion of those articles in Stilgoe, *Metropolitan Corridor*, 87–88.

29. Buder, *Pullman*, 131–33; Alfred Lief, *It Floats: The Story of Procter and Gamble* (New York, 1958), 59; Taylor, *Satellite Cities*, 289.

30. Taylor, *Satellite Cities*, "rushed," 91; "similar skill," 103.

31. Taylor, *Satellite Cities*, "a side issue," 174; "moat," 180; "triumphs," 227; William Z. Foster, *The Steel Strike* (New York, 1920).

32. Steven Ross, *Workers on the Edge*, 284. Cincinnati Milacron, *1884 Cincinnati Milacron 1984, Finding Better Ways* (Cincinnati, 1984), 23–42.

33. See testimony before the U.S. Industrial Commission between 1900–1902, quoted in David M. Gordon, "Capitalist Development and the History of American Cities," in William K. Tabb and Larry Sawyers, *Marxism and the Metropolist* (New York, 1978), 49.

34. Taylor, *Satellite Cities*, "fever," 23; "trade unionism," 101.

35. Weber, *The Growth of Cities*, quoted passage on 205; see also 419.

36. A. E. Dixon, "The Planning and Construction of Power Stations," *Engineering Magazine* 31 (September 1906), 909–10, quoted in Stilgoe, *Metropolitan Corridor*, 114.

37. Weber, *The Growth of Cities*, 205–6; Taylor, *Satellite Cities*, superintendents, 98; large surplus, 21. See also Jackson, *Crabgrass Frontier*, 113.

38. Thomas Stanley Matthews, *Name and Address* (New York, 1960) quoted in Zane L. Miller, *Boss Cox's Cincinnati: Urban Politics in the Progressive Era* (Chicago, 1968), 42.

39. Andrews, *Battle for Chicago*, 111.

40. Lewis Mumford, *Sticks and Stones* (New York, 1924), 105–6. See also the discussion of "money and privacy" in Perry R. Duis, *The Saloon: Public Drinking in Chicago and Boston, 1880–1920* (Urbana, 1983), 205–11.

41. Jackson, *The Crabgrass Frontier*, 76–86, the *World* quoted on 81.

42. In Jackson's words suburbanites were spared the inconvenience "of living near the noxious fumes, deafening noises, and poor people who made the prosperity possible in the first place." Jackson, *Crabgrass Frontier*, chaps. 4–5, quoted passage on 102.

43. The department store, Trachtenberg argues, "disguised links between

goods and factories." Trachtenberg, *The Incorporation of America*, 129–33, quoted passage on 133.

44. Trachtenberg, *The Incorporation of America*, 126–39.

45. Robert Wiebe, *The Search for Order*, chap. 5. Barton Bledstein, *The Culture of Professionalism* (New York, 1976). See also Boyer, *Urban Masses and Moral Order*, chaps. 8–10, which, more than the other works, suggests the role suburbanization played in the transformation of the middle class. See also Stuart M. Blumin, *The Emergence of the Middle Class: Social Experience in the American City, 1790–1900* (New York, 1989), especially chap. 5 on the role of consumption, urban space, and the home in the making of the middle class.

46. Jacob Riis, *How the Other Half Lives* (New York, 1957; reprint), 2, 14.

47. Robert W. DeForest and Lawrence Veiller, *The Tenement House Problem*, vol. 1 (New York, 1903), 1–13; Mumford, *Sticks and Stones*, 110.

48. DeForest and Veiller, *The Tenement House Problem*, 144–45.

49. Robert B. Fairbanks, *Making Better Citizens: Housing Reform and the Community Development Strategy in Cincinnati, 1890–1960* (Urbana, 1988), 13–24; local health official quoted on 15.

50. Chicago Department of Health *Report, 1881–1882*, 47–50; quoted in Edith Abbott, *The Tenements of Chicago, 1908–1925* (Chicago, 1935), 27.

51. Abbott, *The Tenements of Chicago*, passim; DeForest and Veiller, *The Tenemenet House Problem*, 129–34.

52. The fear of fraternization had always outstripped reality, especially in the older commercial cities. On the lack of middle-class sympathy for the railroad strikers of 1877 and other radicals, see Brecher, *Strike!*, chap. 1; Boyer, *Urban Masses and Moral Order*, chap. 8. For an alternative view see Herbert Gutman, "The Workers' Search for Power," and Gutman, *Work, Culture, and Society*, especially 234–92. Of course some members of the middle class came to identify with the poor and to champion their cause. See Christopher Lasch, *The New Radicalism in America 1889–1963; The Intellectual as a Social Type* (New York, 1965). But Lasch uses middle class as a synonym for bourgeois and is referring to "a class of people which derives its income from the ownership of property" (xiii). His new radicals came largely from the traditional antebellum middle class and presumably had a greater allegiance to the pre-industrial order. In any event a key feature of their radicalism was a rejection of precisely that separation of culture and business, or domesticity and public life, that underlay suburbanization.

53. Robert Hartley in New York Association for Improving the Conditions of the Poor, *Annual Report* (1851), 18; Charles Parkhurst, *Our Fight With Tammany* (New York, 1895), 270–76; both quoted in Boyer, *Urban Masses and Moral Order*, Hartley on 90; Parkhurst on 171. Parkhurst appears to have resided in suburban New Jersey.

54. Olmsted, "Public Parks and the Enlargement of Towns," (New York, 1970; reprint of 1870 edition), 20–21.

NOTES TO CHAPTER 2

55. Charles Kellogg, National Conference of Charities and Corrections, *Proceedings* (1887), 134, quoted in Boyer, *Urban Masses and Moral Order*, 149. Charity Organization Society of New York, *Fifth Annual Report* (January 1, 1887), 38; quoted in Roy Lubove, *The Professional Altruist* (Cambridge, Mass., 1965), 5.

56. On the Charity Organization Society, see Boyer, *Urban Masses and Moral Order*, 143–61, especially 153. On Brace, see Thomas Bender, *Toward an Urban Vision* (Lexington, Ky., 1975), 129–58. On the institutional reformers of the Jacksonian era, see David J. Rothman, *The Discovery of the Asylum: Social Order and Disorder in the New Republic* (Boston, 1971) and Boyer, *Urban Masses and Moral Order*, chaps. 1–4.

57. Richard Hofstadter, *The Age of Reform; From Bryan to FDR* (New York, 1955), 8–10.

58. Jane Addams, "The Subtle Problem of Charity," *Atlantic Monthly* 83 (February 1899), 163–78, quoted passage on 163–64. On the poorhouse and the destitute, Jane Addams, *Twenty Years at Hull House* (New York, 1910), 155.

59. Hutchins Hapgood, *Types From City Streets* (New York, 1910), 62–64.

60. Raymond A. Mohl, *The New City: Urban America in the Industrial Age, 1860–1920* (Arlington Heights, Ill., 1985), 40–44. See also Trachtenberg, *The Incorporation of America*, 112–30.

61. Delos F. Wilcox, *Great Cities in America* (New York, 1910), 2–3. Delos F. Wilcox, *The American City; A Problem in Democracy* (New York, 1904), "independence," 6; "standing room," 201; Wilcox, *Great Cities*, "transients," and "well-to-do," 3.

62. Sam Bass Warner, Jr., *Streetcar Suburbs*, (Cambridge, Mass., 1962), 25–27. See also Glen Holt, "The Changing Perception of Urban Pathology: An Essay on the Development of Mass Transit in the United States," in Kenneth T. Jackson and Stanley K. Schultz, ed., *Cities in American History* (New York, 1972), 324–43.

63. Charles H. Cooley, "Social Significance of Street Railways," *Publications of the American Economic Association* 6 (Baltimore, 1891), 72; A. H. Sinclair, "Municipal Monopolies and Their Management," *Street Railway Journal* 7 (October 1891), 519; John R. Commons, *Social Reform and the Church* (New York, 1894), 143; all quoted in Melvin G. Holli, *Reform in Detroit; Hazen S. Pingre and Urban Politics* (New York, 1969), 36.

64. Street railway profits, Kenneth Jackson argues, were "not feasible unless the residential neighborhoods were closely packed." Those who remained in the inner city, Jackson adds, were "forced to compete for housing space where real estate was the most expensive and housing the least desirable." Jackson, *Crabgrass Frontier*, 116–37; quoted passages on 136–37. On the development of the Bronx, see Robert W. DeForest and Lawrence Veiller, *The Tenement House Problem* 42–43. On the development of Roxbury, see Warner, *Streetcar Suburbs*, especially 55–58. On the use of the street railway system by the poor, see Robert DeForest and Lawrence Veiller, *The Tenement House Problem*, 331–32; Theodore Hersh-

berg, Harold E. Cox, Dale Light, Jr., and Richard R. Greenfield, "The Journey-to-Work," in Hershberg et al., *Philadelphia* (New York, 1981); David Hammack, *Power and Society* (New York, 1985), 248.

65. Like the street railway, the telephone industry encouraged the pattern of peripheral expansion and increased congestion at the core. The telephone, its early historian noted, had "made the skyscraper possible" and was "indispens-able" to the national corporations that resided in it. But it was the long-distance call, from city to suburb or between cities, that proved to be "the salvation of the business." Thus the planners in Bell Telephone's "foresight department" had constructed twenty-five million dollars worth of reserve capacity for suburban expansion by 1910. At the same time the corporation had laid enough under-ground cable in Manhattan to accommodate a population of eight million. Un-sure whether it would "scatter" or "concentrate" population, the historian of the "telephonization of city life" recognized that it "helped to create an absolutely new type of city." Herbert N. Casson, *The History of the Telephone* (Chicago, 1910), 173, 199, 200, 232–33, 289–99.

66. Jackson, *Crabgrass Frontier*, 113–14.

67. DeForest and Veiller, *The Tenement House Problem*, 372–73.

68. DeForest and Veiller, *The Tenement House Problem*, 369–77, "erected di-rectly," 375; "hardly one," 369; the building loan operator, 370; *Commercial Ad-vertiser*, 377.

69. DeForest and Veiller, *The Tenement House Problem*, 375–76.

70. Charles W. Cheape, *Moving the Masses* (Cambridge, 1980), 6–7; descrip-tion of generator in Edward Hungerford, "The Human Side of a City Railroad," *Harper's Weekly* 53 (August, 28, 1909), 10–12.

71. E. J. Edward, "The Street Car Kings," *Munsey's* 30 (December 1903), 383–93, quoted passage on 384.

72. Burton J. Henrick, "Street Railway Financiers," *McClure's* 30 (November 1907), 33–48. See also pts. 2 and 3, (December 1907), 236–50 and (June 1908), 323–38; United States Bureau of the Census, *Special Reports, 1902*, 120–21; Ed-ward C. Kirkland, *Industry Comes of Age*, 244–46.

73. Kenneth Jackson argues that some "transit tycoons were less interested in the nickels in the fare box than they were in their personal land development schemes." Jackson, *Crabgrass Frontier*, 120.

74. E. J. Edward, "The Street Car Kings," 384–86. On mileage increasing faster than traffic, see Cheape, *Moving the Masses*, 7.

75. Hurd found that the fluidity of transit in the city was the single most important factor influencing realty values. He noted that in some cases transit extensions did reduce the costs of some parcels of land. Richard Hurd, *Principles of Urban Land Values* (New York, 1905).

76. Doris Dwyer, "A Century of City Building: Three Generations of the Kilgour Family in Cincinnati, 1798–1914," (Miami, Ohio, 1979, copy in Cincin-nati Historical Society), 127–40.

77. Theodore Dreiser, *The Titan* (New York, 1914), 4–5, 11.

78. Burton J. Henrick, "Street Railway Financiers," 35.

79. Metropolitan realty values represented, Lewis Mumford notes, the "mainstay of savings banks and insurance companies." Lewis Mumford, *The Culture of Cities* (New York, 1938), 229. Insurance companies were among the first to build skyscrapers in both New York and Chicago. On New York's notorious Equitable Building, see Seymour Toll, *Zoned American* (New York, 1969), 70–71. The larger speculative builders of tenement houses commonly secured long-term loans from insurance and trust companies. DeForest and Veiller, *The Tenement House Problem*, 372–73.

80. Taylor, *Satellite Cities*, 100.

81. Jackson has argued the street railway was probably the dominant factor of many that determined urban growth. Jackson, *Crabgrass Frontier*, 118–20. Paul Barrett has convincingly argued that habit, "the cost of new housing, and racial and ethnic prejudice worked against transit's decentralization effect on residence." Paul Barrett, *Urban Transit and the Automobile: The Formation of Public Policy in Chicago, 1900–1930* (Philadelphia, 1983), 106. See Thomas L. Philpott, *The Slum and the Ghetto: Neighborhood Deterioration and Middle-Class Reform, Chicago, 1880–1930* (New York, 1978) on the effect of racial prejudice on housing patterns.

82. Edward E. Higgins, "Some of the Larger Transportation Problems in Cities," *Municipal Affairs* 3 (June 1899), 234–55, quoted passages on 234, 236. Edward Dana Durand, "Street Railways Fares in the United States," *Review of Reviews* 31 (February 1905), 171–76, quoted passage on 171. Durand concluded that although the three-cent fare would be "unremunerative," a fare of four cents or six for twenty five could be achieved. W. W. Wheatley, "Transporting New York's Millions," *World's Work* 6 (May 1903), 3422–36, on Union Square see 3428.

83. Wilcox, *The American City*, 31–33.

84. "Lively Times in Chicago," *New York Times* (October 10, 1888).

85. Wilcox, *The American City*, 29.

86. "Blockading the Streets," *New York Times* (March 4, 1886); "Stopping All Cars," *New York Times* (March 5, 1886).

87. "Scenes on Second Avenue," *New York Times* (July 20, 1899).

88. Theodore Dreiser, *Sister Carrie* (New York, 1961), 383.

89. "Stopping All Cars," *New York Times* (March 5, 1886).

90. "Lively Times in Chicago," *New York Times* (October 10, 1888), "Street Cars Tied Up," *New York Times* (October 7, 1888).

91. "The Brooklyn Street-Car Strike," *Harpers' Weekly* (February 2, 1895), 117.

92. James Barnes, "The End of the Strike in Brooklyn," *Harpers' Weekly* (February 9, 1895), 142.

93. Louis F. Post and Fred C. Leubuscher, *Henry George's 1886 Campaign* (reprint, Westport, Conn., 1976), 153.

94. Post and Leubuscher, *George's 1886 Campaign*, platform statement, 13; campaign speech, 28.

95. Post and Leubuscher, *George's 1886 Campaign*, 25–27.

96. Post and Leubuscher, *George's 1886 Campaign*, 8–9. Weber reported that in 1890 more than 93 percent of the residents of Manhattan were tenants. Weber, *The Growth of Cities*, 427.

97. In the wake of the United Labor party campaigns in Cincinnati, the Cox machine employed a similar strategy in building up a durable Republican majority in that city. Fairfield, "Cincinnati's Search For Order," 15–26.

98. Post and Leubuscher, *George's 1886 Campaign*, the threat to home ownership and mortgage-loaning institutions, 64–65; "no fear," 103.

99. Alan Trachtenberg, *Brooklyn Bridge; Fact and Symbol* (Chicago, 1965), 119.

100. George, *Social Problems*, 19.

101. Abram Hewitt, "The Meaning of the Brooklyn Bridge," in Allan Nevins, ed., *Selected Writings of Abram Hewitt* (New York, 1937), 295–311, quoted passages on 298–99.

102. *New York Tribune*, March 12, 1882; *Railroad Gazette* 25 (June 1, 1883), 348; both quoted in Trachtenberg, *Brooklyn Bridge*, 110–13; DeForest and Veiller, *The Tenement House Problem*, 335.

103. Cheape, *Moving the Masses*, 73; Hammack, *Power and Society*, 234–35.

104. Cheape, *Moving the Masses*, 79; Hammack, *Power and Society*, 233–34, 237.

105. Cheape, *Moving the Masses*, 80; Hammack, *Power and Society*, 247–48.

106. Cheape, *Moving the Masses*, 79; Hammack, *Power and Society*, 234.

107. Hammack, *Power and Society*, 249.

108. Hammack, *Power and Society*, 249–50; Cheape, *Moving the Masses*, 81–82.

109. Hammack, *Power and Society*, 246–47.

110. Hammack, *Power and Society*, 250; Cheape, *Moving the Masses*, 80.

111. The composition of the new commission, Hammack has argued, "made it certain that rapid transit planning would take place under the exclusive direction of the city's mercantile elite, as represented in the Chamber of Commerce." Hammack, *Power and Society*, 249–50. See also Cheape, *Moving the Masses*, 81–82.

112. Julius Wilcox, "The New Transit System and the New New York," *The Independent* 55 (September 24, 1903), 2283–86.

113. W. W. Wheatley, "Transporting New York's Millions," *World's Work* 6 (May 1903), 3422–36. On the Long Island Railroad tunnel, see William J. Gaynor, "New York's Subway Policy," *Municipal Affairs* 5 (June 1901), 433–38.

114. One new rapid transit proposal included Ryan's cynical offer to merge his decrepit surface lines with the profitable subways upon a uniform five-cent fare with universal transfers as a way to empty the tenement districts. "Solving

A Great City's Transportation Problem," *World's Work* 15 (November 1907), 9594–99, "this place of discontent" on 9594. On Ryan's proposal and the public response, see James Walker, *Fifty Years of Rapid Transit* (New York, 1970, reprint of 1918 edition), 197–201.

115. Henry Bruere, "Public Utilities Regulation in New York," *Annals of the American Academy of Political and Social Sciences* 31 (May 1908), 535–51, quoted passages on 538.

116. Thomas Mott Osborne, "Public Service Commissions Law of New York," *Atlantic Monthly* 101 (April 1908), 545–54, quoted passage on 554. Without the new law, Public Service Commissioner Bassett wrote later, "the natural growth of the city would have been restricted." Edward M. Bassett, *Autobiography* (New York, 1939), 111.

117. Walker, *Fifty Years of Rapid Transit*, 242.

118. Walker, *Fifty Years of Rapid Transit*, 261.

119. Bassett, *Autobiography*, 112–13.

120. Henry Wright, "The Interrelation of Housing and Transit," *American City* 10 (January 1914), 51–53.

121. Milo Maltbie, "Transportation and City Planning," *Proceedings*, Fifth National Conference on City Planning (Chicago, 1913), 107–19.

Chapter 3

1. Charles H. Cooley, quoted in Adna Weber, *The Growth of Cities in the Nineteenth Century* (New York, 1899), 474. The quotation is not footnoted but is virtually identical to a passage in Cooley, *The Theory of Transportation* (Publication of American Economic Association, May 1894). Gilmore Simms, "The Philosophy of the Omnibus," *Godey's Lady's Book* 23 (September 1841), 105, quoted in Glen E. Holt, "The Changing Perception of Urban Pathology," in Kenneth T. Jackson and Stanley K. Schultz, eds., *Cities in American History* (New York, 1972), 326. I use the term *unrealistic* in both its conventional sense and in the more specific connotation developed in this work.

2. Carroll D. Wright, "Rapid Transit: Lessons From the Census," *Popular Science Monthly* 40 (April 1892), 758–92.

3. Adna Weber, "Suburban Annexations," *North American Review* 166 (May 1898), 612–17, quoted passage on 616–17. See also Weber, *The Growth of Cities in the Nineteenth Century*, 473–75.

4. Paul Barrett, *The Automobile and Urban Transit* (Philadelphia, 1983), 106–10.

5. Barrett explains that what Yerkes actually said during an 1893 stockholders' meeting was that the "short hauls and the people who hang on the straps are the ones we make our money out of. . . . We make no money on the man who has a seat and rides to the end of the line." As in the shorter misquote, the point was

that transit's profitability and its ability to disperse population were incompatible. *Chicago Tribune,* January 11, 1893. See Barrett, *The Automobile and Urban Transit,* 18.

6. In Detroit, where the reform mayor Hazen Pingree began the movement for the three-cent fare, Olivier Zunz has documented surprisingly high rates of home ownership among industrial workers, particularly immigrants. Ironically, the pattern of home ownership initially developed without the benefit of even surface transit on the city's east side. It is possible that cheap rapid transit might have encouraged and spread that pattern, but transit's effect on realty costs would have been a complicating factor. In George's campaign, of course, rapid transit had been linked to the single tax. Melvin Holli, *Reform in Detroit* (New York, 1969), especially chaps. 3 and 6. Olivier Zunz, *The Changing Face of Inequality* (Chicago, 1982), on the lack of street railway service on the east side, 123–25; on home ownership, chap. 6.

7. Frederic C. Howe, *The City; The Hope of Democracy* (Seattle, 1967, reprint of 1905 edition), 69–70.

8. For a modern statement of the importance of public transportation and equal access to the suburb, see K. H. Schaeffer and Elliot Sclalr, *Access for All: Transportation and Urban Growth* (Baltimore, 1975).

9. Howe, *The City,* 123, 51.

10. Barrett, *The Automobile and Urban Transit,* on Dunne 34; on planners and the dream of dispersing population, 10. On professional planners and public transportation, see Mark S. Foster, *From Streetcar to Superhighway* (Philadelphia, 1981).

11. Barrett, *The Automobile and Urban Transit,* 3–7. See also Foster, *From Streetcar to Superhighway.*

12. James J. Flink, *The Car Culture* (Cambridge, 1975), 40.

13. Samuel Haber, *Efficiency and Uplift: Scientific Management in the Progressive Era* (Chicago, 1964) especially x; Daniel T. Rodgers, "In Search of Progressivism," in Stanley Kutler and Stanley Katz, eds., *Reviews in American History; The Promise of American History: Progress and Prospects,* vol. 10 (December 1982).

14. *Chicago Tribune,* February 12, 1906; quoted in Barrett, *The Automobile and Urban Transit,* 23.

15. Among realists, city managers were particularly concerned about keeping costs low. Consider, for example, the chilly reception Richard Childs received when he suggested that managers might one day be known not for "a freakishly low expense per capita" but for their role in "great new enterprises of service." He was quickly advised that "theorists were not welcome" at the managers' meeting. Leonard D. White, *The City Manager* (Chicago, 1927), 149. But Roger Lotchin and Kenneth Fox have shown that municipal reformers and "innovators" (Fox's term) expanded rather than trimmed municipal budgets. Roger Lotchin, "Power and Policy: American City Politics Between the Two World Wars," in

Scott Greer, ed., *Ethics, Machines, and the American Urban Future* (Cambridge, Mass., 1981), 1–50; Kenneth Fox, *Better City Government* (Philadelphia, 1977), especially chap. 5. See also James Weinstein, *The Corporate Ideal in the Liberal State* (Boston, 1968), 113–14 on the willingness of business reformers to venture into the realm of social reform.

16. Miller (who coined the term) argues that the purpose of the new urban discipline was to address the problems of the city "without arousing the divisive emotional, and hysterical responses which helped immobilize municipal statesmen in the 1880's." Zane L. Miller, *Boss Cox's Cincinnati: Urban Politics in the Progressive Era* (Chicago, 1968), 239. I have borrowed the term "the new urban discipline" from Miller's study of urban politics in the Progressive Era because of the close similarity between the movements he describes and those examined here. While my interpretation and definition of the new urban discipline differ from Miller's, they have been influenced in numerous ways by Miller's work. See Miller, *Boss Cox's Cincinnati*, 111–60.

17. On the national effort to stabilize the corporate order, see Weinstein, *The Corporate Ideal in the Liberal State*; Gabriel Kolko, *The Triumph of Progressivism* (Glencoe, 1963). A more moderate version of the argument that de-emphasizes the role of corporate hegemony is Robert Wiebe, *The Search for Order* (New York, 1967).

18. Henry Morgenthau, "A National Constructive Programme For City Planning," First National Conference on City Planning (Washington, D.C., 1909), published as *City Planning; Hearing Before the Committee on the District of Columbia United States Senate on the Subject of City Planning* (Washington, D.C., 1910), 75–79, quoted passage on 78.

19. Robert Anderson Pope, "Some of the Needs of City Planning in America," *City Planning: Hearing*, 59–60.

20. "Labeling themselves neutral experts, engineers professed to work above the din of local politics. Usually they tried to isolate themselves from partisan wrangles, and often succeeded." Stanley K. Schultz and Clay McShane, "To Engineer the Metropolis: Sewers, Sanitation, and City Planning in Late-Nineteenth-Century America," *Journal of American History* 65 (September 1978), 389–411, quoted passage on 399. That is not to imply that such reforms were completely free of political controversy. See Clay McShane, "Transforming the Use of Urban Space: A Look at the Revolution in Street Pavements, 1880–1924," *Journal of Urban History* 5 (May 1979), 279–307; on early conflicts between cyclists and inner-city residents over asphalted streets, see Steven A. Riess, *City Games: The Evolution of American Urban Society and the Rise of Sports* (Urbana, 1989), 63–64.

21. Jon C. Teaford, *The Municipal Revolution in America: Origins of Modern Urban Government, 1625–1825* (New York, 1984). On artisan republicanism see Sean Wilentz, *Chants Democratic: New York City and the Rise of the American Working Class, 1788–1850* (New York, 1984), chap. 2.

22. Teaford, *The Municipal Revolution*; Zane L. Miller, "Scarcity, Abundance, and American Urban History," *Journal of Urban History* 4 (February 1978), 131–56.

23. Zane Miller argues that the machine appeared "at the moment of the transformation of the perception of American cities as residential rather than essentially economic communities." Zane L. Miller, "Bosses, Machines, and the Urban Political Process," in Greer, ed., *Ethnics, Machines, and the American Urban Future*, 60.

24. Ira Katznelson, *City Trenches* (New York, 1981); Amy Bridges, *A City in the Republic: Origins of Machine Politics in Ante-Bellum New York* (New York, 1984).

25. Amy Bridges, *A City in the Republic*, 3.

26. Katznelson, *City Trenches*, 54–65.

27. Louis F. Post and Fred C. Leubuscher, *Henry George's 1886 Campaign* (reprint of 1887 edition, Westport, Conn., 1976), 33.

28. Businessmen's criticism of ULP in Cincinnati from the Cincinnati *Enquirer*, December 15, 1886, quoted in Steven J. Ross, *Workers on the Edge* (New York, 1985), 311; the phrase "Republican-Democratic-capitalist" is Ross's, 312. On opposition to ULP in other cities see John R. Commons et al., *A History of Labour in the United States*, vol. 2 (New York, 1918), 466.

29. Post and Leubuscher, *George's 1886 Campaign*, 172–73.

30. On the social reformer as machine politician see Holli, *Reform in Detroit*, 152–56.

31. Holli, *Reform in Detroit*, bribes, 81; petitions and boycotts, 107–8; the riot, 38–40; Howe's statement is in his introduction to Tom L. Johnson, *My Story* (New York, 1911), xxiv.

32. Ray Ginger, *Altgeld's America* (New York, 1958), 180–83. Allen Davis, *Spearheads for Reform*, 152–62. The quotation is from Carter Harrison, *Stormy Years* (New York, 1935), 191. See also John H. Gray, "The Street Railway Situation in Chicago," *Quarterly Journal of Economics* 12 (October 1897), 83–90; Milo Roy Maltbie, "Street Railways of Chicago; Analysis of Financial Operations," *Municipal Affairs* 5 (June 1901), 441–83.

33. Adna Weber, "The Significance of Recent City Growth," *Annals of the American Academy of Political and Social Sciences* 23 (March 1904), 234–35. For a defense of the "free trade" in franchises, see "Street Railways and Their Relation to the Public," *Municipal Affairs* 1 (1897) 396–97; L. S. Rowe, "Relation of Cities and Towns to Street Railway Companies," *Annals of the American Academy of Political and Social Sciences* 12 (1898), 103–8, "willingness to experiment," 104. Rowe reviewed a Massachusetts report that recommended against regulation, although he personally called for "more careful control over private corporations," 107.

34. Weber, "The Significance of Recent City Growth," 235–36.

35. Johnson, *My Story*, xxii.

36. Wagner quoted in J. Joseph Huthmacher, *Senator Robert Wagner and the*

Rise of Union Liberalism (New York, 1971), 20–21. On Ohio cities see Jean L. Stinchcombe, *Reform and Reaction* (Belmont, Calif., 1968), 30–34.

37. Tom Johnson, *My Story*, xxi, 125.

38. Milo Maltbie, "Municipal Functions; A Study of the Development, Scope, and Tendency of Municipal Socialism," *Municipal Affairs* 2 (December 1898), 577–799; quoted passage on 770.

39. Holli, *Reform in Detroit*, 56–74, quoted passage on 56.

40. Holli, *Reform in Detroit*, 56–63.

41. John Buenker, *Urban Liberalism and Progressive Reform* (New York, 1973), 28–32.

42. Urban liberals, Buenker writes, attacked such problems "as child and female labor, inadequate housing, low wages, excessive hours, dangerous working conditions, industrial accidents, and lack of retirement benefits." Buenker, *Urban Liberalism*, chaps. 2–3, quoted passage on 42.

43. Howe, *The City*, vii.

44. Howe, *The City*, 44–45.

45. Howe, *The City*, 114–23.

46. Post and Leubuscher, *George's 1886 Campaign*, 172–73.

47. Miller, "Scarcity," 141.

48. Frank J. Goodnow, "The Tweed Ring in New York City," in James Bryce, *The American Commonwealth*, vol. 2 (London, 1888), 335.

49. Holli, *Reform in Detroit*, 174–75.

50. Seth Low, "The Government of Cities in the United States," *Century Magazine* 42 (September 1891), 730–36.

51. Seth Low, "The Problem of Municipal Government," Address, Cornell University, March 16, 1887, 11; quoted in Gerald Kurland, *Seth Low* (New York, 1971), 65.

52. Many late-nineteenth century reformers, Miller argues, believed that the city faced a choice "between efficient management and disorder and obsolescence." Miller, "Scarcity," 142. On the National Civic Federation, see Weinstein, *The Corporate Ideal in the Liberal State*.

53. Low, "The Government of Cities in the United States," 730–36.

54. Low, "Municipal Government," Address, Philadelphia Committee of Fifty, January 27, 1892, 12–13; quoted in Kurland, *Seth Low*, 72–73; "few American cities" is from Low, "The Government of Cities," 732.

55. Municipal government as a force for social harmony and economic development was also the strategy Hewitt had proposed in his call for a municipal subway. See chapter 2 in this volume.

56. The call for disenfranchisement continued into the new century. In 1904 Henry Jones Ford argued that "if municipal government is simply a business proposition, then participation in it should be confined to those who have an interest in the business." Recognition of that fact would require the elimination

of "the herds of voting cattle in which our ward politicians traffic," Ford argued, but he did so with little hope that such a proposal would be adopted. Henry Jones Ford, "Principles of Municipal Organization," *Annals of the American Academy of Political and Social Sciences* 23 (March 1904), 195–222; quoted passage on 220.

57. Carl Schurz, "The Task of the Citizens' Union," *Harper's Weekly* 41 (December 11, 1897), 1215.

58. Allen Davis, *Spearheads for Reform* (New York, 1967), especially chap. 8.

59. Robert A. Woods and Albert J. Kennedy, *The Settlement Horizon* (New York, 1922), 39, 59, 227–29.

60. Jane Addams, "Ethical Survivals in Municipal Corruption," *International Journal of Ethics* 8 (April 1898), 273–91, quoted passages on 282 and 291. James Reynolds, "The Settlement and Municipal Reform," *Proceedings*, National Conference of Charities and Correction (Grand Rapids, 1896), 138–42. On municipal reform as a moral problem, see Boyer, *Urban Masses and Moral Order in America, 1820–1920* (Cambridge, Mass., 1978), chap. 11.

61. Woods and Kennedy, *The Settlement Horizon*, 34–39.

62. Jane Addams, "The Settlement as a Factor in the Labor Movement," in *Hull House Maps and Papers* (New York, 1895), 201–2.

63. Graham Taylor, *Pioneering on Social Frontiers* (Chicago, 1930), 7, 116.

64. Woods and Kennedy, *The Settlement Horizon*, 226–27.

65. Woods and Kennedy, *The Settlement Horizon*, 398. The settlement effort to mediate class conflict had its parallel outside the neighborhood in the workplace. "The new profession of industrial counsellor or employment manager is carrying the settlement demand of sympathetic understanding of the workingman's needs as operative, shopmate, householder, and citizen into broad-scale practice," Woods explained. Woods and Kennedy, *The Settlement Horizon*, 397.

66. Woods and Kennedy, *The Settlement Horizon*, 229.

67. John Daniels, *America via the Neighborhood* (New York, 1920), 222–23.

68. Woods and Kennedy, *The Settlement Horizon*, 225–27.

69. Jane Addams, "Why the Ward Boss Rules," *The Outlook* 58 (April 2, 1898), 878–82, quoted passage on 880.

70. Addams, "Ethical Survivals," 291.

71. Woods and Kennedy, *The Settlement Horizon*, 227.

72. Woods and Kennedy, *The Settlement Horizon*, 227–28. On the relationship between Woods and Donovan, see Davis, *Spearheads for Reform*, 148–49.

73. Jane Addams, *Twenty Years at Hull House* (New York, 1910), 319.

74. Daniel Levine, *Jane Addams and the Liberal Tradition* (Madison, Wis., 1971), especially 67. Ray Ginger, *Altgeld's America* (New York, 1973), especially 242. Mary K. Simkhovitch, *Neighborhood* (New York, 1930), 102. Graham Taylor, *Chicago Commons through Forty Years* (Chicago, 1936), 33–36. Woods and Kennedy, *The Settlement Horizon*, 369.

75. Woods and Kennedy, *The Settlement Horizon*, 227–28, 360.

76. Woods and Kennedy, *The Settlement Horizon*, "high professional standard," 228–29; "new type," 228. "Institutionalize," Amos Pinchot, quoted in Roy V. Peel, Introduction to William L. Riordon, *Plunkett of Tammany Hall* (New York, 1948), xli.

77. On Greenwich House, Simkhovitch, *Neighborhood*, 75–76, 149, 160. Gerald Kurland, *Seth Low*, 59, 146. Graham Taylor, *Chicago Commons through Forty Years*, 67–68. Graham Taylor, *Pioneering on Social Frontiers*, 61. Davis, *Spearheads for Reform*, 68–70.

78. Cincinnati Chamber of Commerce, *Sixty-Fifth Annual Report*, 1913, quoted in Miller, *Boss Cox's Cincinnati*, 120–21. On businessmen's interest in reform, see Weinstein, *The Corporate Ideal in the Liberal State*, chap. 4; Samuel P. Hays, "The Politics of Reform in Municipal Government in the Progressive Era," *Pacific Northwest Quarterly* 55 (October 1964), 157–69.

79. Jane Addams, *The Spirit of Youth and the City Streets* (New York, 1909), 98. On settlements and social reform, see the discussion of the Committee on Congestion of Population in chapter 4 of this volume. Also see Davis, *Spearheads for Reform*.

80. Benjamin Flower, *Civilization's Inferno; or Studies in the Social Cellar* (Boston, 1893); quoted in Boyer, *Urban Masses and Moral Order*, 170.

81. Henry G. Foreman, "The Chicago Park System," *World To-Day* 13 (September 1907), 901–12, quoted passage on 905.

82. Ernest Poole, "Chicago's Public Playgrounds," *Outlook* 87 (December 7, 1907), 775–81, quoted passages 776–78.

83. Graham Taylor, "How They Played At Chicago," *Charities and the Commons* 18 (August 3, 1907), 473–74.

84. J. Horace McFarland, "General Recreation Planning," in John Nolen, ed., *City Planning* (New York, 1916), 147.

85. Charles Mulford Robinson, "The Sociology of Street Layout," *Annals of the American Academy of Political and Social Sciences* 51 (January 1914), 192–97, quoted passage on 196–97.

86. Charles Mulford Robinson, *Modern Civic Art; or, The City Made Beautiful* (New York, 1903), 91; quoted in Boyer, *Urban Masses and Moral Order*, 266.

87. Milo Maltbie, "Municipal Functions; A Study of the Development, Scope, and Tendency of Municipal Socialism," *Municipal Affairs* 2 (December 1898), 577–799, quoted passage on 767.

88. Poole, "Chicago's Public Playgrounds," 780–81.

89. In other senses as well the new urban discipline was literally a discipline: a subject that is taught; orderly or prescribed conduct or pattern of behavior; a rule or system of rules governing conduct or activity.

90. Maltbie, "Municipal Function," 762–63. For a contemporary discussion

NOTES TO CHAPTER 3

of costs and fares, see Edward Dana Durand, "Street Railway Fares in the United States," *Review of Reviews* 31 (February 1905), 171–76. For a discussion of the public utility corporation from the point of the view of the private corporation and in terms of marginal and average costs, see Alan D. Anderson, *The Origin and Resolution of an Urban Crisis: Baltimore, 1890–1930* (Baltimore, 1977), 5–9.

91. Maltbie, "Municipal Functions," 770–71.

92. Pingree, Holli argues, urged that compensation "should be taken in the form of low fares that benefitted all the citizens rather than in the form of higher franchise fees that reduced taxation or eliminated the need for tax increases and thus aided the propertied citizens." Holli, *Reform in Detroit*, 52, 112.

93. Barrett argues that "any meaningful engineering judgment about mass transit was inherently political" and hence subject to both public debate and popular rejection. Barrett, *The Automobile and Urban Transit*, 92. On public health and medical professionals, see Alan I Marcus, "Professional Revolution and Reform in the Progressive Era: Cincinnati Physicians and the City Elections of 1897 and 1900," *Journal of Urban History* 5 (February 1979), 183–207. Even Tammany boss Charles Murphy declared public health above politics. See Wiebe, *The Search for Order*, 115–16.

94. See chapter 2 in this volume.

95. New York reformers, David Hammack explains, saw it as a way to reach out "to the aristocracy of labor, whose members might hope for employment in building a new transit system and might even hope to move to a new small house at the end of the line." *Record and Guide*, March 18, 1893, quoted in David Hammack, *Power and Society* (New York, 1985), 246; "aristocracy," 248.

96. Jon C. Teaford, *The Unheralded Triumph* (Baltimore, 1984), chaps. 6–7. The term "extra-legal molders" is Teaford's.

97. Weinstein, *The Corporate Ideal in the Liberal State*, 24–26. Ernest S. Griffith, *A History of American City Government: The Progressive Years and Their Aftermath, 1900–1920* (New York, 1974), 86–89.

98. Bureau of the Census, *Bulletin 20, Statistics of Cities; 1902 and 1903*, 4–5; quoted in Kenneth Fox, *Better City Government*, 73. Emphasis added.

99. Bureau of the Census, *Bulletin 20, Statistics of Cities; 1902 and 1903*, 4–5; quoted in Kenneth Fox, *Better City Government*, 73.

100. Fox explains that Rowe discussed the importance of democratic control "without concern that he was eliminating all controversy over the proper tasks of city government from his conception of municipal democracy." Rowe's "democracy of pleasures" was, Fox argues, an "unfortunate passage" in which "Rowe allowed himself to be carried away by his own rhetoric." Leo S. Rowe, *Problems of City Government* (New York, 1908), 94, 135, 123, 51–52, 204; Fox, *Better City Government*, 130–31.

101. Barrett, *The Automobile and Urban Transit*, passim.

102. Milo R. Maltbie, "Transportation and City Planning" and Alfred Bettman, "Comments," *Proceedings*, Fifth National Conference on City Planning
(Chicago, 1913), 107, 127–28.

103. The best study of the rapid transit debate is Eva Jane Kartye, "Rapid
Transit in Cincinnati, 1900–1939," (M.A. thesis, University of Cincinnati,
1963). On the early history of mass transit in Cincinnati, see Doris Dwyer, "A
Century of City-Building; Three Generations of the Kilgour Family in Cincinnati, 1798–1914," (Ph.D. dissertation, Miami University, 1979), 102–3. For an
account of the charter movement, see Charles P. Taft, *City Management: The
Cincinnati Experiment* (Port Washington, N.Y., 1933) For a more detailed discussion of those issues, see John D. Fairfield, "Cincinnati's Hole in the Ground:
Rapid Transit, City Planning, and the New Urban Discipline," *The Old Northwest* (Fall 1988).

104. *Sixth Annual Report* of the Cincinnati Anti-Tuberculosis League (Cincinnati, 1913), 11–12. See also Robert B. Fairbanks, *Making Better Citizens* (Urbana,
1989), 28; Zane Miller, *Boss Cox's Cincinnati*, 220–21; Cincinnati Traction Company, *Press Clippings and Scrapbooks* vols. 93–94, in Cincinnati Historical Society.
Elliott Hunt Pendleton, "Cincinnati's Traction Problem," *National Municipal Review* 2 (October 1913), 617–28, quoted passage on 617.

105. Miller, *Boss Cox's Cincinnati*, 221–22; Pendleton, "Cincinnati's Traction
Problem," 623–25.

106. *Cincinnati Post*, April 22, 1913. A clipping file of accounts of the strike
taken from the local newspapers may be found at the Cincinnati Public Library.
See also the Cincinnati Traction Corporation scrapbooks at the Cincinnati Historical Society.

107. *Cincinnati Times-Star*, April 22, 1913.

108. *Cincinnati Enquirer*, April 30, 1913, May 3, 1913; the Trades Union Municipal Ownership League included representatives from the city's streetcar and
brewery workers, iron molders and pattern makers, among others.

109. *Cincinnati Post*, May 8, 1913.

110. *Cincinnati American*, May 8, 1913.

111. *Cincinnati Times-Star*, May 14, 1913; *Cincinnati Enquirer*, May 15, 1913.

112. *Cincinnati Times-Star*, May 17, 1913. See also *Cincinnati Times-Star*,
May 16–17, 1913; *Cincinnati Post*, May 16, 1913; Marc N. Goodnow, "Motor-
man and Mayor in Strike Strategy," *Survey* 30 (July 28, 1913), 432–33.

113. *Cincinnati Times-Star*, May 17–18, 1913.

114. *Cincinnati Times-Star*, May 17, 1913.

115. John R. Holmes to Mary L. Holmes, May 19, 1913 in Cincinnati Historical Society.

116. *Cincinnati Enquirer*, May 28, 1913.

117. "Speech of Herbert Bigelow at Race and Fifth Streets," July 26, 1913,

NOTES TO CHAPTER 3

Cincinnati Historical Society; Pendleton, "Cincinnati's Traction Problems," 623–28; Kartye, "Rapid Transit in Cincinnati," 81; Miller, *Boss Cox's Cincinnati*, 220–24.

118. Landon Warner, "Henry T. Hunt and Civic Reform in Cincinnati," *Ohio State Archaeological and Historical Quarterly* 62 (April 1953), 146–61.

119. *Citizens' Bulletin*, November 15, 1913, and November 22, 1913; Miller, *Boss Cox's Cincinnati*, 237–38.

120. Kartye, "Rapid Transit in Cincinnati," 76–86.

121. Kartye, "Rapid Transit in Cincinnati," 86–113.

122. *Citizens' Bulletin*, August 8, 1913.

123. Miller, *Boss Cox's Cincinnati*, 230–39.

124. Fairbanks, *Making Better Citizens*, 42–43. Bettman's papers in the University of Cincinnati Archives, Urban Studies Collection, include extensive documentation of the activities of the United City Planning Committee.

125. United City Planning Committee of Cincinnati, "Statement and Evidence on Pending Zoning Ordinance to City Council of Cincinnati (January 24, 1924), 15–17, 31–32; in Archives of Public Library of Cincinnati and Hamilton County.

126. "Report Dated May 18th, 1926 on Rapid Transit Commission of Cincinnati By Third Member (Chairman) of Law Committee—Murray Seasongood," in Urban Studies Collection of University of Cincinnati Archives.

127. "Report Dated May 18th, 1926 on Rapid Transit Commission of Cincinnati By Third Member (Chairman) of Law Committee—Murray Seasongood," in Urban Studies Collection of University of Cincinnati Archives.

128. City Planning Commission, *The Official City Plan of Cincinnati, Ohio* (Cincinnati, 1925), 128. On downtown congestion see 91–109, on radial thoroughfares see 55–90.

129. *Official City Plan*, 25–54.

130. United City Planning Committee, "Statement of Evidence," 13.

131. *Official City Plan*, 50–51; see also Mel Scott, *American City Planning Since 1890* (Berkeley, 1971), 228–29.

132. United City Planning Committee. "Statement of Evidence," 24, 29.

133. Anderson argues in the case of Baltimore that the automobile provided the resolution of an urban crisis caused by the growing cost of urban services. Certainly, automobility allowed municipal governments to escape the cost of public transit and other urban services, but at a cost to those urbanites without access to the automobile and the suburban periphery. Anderson, *The Origin and Resolution of an Urban Crisis*.

134. Fairbanks, *Making Better Citizens*, especially 25–70; Bettman quoted on 42–43.

135. United City Planning Committee, "Statement of Evidence," Bettman,

280

5; civil engineering, 47; "peace and contentment," 40; labor leader, 34; "worker who retires," 15.

136. United City Planning Committee, "Statement of Evidence," 17.

137. Fairbanks, *Making Better Citizens*, especially 58–70.

138. Leaving economic inequality unresolved was particularly true of zoning. Argues planning historian Don Kirschner, "For those who rejected social re-form, the great advantage of zoning was that it could be used like a laser to target a limited, concrete objective without disturbing the wider network of social re-lations around it." Don Kirschner, *The Paradox of Professionalism* (Westport, Conn., 1986), 60–61.

139. Charles A. Beard, *American City Government; A Survey of Newer Tenden-cies* (New York, 1912), 386. I am indebted to Zane Miller for the reference.

Chapter 4

1. An excellent biography of Burnham is Thomas S. Hines, *Burham of Chi-cago: Architect and Planner* (New York, 1974). The phrase "architect of capitalism" is Hines's.

2. Daniel Burnham and Edward H. Bennett, *Plan of Chicago* (Chicago, 1908), 1.

3. Homer Hoyt, *One Hundred Years of Land Values in Chicago* (New York, 1970; reprint of 1933 edition), 327–48; on 1877–92, 185; on 1894–1910 see charts on 345–46. See also Richard M. Hurd, *Principles of City Land Values* (New York, 1903).

4. Burnham, *Plan of Chicago*, "metropolis," 32; "illimitable," 80.

5. Burnham, *Plan of Chicago*, concentric and arterial highways, 40–41; "traf-fic," 91.

6. Barrett argues that the *Plan of Chicago* represented a turning point in ur-ban transportation in Chicago and "marks the transfer of the center of attention from transit planning to street planning." Barrett, *The Automobile and Urban Transit* (Philadelphia, 1983), 80.

7. Burnham, *Plan of Chicago*, 80–88, "new streets," 80; "remorseless," 88; "circulation," 86.

8. Burnham, *Plan of Chicago*, 61–74, "clearing house," 61; "complete ma-chine," 65; "many times," 74. See also Barrett, *The Automobile and Urban Tran-sit*, 80.

9. Burnham, *Plan of Chicago*, 64. Carter Harrison, in describing the 1897 teamsters' strike, recalled the teamsters as "at best a scrappy lot." The stockyard teamsters in particular "were the type of human animal that feeds on raw meat." As that was the recollection of one of their supporters, it is not difficult to imag-

ine their reputation among their opponents. Carter H. Harrison, *Stormy Years* (Indianapolis, 1935), 212.

10. Burnham, "Plan of Chicago, "nerves," 74; "effectiveness," 86; wealthy spending, 8; "good labor market," 46–47.

11. Burnham, *Plan of Chicago*, "lakefront," 50; "burden," 53; "parades," 111. The park and the boulevard, in Burnham's view, offered something of the same relief once associated with rapid transit and the suburban home.

12. Burnham, *Plan of Chicago*, 36.

13. Hines, *Burnham of Chicago*, chap. 1.

14. "Beauty pays," quoted in Paul S. Boyer, *Urban Masses and Moral Order in America, 1820–1920* (Cambridge, 1978), 275; Burnham, *Plan of Chicago*, "higher emotions," 30.

15. Burnham, *Plan of Chicago*, "good citizenship," 120–23. See Boyer, *Urban Masses and Moral Order*, 271–75.

16. William H. Wilson, *The City Beautiful Movement* (Baltimore, 1989), 37, 41–45.

17. Boyer, *Urban Masses and Moral Order*, chap. 18; Charles Mulford Robinson, *Modern Civic Art; or The City Made Beautiful* (New York, 1903), quoted in Boyer, *Urban Masses and Moral Order*, 266.

18. Burnham, *Plan of Chicago*, 109.

19. Burnham, *Plan of Chicago*, "habits," 84; Haussmann's Paris, 15; "menace," 108.

20. Burnham, *Plan of Chicago*, "assemble for discussion," 88; "dignity and importance," 115; "good order," 4; "a long step," 29; "teach," "impressive height," 116.

21. Wilson has shown that the conflict between proponents and opponents of the city beautiful often reflected differences in their perception of the city as a complex social organism or an economic mechanism. Wilson, *The City Beautiful Movement*, pts. 2 and 3.

22. On the failure of city beautiful advocates to grasp the economic realities of metropolitan development, see John R. Stilgoe, *Metrpolitan Corridor* (New Haven, 1983), 215.

23. Robert Wiebe, *The Search for Order* (New York, 1967); Robert Wiebe, *Businessmen and Reform* (New York, 1962); Christopher Lasch, *The New Radicalism in America* (New York, 1965).

24. Gabriel Kolko, *The Triumph of Conservatism* (New York, 1963); James Weinstein, *The Corporate Ideal in the Liberal State* (Boston, 1968); for an application of the argument concerning big business's support for government regulation to the field of city planning, see M. Christine Boyer, *Dreaming the Rational City* (Cambridge, Mass., 1983).

25. Frederick Law Olmsted, Jr., "Introductory Address on City Planning," in *Proceedings*, Second National Conference on City Planning (Philadelphia, 1910), 16–17.

26. John Dewey, "Intelligence and Morals," in *The Influence of Darwin on Philosophy* (Bloomington, 1965; reprint of 1911 edition), 74; for a fuller discussion of the intellectual underpinnings and practical application of "positive environmentalism," see Boyer, *Urban Masses and Moral Order*, especially chaps. 15–17. The term "positive environmentalism" is Boyer's.

27. At least some middle-class professionals worried about questions of efficiency and democracy. See, for example, Patricia Mooney-Melvin, *The Organic City* (Lexington, Ky., 1977) for a discussion of Wilbur Phillips, creator of the social unit idea. See also Fox, *Better City Government* (Philadelphia, 1977), especially chapt. 6; and Samual Haber, *Efficiency and Uplift* (Chicago, 1964).

28. George Ford, "The City Scientific," *Proceedings*, Fifth National Conference on City Planning, 31.

29. See, for example, Herbert Gutman's analysis of the origins of the welfare state in New Jersey. Herbert Gutman, *Work, Culture, and Society* (New York, 1976), especially 261.

30. Benjamin C. Marsh, "City Planning in Justice to the Working Population," *Charities* 19 (February 1, 1908), 1514–18, quoted passage on 1514.

31. Wilson, *The City Beautiful Movement*, 285–90.

32. Robert A. Pope, "Some of the Needs of City Planning in America," *City Planning; Hearing Before the Committee on the District of Columbia* (Washington, D.C., 1910), 75–77. The volume, hereafter cited as *City Planning Hearing*, included the proceedings of the First National Conference on City Planning. George Hooker and a few others did comment favorably on the city beautiful movement at the conference. George Hooker, "Report on City Planning in Chicago," *City Planning Hearing*, 96–98. "Politically the group found equilibrium in the moderate left," writes Wilson of the first national conference. Wilson, *The City Beautiful Movement*, 286.

33. Mary Simkhovitch, "Address," *City Planning Hearing*, 101–4, quoted passage on 104; on "anti-urban" attitudes within the CCP see Allen Davis, *Spearheads for Reform* (New York, 1967), 70–73.

34. Simkhovitch, "Address," 104; Benjamin Marsh, *Introduction to City Planning* (New York, 1909); on death rates and congestion, 12–13, quoted passage, 27.

35. Benjamin C. Marsh, "Economic Aspects of City Planning," *City Planning Hearing*, 104–5, quoted passage on 105.

36. Mary Simkhovitch, *Neighborhood* (New York, 1938), 127; on her neighbor's love of urban life, see "Address," *City Planning Hearing*, 103.

37. Lillian Wald, *The House on Henry Street* (New York, 1915), 249.

38. Marsh, *Introduction to City Planning*, 27.

39. Charles A. Beard, *American City Government: A Survey of Newer Tendencies* (New York, 1912), 376–79. The commission's report is included as an appendix.

40. Huthmacher, *Senator Robert Wagner and the Rise of Urban Liberalism* (New

York, 1971), chap. 1. See especially Huthmacher's description of Wagner physically crawling through a hole in a factory wall labeled "fire escape," 6. See also Buenker, *Urban Liberalism and Progressive Reform* (New York, 1973), 48–49.

41. Quoted in Huthmacher, *Senator Robert Wagner*, 9.

42. Zoning served to separate city planners, Mel Scott has argued, "more and more from groups attempting to improve social and economic conditions." Mel Scott, *American City Planning Since 1890* (Berkeley, 1971), 117.

43. Sam Bass Warner, Jr., *The Urban Wilderness* (New York, 1972), 230–31.

44. Roy Lubove, *Community Planning in the 1920's* (Pittsburgh, 1963).

45. Mumford quoted by the editor, *Survey Graphic* 54 (May 1, 1925).

46. Mumford actually had a rather low opinion of Henry George's contribution; see, for example, Lewis Mumford, *The Culture of Cities* (New York, 1938), 156, 394. But since George influenced the work of both Ebenezer Howard and Patrick Geddes, who in turn influenced Mumford, it seems fair to argue that Mumford worked in a tradition shaped by George. Moreover, Charles Whitaker, editor of the *Journal of the American Institute of Architects* and an ardent single-taxer, sponsored some of Mumford's first writings. Daniel Schaffer, *Garden Cities for America: The Radburn Experience* (Philadelphia, 1982), 34–36. Of course it was Mumford who helped Americans rediscover Olmsted, another member of the republican tradition, in the 1930s. Howard, while acknowledging a debt to George, pointed to the greater influence of Edward Bellamy and his utopian novel *Looking Backward*. But the communal ownership of land, a variation on George's single tax, was integral to Howard's scheme. Ebenezer Howard, *Garden Cities of To-morrow* (London, 1902), on the communal ownership of land, 28; on his debt to Henry George, 123–24.

47. "To be built successfully, the garden city should be the product of a regional authority," Mumford wrote later in explaining the failure of the garden city movement in America. "The garden city can take form, in other words, only when our political and economic institutions are directed toward regional rehabilitation." Lewis Mumford, *The Culture of Cities*, 401.

48. Lewis Mumford, "Regions—To Live In," *Survey Graphic* 54 (May 1, 1925), 151–52.

49. Clarence Stein, "Dinosaur Cities," *Survey Graphic* 54 (May 1, 1925), 134–38, quoted passage on 135.

50. Alfred Smith, "Seeing a State Whole," *Survey Graphic* 54 (May 1, 1925), 158.

51. *Report of the Commission on Housing and Regional Planning* (March 1, 1925), on new and old tenements, 10–11; on financing costs, 26; "responsible officers," 35; "real hopes," 36. See also Clarence Stein, "Housing New York's Two-Thirds," *The Survey* 51 (February 15, 1924), 509–10.

52. *Report of the Commission on Housing and Regional Planning* (March 1, 1925), "adequate capital," 11; tax exemptions, 37.

53. Roy Lubove, *Community Planning in the 1920's*, 35.

54. Lewis Mumford, "Houses—Sunnyside Up," *The Nation* 120 (February 4, 1925), 115–16. Henry Wright, "The Road to Good Houses," *Survey Graphic* 54 (May 1, 1925), 165–68. See also Lubove, *Community Planning in the 1920's*.

55. Mumford, "Houses—Sunnyside Up," 115.

56. *Report of the Commission on Housing and Regional Planning* (February 18, 1926), "for wage earners," 6; state housing bank, 7, 50–52.

57. Lewis Mumford, "The Next Twenty Years in City Planning," *Proceedings*, Nineteenth National Conference on City Planning (Washington, D.C., 1927), 45–56, quoted passages, 48–50.

58. Benjamin Marsh, *Lobbyist for the People* (Washington, D.C., 1953), 18–35; "land speculators," 28; Pratt, 24; DeForest, 35.

59. Testimony of Benjamin Marsh, *City Planning Hearing*, 5–14.

60. John Nolen, "The Subdivision of Land," and Frederick Law Olmsted, Jr., "City Planning," in John Nolen, ed., *City Planning* (New York, 1916), 35, 15.

61. Arthur Tuttle, "The Enforcement of a Street Plan," *Proceedings*, Thirteenth National Conference on City Planning (Pittsburgh, 1921), 72.

62. Robert Pope, "Some of the Needs of City Planning," 78.

63. George F. Swain, "The Attitude of the Engineer Toward City Planning," *Proceedings*, Fourth National Conference on City Planning (Boston, 1912), 30–34.

64. Frederick Law Olmsted, Jr., "Introductory Address on City Planning," *Proceedings*, Second National Conference on City Planning (Rochester, 1910), 23. On the role of the engineer in the development of the early city planning movement, see Stanley K. Schultz and Clay McShane, "To Engineer the Metropolis: Sewers, Sanitation, and City Planning," *Journal of American History* 65 (September 1978), 389–411.

65. George Ford, "The City Scientific," 31.

66. Nelson P. Lewis, *Planning the Modern City* (New York, 1916), 1, 18.

67. Mel Scott, *American City Planning since 1890*, 163–66. Don Kirschner, *The Paradox of Professionalism* (Westport, Conn., 1986), 60–61.

68. Nolen, ed., *City Planning*.

69. Ford, "City Scientific," quoted in Scott, *American City Planning since 1890*, 121–22. Professionals tended to ignore, Scott argues, that "resistance to a planner's proposal might . . . stem from his own failure to appreciate local traditions." Scott suggests that planners had begun to lose sight of "the importance of plumbing the desires, feelings, hopes, and aspirations of community and neighborhood—and of taking them into account in planning."

70. Bruno Lasker, "Bolshevik Cities; An Undelivered Speech at the Eleventh National Conference on City Planning," *Survey* 42 (June 14, 1919), 423–25.

71. *Proceedings*, Thirteenth National Conference on City Planning, 204. Robert Whitten, "Zoning and Living Conditions," *Proceedings*, Thirteen National

Conference on City Planning. Henry V. Hubbard, "The Profession of City Planning," *City Planning* (July 1927), 201–3; Kirschner, *The Paradox of Professionalism*, 60–61.

72. Scott, *American City Planning since 1890*, 162. E. M. Bassett, *Autobiography* (New York, 1939), 131. Kirschner, *The Paradox of Professionalism*, 60–61.

73. John Taylor Boyd, Jr., "The New York Zoning Resolution and Its Influence on Design," *The Architectural Record* 48 (December 1920), 194.

74. Marsh, *Introduction to City Planning*, 41–56. See, for example, Frederick Law Olmsted, Jr., "The Scope and Results of City Planning in Europe," *City Planning Hearing*, 66–68. On the German example see also William Harbutt Dawson, *Municipal Life and Government in Germany* (New York, 1944).

75. Frederic Howe, "City Building in Germany," *Scribner's* 47 (May 1910), 601–14. See Seymour I. Toll, *Zoned American* (New York, 1969), 128–40.

76. Toll, *Zoned American*, especially chaps. 3–4.

77. Abram I. Elkus, "Working Conditions in Factories," *Independent* 74 (April 3, 1913), 737; "Lawson Purdy," *American Magazine* 72 (July 1911), 310; Toll, *Zoned American*, 148–50.

78. E. M. Bassett, "Discussion," *Proceedings*, Fifth National Conference on City Planning, 126.

79. Heights of Buildings Commission, *Report of the Heights of Buildings Commission to the Committee on the Height, Size and Arrangement of Buildings of the Board of Estimate and Apportionment of the City of New York* (New York, 1913), 3; hereafter the 1913 *Report*. On the composition of the Heights of Buildings Commission, see S. J. Makielski, Jr., *The Politics of Zoning* (New York, 1966), 16, 200 n. 31.

80. The commission worked, Scott argues, "in an atmosphere dominated by the financial and commercial interests of the city." Scott, *American City Planning since 1890*, 155.

81. 1913 *Report*, 18. Toll, *Zoned American*, 153.

82. 1913 *Report*, 19–20.

83. E. M. Bassett, Speech to the Chicago Real Estate Board, November 13, 1922, (Chicago, 1923), quoted in Makielski, *The Politics of Zoning*, 24. On the instability of realty values, see Edwin H. Spengler, *Land Values in New York in Relation to Transit Facilities* (New York, 1930); see 135–37 for Spengler's Georgist recommendations.

84. "Reminiscences of Lawson Purdy," Columbia University of Oral History Collection, 28; quoted in Toll, *Zoned American*, 150.

85. 1913 *Report*, 7.

86. Edward M. Bassett, *Zoning* (New York, 1940), 113. On the Supreme Court case, see Toll, *Zoned American*, 182–83.

87. Cooke in the *New York Times*, April 6, 1913, and Burton in the *New York Times*, December 31, 1916; both quoted in Toll, *Zoned American*, 151, 177.

88. 1913 *Report*, 28.

89. *Final Report of the Commission of Building Districts and Restrictions* (New York, 1916); on legal difficulties with the restrictive covenant, see testimony of Edward M. Bassett, 82–85.
90. Ernest Freund, quoted in 1913 *Report*, 9.
91. 1913 *Report*, 27.
92. E. M. Bassett, *Autobiography*, 120–21.
93. *A Standard State Zoning Enabling Act* (rev. ed.; U.S. Dept. of Commerce, 1926), 5; quoted in Toll, *Zoned American*, 202.
94. Stanley K. Schultz, *Constructing Urban Culture: American Cities and City Planning, 1800–1920* (Philadelphia, 1989), 89.
95. Lewis Mumford, "Botched Cities," *American Mercury* 18 (1929), 144–48, quoted passages on 147. See also Toll, *Zoned American*, especially 198–210.
96. Howard, *Garden Cities of To-morrow*, passim.
97. Toll, *Zoned American*, 205.
98. Thomas Lee Philpott, *The Slum and the Ghetto* (New York, 1978), 246–47.
99. Zoning complemented the efforts of the corporate "captains of consciousness" discussed in Stewart Ewen, *Captains of Consciousness* (New York, 1976).
100. Zoning proponents, Scott argues, were "inclined to give legal sanction to the status quo, to prevent only gross disorder, and to ignore long-term changes that might be socially desirable." Scott, *American City Planning since 1890*, 155.
101. John Ihdler, "The City Plan and Living and Working Conditions," *Proceedings*, Thirteenth National Conference on City Planning (Pittsburgh, 1921), 9.
102. George Ford, "Regional and Metropolitan Planning," *Proceedings*, Fifteenth National Conference on City Planning (Baltimore, 1923), 15.
103. Robert Whitten, "Zoning and Living Conditions," 27–28.
104. Walter Moody, *What of the City?* (Chicago, 1919), 42, 87.
105. Thomas Adams, "The Making of the New York Regional Plan," *Proceedings*, Seventeenth National Conference on City Planning (New York, 1925), 216.
106. Bartholomew quoted by Clarence Platt, *Proceedings*, Twenty-Third National Conference on City Planning (Rochester, 1931), 196.
107. "Discussion," *Studies on Building Height Limitations in Large Cities* (Chicago, 1923), 128.
108. Address by Bassett, Nov. 14, 1922, to the Chicago Real Estate Board, *Studies on Building Height Limitations in Large Cities*, 155–56.
109. Makielski, *The Politics of Zoning*, 134, 157–58.
110. *Ambler Realty Co. v. Village of Euclid*, 297 Fed. 314 (D.C.N.D., Ohio, 1924), 316. See Schultz, *Constructing Urban Culture*, 85–86. Anthony Downs would later employ an argument similar to Westenhaver's. Exclusionary zoning, Downs argued, "benefits the wealthy and the middle class at the expense of load-

ing large costs onto the very poor." The situation was "not a 'natural' result of 'free market forces.' On the contrary, it is created, sustained, and furthered by public policies and laws that prevent free markets from operating." Anthony Downs, *Opening Up the Suburbs: A Strategy for Urban America* (New Haven, 1973), 11.

111. *Village of Euclid et al. v. Ambler Realty Company*, 272 U.S. 378.

112. Makielski, *The Politics of Zoning*, 134, 157–58.

113. The attitudes of labor leaders discussed by Charles H. Cheney, "Zoning in Practice," *Proceedings*, Eleventh National Conference on City Planning (Buffalo, 1919), 162.

114. "Possession is nine-tenths of the law" goes the popular saying. Perhaps that refers to a belief that physical possession is often more important than the legal right. But it also reflects the fact that the rights of property largely define the essence and limits of the law in America.

115. Schultz, *Constructing Urban Culture*, on the Louisville case, 236, n. 60. The case was *Buchanan v. Warley*, 245 U.S. 60 (1917). On the *Euclid* case see Justice Sutherland's majority opinion, 272 U.S. 387. This entire section on the legal history of zoning owes a great deal to Schultz's work if not always to his interpretation.

116. On the zoning board of appeals, see Edward M. Bassett, *Zoning: The Laws, Administration, and Court Decisions during the Last Twenty Years* (New York, 1972; reprint of 1936 edition), chap. 6.

117. George Ford, "What Planning Has Done for Cities," *Proceedings*, Sixteenth National Conference on City Planning (Los Angeles, 1924), 19.

118. John Taylor Boyd, Jr., "Zoning and Wage-Earners Housing." *The Architectural Record* 60 (August 1926), 182.

119. Robert Fitch, "Planning New York," in Roger Alcaly and David Mermelstein, *The Fiscal Crisis in American Cities* (New York, 1976), 250–55.

120. On the conflicting needs of various forms of property and the struggle over the built environment, see David Harvey, *Consciousness and the Urban Experience: Studies in the History and Theory of Capitalist Urbanization* (Baltimore, 1985), 36–62.

121. Henry Morgenthau, "A National Constructive Programme for City Planning," *City Planning Hearing*, 60. Robert Fitch, "Planning New York". The term "city rentable" is Fitch's.

122. Robert M. Haig, "Economic Conditions," *Regional Survey of New York and Its Environs*, vol. 1 (New York, 1927), 31–33; Fitch, "Planning New York," 268–70.

123. Haig, "Economic Conditions," 31–32; Fitch, "Planning New York," 268–72.

124. Thomas Adams, "Introduction," *The Graphic Regional Plan*, vol. 1 (New York, 1928), viii. Scott, *American City Planning since 1890*, 170–74.

125. Charles Cheney, "Zoning in Practice," *Proceedings*, Eleventh National

Conference on City Planning (Buffalo, 1919), 162. United City Planning Committee document, April 5, 1923; Bettman papers, University of Cincinnati, box 1, folder 1. George Ford, "What Planning Has Done For Cities," 27.

126. John Nolen, "Planning Problems of Industrial Cities," *Proceedings*, Eleventh National Conference on City Planning (Buffalo, 1919), 22. Lawrence Veiller, "The Housing Situation and the Way Out," *The Architectural Record* 48 (December, 1920), 531. Lawrence Veiller, "Slumless America," *Proceedings*, Twelfth National Conference on City Planning (Cincinnati, 1920), 156–59. John Ihdler, "Housing and Transport with Labor Placement," *Annals of the American Academy of Political and Social Sciences* 81 (1919), 53.

127. Lawrence Veiller, "Are Great Cities A Menace?", *Architectural Record* 51 (February 1922), 175–84.

128. George Ford, "Regional and Metropolitan Planning," 13–14.

129. Haig, "Economic Conditions," 18, 24–25.

130. See Mumford's scathing review of the RPNYE; *New Republic* (June 15 and 22, 1932).

131. Haig, "Economic Conditions," 18, 24–25; George Ford, "The City Scientific," 36.

132. Haig, "Economic Conditions," 18–21.

133. *New York Times* (December 13, 1931), sec. 9, 5.

134. Allan Nevins, *Ford*, vol. 2 (New York, 1954), 282, 288, 296–97.

135. Simkhovitch, "Address," 103. To the editor, *New York Sun*, April 11, 1923, 20. On "metropolitan scurry" see Stilgoe, *Metropolitan Corridor: Railroads and the American Scene* (New Haven, 1983), 21–26, passim.

136. Harry Braverman, *Labor and Monopoly Capital: The Degradation of Work in the Twentieth Century* (New York, 1974), 87.

137. Charles W. Leavitt, "Street Widenings for Bridge Approaches," Proceedings, Sixteenth National Conference on City Planning (Los Angeles, 1924), 188–92.

138. Lewis Mumford, "The Next Twenty Years in City Planning," 45–50.

139. Thomas Fitzgerald, "Mass Transportation on the City Streets," *Proceedings*, Twenty-Third National Conference on City Planning (Rochester, 1931), 26.

140. Charles H. Cheney, "Sacrificing Beauty to Traffic," *Literary Digest* 49 (April 12, 1930), 105.

141. Ford, "What City Planning Has Done for Cities," 9; Morris Knowles, "City Planning As a Permanent Solution of the Traffic Problem," *Proceedings*, Seventeenth National Conference on City Planning (New York, 1925), 57–61.

142. Clay McShane, "Transforming the Use of Urban Space: A Look at the Revolution in Street Pavements, 1880–1924," *Journal of Urban History* 5 (May 1979), 279–307.

143. "Graphic Records of Traffic Accidents," *American City* 35 (July 1926), 84–85; Albert W. Whitney, ed., *Man and Motor Car* (New York, 1936), 168, 212.

144. George Duhamel, *America; The Menace* (Cambridge, 1931), 75–76.

145. Adams, "Introduction," *The Graphic Regional Plan*, vol. 1, x.

146. H. A. Overstreet, "Arousing the Public Interest in City Planning," *Proceedings*, Twentieth National Conference on City Planning (Dallas, Ft. Worth, 1928), 125–131.

147. H. A. Overstreet, "Arousing the Public Interest in City Planning," 125–131.

Chapter 5

1. Harvey Zorbaugh, *The Gold Coast and the Slum* (Chicago, 1929), 252–69, quoted passages on 269–70.

2. Zorbaugh, *The Gold Coast and the Slum*, 272–73.

3. Zorbaugh, *The Gold Coast and the Slum*, 254–58.

4. Zorbaugh, *The Gold Coast and the Slum*, 258–60.

5. Zorbaugh, *The Gold Coast and the Slum*, 271–74.

6. Zorbaugh, *The Gold Coast and the Slum*, 261, 272.

7. Zorbaugh, *The Gold Coast and the Slum*, 274–79.

8. Robert E. Park, Introduction to Zorbaugh, *The Gold Coast and the Slum*, ix–x.

9. Beardsley Ruml, a "loyal alumnus of the University of Chicago and an admirer of Merriam," directed the Rockefeller Foundation's General Education Fund. Barry Deal Karl, *Charles E. Merriam and the Study of Politics* (Chicago, 1974), 132–36.

10. Charles E. Merriam, *New Aspects of Politics* (Chicago, 1925), 207. See also Karl, *Merriam and the Study of Politics*, chaps. 4–8 and Charles E. Merriam, *A More Intimate View of Urban Politics* (New York, 1929), 22.

11. Merriam, *New Aspects of Politics*, 6, 17–18.

12. Merriam, *A More Intimate View of Urban Politics*, 102.

13. Merriam, *A More Intimate View of Urban Politics*, 70–75.

14. Merriam, *New Aspects of Politics*, on the use of experts and Lippmann's proposal, 163–71, quoted passages on 178.

15. On Merriam's views on social planning, see the epilogue in this volume.

16. On the spate of urban utopias, see Stanley Schultz, *Constructing Urban Culture: American Culture and City Planning, 1800–1920* (Philadelphia, 1989), chap. 1.

17. Winifred Raushenbush, *Robert E. Park: Biography of a Sociologist* (Durham, N.C., 1979), 20.

18. Robert E. Park, "Autobiographical Note," *Collected Works of Robert E. Park*, vol. 1 (New York, 1974), v–vi. Park's statement in 1936 that he had set out to "reform the newspaper, by making it more accurate and scientific, something like *Time* and *Fortune*" might puzzle current readers of those journals. It also

suggests something of the weakness of Park's pragmatism, the tendency to confuse power with truth. Raushenbush, *Robert E. Park*, 158.

19. Park's January 20, 1936, letter to Howard Odum quoted in Raushenbush, *Robert E. Park*, 158.

20. Fred H. Matthews, *Quest for an American Sociology: Robert E. Park and the Chicago School* (Montreal, 1977), 36–39.

21. Matthews, *Quest for an American Sociology*, 39–52.

22. Like Simmel, Park was concerned to show, as Fred Matthews has argued, "how important was the fact of sociability, of relatedness, in shaping action." Matthews, *Quest for an American Sociology*, 39–52, quoted passage on 42.

23. Robert E. Park, *The Crowd and the Public and Other Essays* (Chicago, 1972), 12–22.

24. Park, *The Crowd and the Public*, 25–31.

25. Park, *The Crowd and the Public*, 31–39.

26. Park, *The Crowd and the Public*, on the general will, 63–81, quoted passages on 76; on collective attention, 44–46; "crowd and public," 78.

27. Park, *The Crowd and the Public*, 46–48.

28. Park, *The Crowd and the Public*, 46–49.

29. Park, *The Crowd and the Public*, 57.

30. Park, *The Crowd and the Public*, 50–61.

31. Park, *The Crowd and the Public*, 79–81.

32. Despite his warnings Simmel, Matthews argues, had "made it all too easy for his followers to build a complete sociology upon formal interaction, while neglecting the element of 'interest,' the degree to which all social life is affected by inequalities of political power and wealth." Matthews, *Quest for an American Sociology*, 42–44, quoted passage on 44.

33. Park quoted in Matthews, *Quest for an American Sociology*, 62–67.

34. Matthews, *Quest for an American Sociology*, 80–85, quoted passage on 80.

35. On Chicago's black population see William M. Tuttle, Jr., *Race Riot: Chicago in the Red Summer of 1919* (New York, 1978), 75–76, n. 4.

36. Robert E. Park, "The City: Suggestions for the Investigation of Human Behavior in the Urban Environment," reprinted in Park and Ernest W. Burgess, *The City* (Chicago, 1925), 1–2. On human ecology see also R. D. McKenzie, "The Ecological Approach to the Study of the Human Community," in Park and Burgess, *The City*.

37. Park, "The City," secondary relations and forms of social control, 22–39.

38. Park, "The City," the segregated neighborhood, 9–14.

39. Alma Herbst, *The Negro in the Slaughtering and Meat-Packing Industry In Chicago* (Boston, 1932), 13–17; Tuttle, *Race Riot*, 110–14. "In 1902, the University of Chicago imported eighty nonunion black laborers from Tuskegee Institute to break a strike at a campus construction site." Tuttle, *Race Riot*, 113.

40. On the issue of black resistance to unionization and white antagonism,

see Tuttle, *Race Riot*, 142–56; Sterling D. Spero and Abram L. Harris, *The Black Worker* (New York, 1968, reprint of 1931 edition); Ray Marshall, *The Negro and Organized Labor* (New York, 1965).

41. Tuttle, *Race Riot*, 114–21; Herbst, *The Negro in the Slaughtering and Meat-Packing Industry*, 24–27.

42 Tuttle, *Race Riot*, 124–39; Herbst, *The Negro in the Slaughtering and Meat-Packing Industries*, 40–45.

43. Tuttle, *Race Riot*, on violence in the stockyards during the riot, 35, 37, 44, 46; on the return of black workers, 57–63; Herbst, *The Negro in the Slaughtering and Meat-Packing Industry*, 45–50.

44. Tuttle, *Race Riot*, 117–18; Herbst, *The Negro in the Slaughtering and Meat-Packing Industries*, 123–27.

45. Rosenwald quoted in Carl Sandburg, *The Chicago Race Riots* (New York, 1919), 77.

46. Charles S. Johnson quoted in E. Franklin Frazier, *The Negro Family in Chicago* (Chicago, 1932), 70; population estimate in Illinois Commission on Race Relations, *The Negro in Chicago* (Chicago, 1922), 79.

47. Rosenwald quoted in Sandburg, *Chicago Race Riots*, 76; Dr. Willis N. Huggins quoted in "Why the Negro Appeal to Violence," *Literary Digest* 62 (August 9, 1919), 11; *The Negro in Chicago*, 165; Sandburg, *Chicago Race Riots*, 8.

48. *The Negro in Chicago*, 205–11.

49. *The Negro in Chicago*, 204–11.

50. *The Negro in Chicago*, 116–22, Hyde Park Property Owners Association quoted on 210.

51. *The Negro in Chicago*, 220–21.

52. Hyde Park resident quoted in *The Negro in Chicago*, 120; the terms "non-adjusted" et al. are those of the Illinois Commission on Race Relations, informally supervised by Park, and of the Chicago school. The term "invasion" was also used extensively by white property owners themselves. Duke quoted in Sandburg, *Chicago Race Riots*, 20. See also Thomas Lee Philpott, *The Slum and the Ghetto* (New York, 1978), 213–15, 218.

53. Sandburg, *Chicago Race Riots*, 46.

54. *The Negro in Chicago*, 120–21.

55. *The Negro in Chicago*, 122–24.

56. Residents quoted in *The Negro in Chicago*, 172, 181; on the segregation on vice, 342–44.

57. *The Negro in Chicago*, 241–97; "little benefit," 273, "retarded" students, 266, "the atmosphere," 274. On the attitudes of park officials and settlement and other reformers, who discouraged the integration of public facilities, see Philpott, *The Slum and the Ghetto*, chaps. 13–14.

58. The best account of the race riot is William M. Tuttle, *Race Riot*, cited above. For Tuttle's account of the beach incident, see 3–10.

59. Frederic Thrasher, *The Gang* (Chicago, 1927), "broad twilight zone," 3;

"the spontaneous effort," 37; "the group," 288; "family larder," 263; "loyalty," 34.

60. *The Negro in Chicago*, trolley incident, 22; white policeman, 451; black
veteran, 481.

61. Placard and Amalgamated Meat Cutters and Butcher Workmen organizer
C. Ford quoted in Tuttle, *Race Riot*, 136–37.

62. Tuttle, *Race Riot*, on union organizing outside the stockyard entrances,
136; on packers dispersing crowds, 138–39.

63. George Edwin Haynes quoted in Sandburg, *Chicago Race Riots*, 23. Amalgamated Meat Cutters and Butcher Workmen organizer A. K. Foote quoted in
Sandburg, *Chicago Race Riots*, 54.

64. Quoted in *The Negro in Chicago*, 45.

65. Seligmann, *The Negro Faces America*, 302.

66. The best overview of the work of the Illinois Commission on Race Relations is in Arthur I. Waskow, *From Race Riot to Sit-In, 1919 and the 1960s* (Garden
City, N.Y., 1966), chap. 5; on the formation of the commission, see 63–72,
80–81, 87. The commission's final report was published as Illinois Commission
on Race Relations, *The Negro in Chicago* (Chicago, 1922).

67. As codirectors of the study, the ICRR chose Park's black graduate student
Charles S. Johnson and Graham R. Taylor, son of the settlement leader. Several
of Park's other students served on the staff, and the members of his seminar on
"The Crowd and the Public" conducted the research for the longest section of
the report on public opinion.

68. *The Negro in Chicago*, 22–25.

69. *The Negro in Chicago*, 22–25.

70. *The Negro in Chicago*, 640–41.

71. Waskow, *From Race Riot to Sit-In*, 83–87, quoted passages on 83.

72. Waskow, *From Race Riot to Sit-In*, 83–87.

73. Irving Louis Horowitz, *Professing Sociology: Studies in the Life Cycle of
Social Science* (Chicago, 1968), 283. Horowitz points to the New Deal as the
crucial period for the development of the elite policy-making style. See Barry
Dean Karl, *Executive Reorganization and Reform in the New Deal: The Genesis of
Administration Management, 1900–1939* (Cambridge, 1963).

74. Waskow argues that the commission gave no suggestion "to Negroes on
how to take the progress that the commission was urging should be given them."
Waskow, *From Race Riot to Sit-In*, 99.

75. *The Negro in Chicago*, 646–47; "servants of families" on 594.

76. *The Negro in Chicago*, 437.

77. *The Negro in Chicago*, 643–50.

78. Walter Lippmann, Introduction to Sandburg, *Chicago Race Riots*, xix;
Graham Taylor, "Chicago in the Nation's Strife," *Survey* 42 (August 9, 1919),
696; Seligmann, *The Negro Faces America*, 38.

79. The ICRR's report lacked an analysis, Waskow argues, "of the ways in

which the pattern of race relations in Chicago fit into the political structure of the city." Waskow, *From Race Riot to Sit-In*, 98.

80. *The Negro in Chicago*, 640–49.

81. Waskow cites interviews with a "white expert on Chicago race relations, a Negro journalist, two former members of the commission's research staff, and a Negro lawyer who had pressed some damage suits on behalf of Negroes hurt in the 1919 riot [who] all agree that *The Negro in Chicago* had little effect on racial practices." Waskow, *From Race Riot to Sit-In*, 103. See also St. Clair Drake and Horace R. Cayton, *Black Metropolis; A Study of Negro Life in a Northern City* (New York, 1945), 78–83, 212. On the continuation of the color line in housing, see Arnold R. Hirsch, *Making the Second Ghetto: Race and Housing in Chicago, 1940–1960* (New York, 1983).

82. Waskow, *From Race Riot to Sit-In*, 97–103; "fear of future violence," 100; Lowden quoted on 100; creation of permanent race-relations body, 103; *The Negro in Chicago*, xiv.

83. Waskow, *From Race Riot to Sit-In*, Mary White Ovington quoted on 47.

84. Hirsch, *Making the Second Ghetto*, passim; on racial violence see chap. 2.

85. *The Negro in Chicago*, 436.

86. W. E. B. Dubois, "Chicago," *The Crisis* 21 (January 1921), 102; quoted in Philpott, *The Slum and the Ghetto*, 209.

87. *Chicago Daily News*, August 7, 1919, quoted in Philpott, *The Slum and the Ghetto*, 219; on the commission and voluntary segregation, 209–27, especially 223–24.

Chapter 6

1. George Duhamel, *America; The Menace* (Cambridge, 1931), 79.

2. Donald Slesinger, "Chicago: The Second Century," *Survey Graphic* 23 (October 1934), 460–62, 512–13.

3. Robert E. Park, "Community Organization and Juvenile Delinquency," in Robert E. Park, Ernest W. Burgess, and Roderick D. McKenzie, *The City* (Chicago, 1925), 109.

4. Waskow argues that the Illinois Commission on Race Relations believed it was up to blacks to change "whichever of their own values and behavior were incompatible with that society." Arthur Waskow, *From Race Riot to Sit-In: 1919 and the 1960s* (Garden City, N.Y., 1966), "indigestible," 96; "incompatible," 101.

5. If Park entertained any reservations about the social responsibility of private economic interests, they did not figure prominently in his work. Perhaps he took the advice of his former teacher John Dewey. To be effective, Dewey argued, academic critics must avoid statements that might "rasp the feelings of everyone exercising the capitalist function." Park's students at the University of Chicago recalled "the milieu within which they functioned at the time as apoliti-

cal, and determinedly so." Several reported that "an overriding concern at the time was to distinguish sociology from socialism—which meant that the discipline could not risk being political." The effort was successful; few could have confused the Chicago school of urban sociology with socialism. John Dewey, "Academic Freedom," *Educational Review* 23 (January 1902), 1–14, quoted passage on 7; interviews with Park's students from James T. Carey, *Sociology and Public Affairs: The Chicago School* (Beverly Hills, Calif., 1975), 154; Dewey article quoted on 58.

6. Ernest Burgess, "Can Neighborhood Work Have a Scientific Basis?" Park and Burgess, *The City*, 142–55.

7. Robert E. Park and Ernest W. Burgess, *Introduction to the Science of Sociology* (Chicago, 1921, 2d ed. 1924), quotations are from the second edition. On the influence of the textbook, see Robert E. L. Faris, *Chicago Sociology, 1920–1932* (San Francisco, 1967), especially 37, and Edward Shils, "Robert E. Park 1864–1944," *The American Scholar* (Winter 1990), 120–27. Shils uses the term "green bible."

8. Park and Burgess, *Introduction*, 23–24.

9. Park and Burgess, *Introduction*, 27–33, 36.

10. Park and Burgess, *Introduction*, 34–39.

11. Park and Burgess, *Introduction*, 785.

12. Park and Burgess, *Introduction*, 56–57.

13. On such reform efforts see Paul S. Boyer, *Urban Masses and Moral Order in America, 1820–1920* (Cambridge, 1978), especially chap. 3, 6–7.

14. Charles L. Brace, *The Best Method of Disposing of Our Pauper and Vagrant Children* (New York, 1859), 3, 11–13, quoted in Thomas Bender, *Toward an Urban Vision* (Lexington, Ky., 1975), 143–44.

15. See Boyer's discussion of "positive environmentalism" and those intellectuals who exhibited "not merely an interest in studying social groups, but also in controlling them through the benevolent manipulation of their environment." Paul Boyer, *Urban Masses and Moral Order*, chap. 15; quoted passage on 224. On Brace, see Thomas Bender, *Toward an Urban Vision* (Lexington, Ky., 1975), chap. 6.

16. Clarence Rainwater, *The Play Movement in the United States* (Chicago, 1922), 125–35, quoted passage on 132.

17. Rainwater, *The Play Movement*, quoted passage on 134.

18. Rainwater, *The Play Movement*, "harmonize," 290; "little democracy" and "self-government," 303.

19. Rainwater, *The Play Movement*, "transition," 253; "towards institutionalization," 306; "efficiency tests," 250, 319; "correlated schedules," 328. The anecdote from the 1910 Playground Association of America Conference is from Harriet Lusk Childs, "The Fourth Annual Play Congress," *American City* 3 (July 1910), 20; quoted in Boyer, *Urban Masses and Moral Order*, 244. See also the dis-

cussion of organized youth sport in Steven A. Riess, *City Games: The Evolution of American Urban Society and the Rise of Sports* (Urbana, 1989), especially 164–68.

20. Frederic Thrasher, *The Gang* (Chicago, 1927), "spontaneous effort," 37; "deliberation" and codes of ethics, 284–88.

21. Thrasher, *The Gang*, "movement and change," 85; "flight," 82; "failure" and "Greeks," 308.

22. Robert E. Park, Introduction in Thrasher, *The Gang*, x–xi.

23. Thrasher, *The Gang*, importance of regulating gangs, 304–7; "organize the play," 494; "rational scheme of life," 524.

24. Thrasher, *The Gang*, 520–22. For a similar argument regarding Judge Ben Lindsay's efforts to reform gangs, see Christopher Lasch, *The New Radicalism in America* (New York, 1965), 154–55.

25. E. T. Hiller, *The Strike; A Study in Collective Action* (Chicago, 1928), 3.

26. Hiller, *The Strike*, 277.

27. Hiller, *The Strike*, 27–29.

28. Hiller, *The Strike*, 27–29.

29. Hiller, *The Strike*, 30–37.

30. Hiller, *The Strike*, 41.

31. Hiller, *The Strike*, general strike, 250–61.

32. Hiller, *The Strike*, 156–91; "social medium," 156; "decisive factor," 191.

33. Park's introduction to Hiller, *The Strike*, viii.

34. Hiller, *The Strike*, 269.

35. Hiller, *The Strike*, 29–37.

36. The best introduction to the Hawthorne experiments is Elton P. Mayo, *The Human Problems of an Industrial Civilization* (New York, 1933).

37. Passages from Mayo, *The Human Problems of a Industrial Civilization* quoted in Robert E. Park, "Industrial Fatigue and Group Morale," *American Journal of Sociology* 40 (November 1934), 349–56; reprinted in Robert E. Park, *Society* (Glencoe, Ill., 1955), 293–300; quoted passages on 295–96. Park was acquainted with Mayo's studies of fatigue as early as 1924; see Park and Burgess, *Introduction to the Science of Sociology*, 925–26. Mayo had been impressed with Clifford Shaw's studies of the delinquency areas and Ruth Cavan's investigation of suicide.

38. Park, *Society*, 295. On stints and quotas and the ethic of manliness, see David Montgomery, "Workers' Control of Machine Production in the 19th Century," *Labor History* 17 (Fall 1971), 485–509. On the logic of scientific management, see Harry Braverman, *Labor and Monopoly Capital: The Degradation of Work in the Twentieth Century* (New York, 1974).

39. Mayo quoted in Park, *Society*, 295. Former counselor quoted in Loren Baritz, *Servants of Power* (Middletown, Conn., 1960), 105. See also Mayo, *The Human Problems of an Industrial Civilization* and Braverman, *Labor and Monopoly Capital*, especially 87, 144–45.

40. Park, *Society*, "political remedy," (Park's words) and "human affairs,"

(Mayo quoted), 296; "better methods," (Mayo quoted) and "ills," (Park's words), 299.

41. Park, *Society*, "industrial folkways," 296; "a body of mores," 298; "formulate," 299; "some sort of consensus," 295.

42. Park, *Society*, 299; "rivalries," in Robert E. Park, "The Immigrant," Robert E. Park, *Collected Works*, vol. 1 (New York, 1974), 19. Robert E. Park, Ernest W. Burgess, and Roderick D. McKenzie, *The City* (Chicago, 1925).

43. Robert E. Park, "The City; Suggestions for the Investigation of Human Behavior in the Urban Environment," in Park, Burgess, and McKenzie, *The City*, the individual, 41; "Strikes," 22; "easy means," 9.

44. Park, "The City," 23–38. Park's view of human relationships in the city was in part shaped by Georg Simmel. See Georg Simmel, "The Metropolis and Mental Life," in Richard Sennett, ed., *Classic Essays on the Culture of Cities* (Englewood Cliffs, N.J., 1969), 47–60. See also Park Dixon Goist, *From Main Street to State Street: Town, City, and Community in America* (Port Washington, N.Y., 1977), especially 114–20, for an analysis of the tension in Park's work between his interest in spatially based forms of social control and those based upon a community of interests.

45. Park, "The City," "instinctive and spontaneous," 30–31; "practical methods," 21.

46. Park, "Community Organization and Juvenile Delinquency," 109–12.

47. Shelby Harrison, "Community Participation in City and Regional Planning," in Ernest W. Burgess, ed., *The Urban Community* (Chicago, 1926), 209–10.

48. Thus the Chicago sociologists reflected what Boyer described as "a fundamental shift of interest away from the individual to the group" in the early twentieth century. Boyer, *Urban Masses and Moral Order*, "mold," 282–83; "shift," 224.

49. Robert E. Park, "The Urban Community as a Spatial Pattern and a Moral Order," in Burgess, ed., *The Urban Community*, 3–18. For a recent discussion of some of the same issues from a Marxist perspective, see David Harvey, *The Urbanization of Capital: Studies in the History and Theory of Capitalist Urbanization* (Baltimore, 1983). Harvey examines the geographic aspect of the capitalist city and focuses on the twin processes of accumulation and class struggle.

50. Park "The Urban Community as a Spatial Pattern and a Moral Order," 3–18.

51. Harvey Zorbaugh, "The Natural Areas of the City," in Burgess, ed., *The Urban Community*, 219–24.

52. Zorbaugh, "The Natural Areas of the City," 224–26.

53. Zorbaugh, "The Natural Areas of the City," 226–29.

54. Harrison, "Community Participation," 209.

55. Harrison, Introduction to Clarence Arthur Perry, "The Neighborhood Unit," one of three monographs in *Regional Survey of New York and Its Environs*, vol. 7, *Neighborhood and Community Planning* (New York, 1929), 22–24.

56. Harrison, "Introduction," 22–24.

57. While at times Park and his colleagues insisted that the old village forms of social control could not be recreated in the urban environment, their work with small groups seemed to be based on just such an effort. For a discussion of the problem, see Ernest W. Burgess, "Can Neighborhood Work Have a Scientific Basis?" in Park, Burgess, and McKenzie, *The City*, 142–55. "There are those who are convinced that the function of the neighborhood center is passing with the decay of the neighborhood in the city," wrote Burgess (154). "For myself, I am not so certain."

58. Clarence Arthur Perry, "The Local Community as a Unit in the Planning of Urban Residential Areas," in Burgess, ed., *The Urban Community*, 238–41.

59. Clarence Arthur Perry, "The Neighborhood Unit," in *Regional Survey of New York and Its Environs*, vol. 7, *Neighborhood and Community Planning*, 25–30; Perry quotes Burgess, "Can Neighborhood Work Have a Scientific Basis," on 115–16.

60. Perry, "The Neighborhood Unit," factors, 31–33, criticism of zoning, 114–17.

61. Perry, "The Neighborhood Unit," 123.

62. Perry, "The Neighborhood Unit," 123–26.

63. Perry, "The Neighborhood Unit," 126–28.

64. President's Conference on Home Building and Home Ownership, *Housing and the Community—Home Repair and Remodeling* (Washington, 1932), vol. 8, 87–104.

65. *Address of Herbert Hoover at the Opening Meeting of the President's Conference on Home Building and Home Ownership* (Washington, 1931), 2; President's Conference on Home Building and Home Ownership, *Housing and the Community—Home Repair and Remodeling* (Washington, 1932), vol. 8, 87–104.

66. President's Conference on Home Building and Home Ownership, *Housing and the Community—Home Repair and Remodeling*, vol. 8, 87–104.

67. President's Conference on Home Building and Home Ownership, *House Design, Construction and Equipment* (Washington, 1932), vol. 5, 2–3; President's Conference, *Housing and Citizenship* (Washington, 1932), 99.

68. Colonel Starrett of the Starrett Corporation quoted in President's Conference on Home Building and Home Ownership, *Slums, Large-Scale Housing and Decentralization* (Washington, 1932), vol. 3, 91–92.

69. Frederick Delano, "National Planning and the American Civic Association," *Proceedings*, Twenty-fifth National Conference on City Planning (Baltimore, 1933), 63; Edwin Burdell, "The Social Problem Involved in Securing the Social Benefits of Slum Elimination," *Proceedings*, Twenty-fifth National Conference on City Planning, 131.

70. John Ihdler, "A Constructive Housing Program From the Community Point of View," *Proceedings*, Twenty-fourth National Conference on City Planning (New York, 1932), 33–34. Ihdler had attended the president's conference as a member of the Committee on Blighted Areas and Slums.

71. Ihdler, "Constructive Housing Program," 34; Burdell, "The Social Problem," 139–41.

72. Burdell, "The Social Problem," 139–41; Ihdler, "Comments," Twenty-fifth National Conference on City Planning, 144; Fredrick Bigger, "Comments," Twenty-fifth National Conference on City Planning, 143.

73. For a similar critique of city planners in the Progressive Era, see Boyer, *Urban Masses and Moral Order*, 282–83.

74. Cincinnati Metropolitan Housing Authority, *Tenant Code* (Cincinnati, n.d.), 3–5; quoted in Robert B. Fairbanks, *Making Better Citizens: Housing Reform and the Community Development Strategy in Cincinnati, 1890–1960* (Urbana, 1988), 105.

75. Robert E. Park, "The Mind of the Hobo: Reflections upon the Relation Between Mentality and Locomotion," in Park, Burgess, and McKenzie, *The City*, 156–60. For an interpretation of Park's career that stresses his search for a new basis of community, see Goist, *From Main Street to State Street*.

76. Robert E. Park, "Community Organization and the Romantic Temper," in Park, Burgess, and McKenzie, *The City*, 118.

77. Park, "Community Organization and Juvenile Delinquency," 106.

78. Park, "Community Organization and the Romantic Temper," 114–22.

79. Park, "Community Organization and the Romantic Temper," 114–22.

80. Park, "Community Organization and the Romantic Temper," 113–14.

81. Park, "The City," 33–39. Chicago's resilient Thompson machine influenced Park's critique of it. An unusually irresponsible politician (as his behavior in the 1919 race riot would suggest), Thompson spent so little time in Chicago that the *Tribune* dubbed him "one of Chicago's most frequent visitors." Yet Thompson managed to maintain the allegiance of his constituents. Exhibiting the machine politician's usual tactics, Thompson was always ready to "dig his hand down into his pocket and order coal, food, or clothing" and to engage "in a homely charity and . . . helpfulness, which no social agency has ever been able to approximate or duplicate." John Bright, *Hizzoner Big Bill Thompson* (New York, 1930), "frequent visitors," 97; "dig his hand," 5; "homely charity," from Harry Elmer Barnes's introduction, xxii.

82. Park, "Industrial Fatigue and Group Morale," 298.

83. Roderick McKenzie, *The Metropolitan Community* (New York, 1933), 70.

84. McKenzie, *The Metropolitan Community*, 71–83; "increased mobility" and "closely-knit" are from McKenzie's summary of his findings in President's Research Committee on Social Trends, *Recent Social Trends* (New York, 1933), 445.

85. McKenzie, *The Metropolitan Community*, "the will to grow," 160; on met-

ropolitan problems, see especially the chapter on "Metropolitan Government" contributed by Thomas H. Reed, 303–10; "common observation," 182; on annexation, 191–98, 306–7.

86. McKenzie, *The Metropolitan Community*, 311–18; on city planning, see contribution of Shelby Harrison and Flavel Shurtleff on "City and Regional Planning," 293–302; Reed on "Metropolitan Government," 303–10.

87. McKenzie, *The Metropolitan Community*, 311–18.

Chapter 7

1. Hoover, "Foreword," and Mitchell, "Review of Findings," in President's Research Committee on Social Trends, *Recent Social Trends* (New York, 1933), v, xi.

2. Barry Dean Karl argues that for Hoover the "transference of the industrial model to social organization seemed as obvious as it was urgent." Barry Dean Karl, *Charles E. Merriam and the Study of Politics* (Chicago, 1974), 209.

3. Charles Beard, "Fact, Opinion, and Social Values," *Yale Review* 22 (March 1933), 595–97. On the debate within the committee, see Karl, *Charles E. Merriam and the Study of Politics*, 221.

4. Harold Buttenheim, "Where City Planning and Housing Meet," *Proceedings*, Twenty-first National Conference on City Planning (Buffalo, 1929), 117–20; Lawrence Veiller, "Light," *Proceedings*, Twenty-first National Conference on City Planning, 125, 138.

5. Harland Bartholomew, "Is City Planning Effectively Controlling City Growth in the U.S.?" *Proceedings*, Twenty-third National Conference on City Planning, (Rochester, 1931), 7–12, "there is beauty" is Bartholomew quoting the architect Louis LaBlume; Bartholomew, "A Program to Prevent Economic Disintegration in American Cities," *Proceedings*, Twenty-fourth National Conference on City Planning (Philadelphia, 1932), 5.

6. Harold Ickes, "Federal Emergency Administration of Public Works," *Proceedings*, Twenty-fifth National Conference on City Planning (Baltimore, 1933), 24; the conference's resolution, 52–53.

7. Alfred Bettman, "City and Regional Planning in Depression and Recovery," *Proceedings*, Twenty-fifth National Conference on City Planning, 9–10. The National Resources Planning Board was originally called the National Planning Board and later the National Resources Committee. I have employed its most commonly used name and the one employed in Marion Clawson, *New Deal Planning: The National Resources Planning Board* (Baltimore, 1981).

8. Adolf Berle, "The Trend of the Turn," *Saturday Review of Literature* 9 (April 15, 1933), 533–35. On the profession's difficulties see F. Stuart Chapin, "The Present State of the Profession," and Ellsworth Faris, "Too Many Ph.D.'s," *American Journal of Sociology* 39 (January 1934), 509–12.

9. Clawson, *New Deal Planning*, 43 and passim.

10. Furthering the work of the Committee on Recent Social Trends, the Na-

tional Resources Planning Board, developed a "system and order committed to an articulate and articulated doctrine of welfare capitalism," argues Barry Dean Karl. Merriam and his Chicago colleagues played an important role "in the training and staffing of the new bureaucracy." Barry Dean Karl, *Charles E. Merriam and the Study of Politics*, "system," 248; "training," 226. Merriam thus helped turn a profession facing a crisis of unemployment into an influential force within the federal government.

11. National Resources Planning Board, Research Committee on Urbanism, *Our Cities: Their Role in the National Economy* (Washington, D.C., 1937), xiii, 75.

12. NRPB, *Our Cities*, vi–vii. On the more progressive orientation of the national administration, see William E. Leuchtenburg, *Franklin D. Roosevelt and the New Deal* (New York, 1963). Paul Conkin, *The New Deal* (Arlington Heights, Ill., 1975) questions the progressive orientation of the Roosevelt administration. For a discussion of labor violence in the 1930s, see Jeremy Brecher, *Strike!* (Boston, 1972).

13. NRPB, *Our Cities*, "democracy," vi; "harmonious," xii; "equalization," x.

14. NRPB, *Our Cities*, 73, 77.

15. NRPB, *Our Cities*, 76, 81.

16. NRPB, *Our Cities*, 75–76, 81–82.

17. NRPB, *Our Cities*, 73–74.

18. NRPB, *Our Cities*, 78–79.

19. Howard Ward, "Cities that Consume Men," *The Nation* 145 (January 22, 1938), 91–93.

20. NRPB, *Our Cities*, "social and political coherence," 85. Mark I. Gelfand, *A Nation of Cities* (New York, 1975), 96–98. Ellis Hawley blames the failure of New Deal antitrust proposals at least in part on lack of a mass constituency for antitrust legislation. Ellis Hawley, *The New Deal and the Problem of Monopoly* (Princeton, 1966), especially 443–49.

21. Gelfand, *A Nation of Cities*, 96–98; Roosevelt's address in dedicating the Bonneville Dam quoted on 96. There is considerable evidence, Irving Horowitz argues, "for the conclusion that [social scientific] information is used when it suits policy-makers and discarded when it does not 'fit' political plans." The fate of *Our Cities* added to that body of evidence. Irving Louis Horowitz, *Professing Sociology* (Chicago, 1968), 272.

22. Louis Wirth, "Urbanism as a Way of Life," *The American Journal of Sociology* (July 1938), 1–24; quoted passages on 4.

23. Wirth, "Urbanism as a Way of Life," 12–13.

24. Wirth, "Urbanism as a Way of Life," 15–17, 22.

25. Georg Simmel, "The Metropolis and Mental Life," in Richard Sennett, ed., *Classic Essays on the Culture of Cities* (Englewood Cliffs, N.J., 1969).

26. Wirth, "Urbanism as a Way of Life," 22–24.

27. The concept of urbanism, Fred Matthews argues, was developed espe-

cially by American scholars who "often seemed reluctant to accept a theory which made the distribution of political and economic power primary." Fred H. Matthews, *Quest for an American Sociology: Robert E. Park and the Chicago School* (Montreal, 1977), 124.

Epilogue

1. Louis Wirth, "Urbanism as a Way of Life," *American Journal of Sociology* (July 1938), 7.

2. Eric Lampard, "American Historians and Urbanization," *American Historical Review* 67 (October 1961), 49–61.

3. Sam Bass Warner, Jr., *The Urban Wilderness* (New York, 1972), 60. While I hesitate to take issue with a historian who has done more than most to clarify our urban past, Warner occasionally has missed the opportunity to explore the way in which political conflicts have shaped the development of the American city. In his excellent study, *The Private City*, Warner suggested that "the successes and failures of American cities have depended upon the unplanned outcomes of the private market." Warner has stated that he used the term "privatism" as a less controversial synonym for capitalism, but in doing so he has misrepresented the character of the American economic experience. Certainly, there is much truth in Warner's assertion that the private search for wealth has been a crucial part of the American urban experience; but urbanites have often pursued wealth and other goals as members of more or less conscious social groups.

In his analysis of revolutionary Philadelphia, for example, Warner documented the struggle between an international coalition of merchants and local artisan militias over the implementation of price controls. In his examination of mid-nineteenth century Philadelphia, he focused on the conflict over the introduction of the factory system between innovative industrialists eager to tap larger markets and traditional craftsmen jealous of their control of the labor process, a conflict that culminated in a series of violent strikes. Warner's own evidence suggested the ways in which social groups attempted to shape to their own needs the market and its technology, and consequently the city. Sam Bass Warner, Jr., *The Private City* (Philadelphia, 1968), "successes and failures," x; passim. On "privatism" as a synonym for "capitalism," see Bruce M. Stave, "A Conversation with Sam Bass Warner, Jr.," *Journal of Urban History* 1 (November 1974), 85–110.

4. Social criticism and political activity are involved in "two-way intellectual traffic," writes T. B. Bottomore. "The social movements produce new ideas about their problems and about their possible solutions, while the critics seek to interpret on a broader scale the meaning of the social conflicts in which the movements are involved." T. B. Bottomore, *Critics of Society: Radical Thought in North*

America (New York, 1968), 88. See also the discussion of Bottomore in Christopher Lasch, *The Agony of the American Left* (New York, 1969), 43–47.

5. John L. Thomas, *Alternative America* (Cambridge, 1983). See also Lasch's discussion of "populism" (not to be confused with the Populist party) in *The Agony of the American Left*, 12–18.

6. "Since the First World War, the social critic in America, deprived of the advantages of the sustained tradition of criticism that would have evolved in connection with a broad movement for radical change, tends to present his ideas 'as extremely personal judgements upon the state of society.'" Lasch, *The Agony of the American Left*, 46. The quoted phrase is Bottomore's. As was suggested in chapter 1 in this book, Henry George was not entirely free from that tendency.

7. Lasch, *The Agony of the American Left*, 1–43.

8. For an analysis of the role the liquor question played in shattering such cross-class coalitions, particularly the post–Civil War Prohibition party, and in binding intellectuals to the corporate order, see John J. Rumbarger, *Profits, Power, and Prohibition: Alcohol Reform and the Industrializing of America, 1800–1930* (Albany, 1989), especially 57–154.

9. Christopher Lasch, *The New Radicalism in America, 1889–1963* (New York, 1965); Lasch, *The Agony of the American Left*, 9–11. Christopher Lasch, *The True and Only Heaven: Progress and Its Critics* (New York, 1991).

10. Gompers quoted in Carl N. Degler, *Out of Our Past* (New York, 1984), 290. See also Lasch, *The Agony of the American Left*, 17.

11. Steve Fraser, "The 'Labor Question'," in *The Rise and Fall of the New Deal Order, 1930–1980* (Princeton, 1989).

12. Lasch, *The New Radicalism*, 168–69, passim. See also Boyer, *Urban Masses and Moral Order*, 220–32.

13. Edward A. Ross, *Social Control: A Survey of the Foundations of Order* (New York, 1916), 88; quoted in Lasch, *The New Radicalism*, 174.

14. The best starting points for an investigation of the debates surrounding the progressive movement are essays by Peter Filene, "An Obituary for the Progress Movement," *American Quarterly* (Spring 1970), and Daniel T. Rodgers, "In Search of Progressivism," *Reviews in American History; The Promise of American History: Progress and Prospects* 10 (December 1982).

15. Morris Janowitz, "The Intellectual History of 'Social Control'", in Joseph S. Roucek, *Social Control for the 1980s: A Handbook of Order in a Democratic Society* (Westport, Conn., 1978), 22–25. On stints and quotas and the ethic of manliness, see David Montgomery, "Workers' Control of Machine Production in the 19th Century," *Labor History* 17 (Fall 1971), 485–509.

16. Ross, *Social Control*, "passiveness," 415; "coalescence," 178–79; "ethical elite," 363; "impose," 415–16; the first passage is quoted in Boyer, *Urban Masses and Moral Order*, 226; the second is quoted in Lasch, *The New Radicalism*, 175. Ross, it seems, has become the preferred whipping boy of contemporary histo-

rians. Consider as a further example Robert Sklar's discussion of Ross's lecture "What the Films Are Doing to Young America," in which Ross blames the movie culture for the younger generation's absorption in sex and, Sklar writes, "fell just short of accusing the movies of having invented the automobile so that young people could have a place where their sex-excitement could be expressed." Indeed Ross's own comment that "this is not the place to cite evidence . . . and I am not going to cite any" invites such ridicule. I feel somewhat abashed at jumping on the bandwagon. But since Ross was an influential figure who had his hands in a variety of reform experiments (including a vice-presidency of the prohibitionist Committee of Sixty) and was also the major early theorist of the science of social control, his presence in this argument is essential. Robert Sklar, *Movie-Made America* (New York, 1975), 137–38; on the Committee of Sixty, see Rumbarger, *Profits, Power, and Prohibition*, 181.

17. W. I. Thomas and Florian Znaniecki, *The Polish Peasant in Europe and America*, vol. 1 (Boston, 1918–1920), I, 1–2.

18. Walter Lippmann, *Public Opinion* (New York, 1965 reprint), 11, 48, 195; see also the discussion of Lippmann's book and of the larger "war for the American mind" in David M. Kennedy, *Over Here: The First World War and American Society* (New York, 1980), 45–92. On Lippmann's work as a propagandist, see Ronald Steel, *Walter Lippmann and the American Century* (Boston, 1980), 141–54.

19. Merriam, *The New Aspects of Politics* (Chicago, 1925), 18–19, 82, 147. The most important scholarly account of Merriam's career, Barry Dean Karl, *Charles E. Merriam and the Study of Politics* (Chicago, 1974), does not discuss *The New Aspects of Politics*.

Index

New York State Tenement House
Commission, 67
New York Times, 52–53, 71–72, 152
New York Tribune, 76
New York World, 60
Nolen, John, 134, 136, 149
"No Mean City" (Lloyd), 46–47
Norton, Charles, 147

Ohio Mechanics' Institute, 116
Olmsted, Frederick Law, 4, 7, 15,
17–21, 24, 47, 60, 124; city planning, 125, 134–35; parks, 7,
19–20, 25–26, 42, 44, 53; republican ideals, 24–25, 28, 252n, 254n,
257n; social control, 44; suburbs,
20–21, 60; World's Columbian Exposition, 42
*Our Cities: Their Role in the National
Economy*, 226, 230–31
Overstreet, H. A., 155–56
Ovington, Mary White, 187
Ownership: corporate, 33; municipal,
40, 78

Park, Robert E., 5–6, 8–10, 158, 161,
163, 231, 244; black migration,
170–81; concepts, 8–9; education,
164–65, 282n; metropolitan community, 219–22; mobility, 218–21;
muckraking, 164–65; neighborhood community, 218–21; pragmatism, 166, 291n; segregation,
186–88; social development,
164–66; social dynamics, 166–70,
201–4; space, 204–7; students,
193–98, 214; University of Chicago, 190–98; urban sociology,
161, 164–65
Parkhurst, Rev. Charles, 62
Parks, 24, 43, 102–3; Chicago, 103,
122; graft, 25; neighborhood, 103;
urban, 18, 20

Paternalism, 56–57, 104, 173, 217
Pennsylvania Railroad, 52–53, 79
Periphery, urban, 2, 48, 50, 53, 85,
268n, 280n
Perkins, Frances, 101
Perry, Clarence, 209–15
Phillips, Wendell, 16
Philpott, Thomas, 187
Pinchot, Amos, 101
Pingree, Hazen, 40, 91, 94, 105, 261n,
272n, 278n
Pinkertons, 56
Planners, professional, 11, 65, 108,
117, 144, 156, 225–31
Planning, 3; anti-planners, 12; city,
83; corporate, 3; debate, 125–29;
private, 77; professional, 3, 118,
223; public, 7–8; rapid transit, 79,
81, 270n; regional, 131, 147, 150,
223; residential, 132; social, 125,
201, 225; urban, 6–7
Plan of Chicago (Burnham), 26,
119–22, 124, 147, 160, 162, 171,
281n
Playground Association of America,
194
Playground movement, 102–3, 117,
193–94, 203
Play groups, 193–94
*Play Movement in the United States,
The* (Rainwater), 193
Plumber and Sanitary Engineer, 61
Police power, 141, 146
Political corruption, 16, 31, 44,
54–55, 64, 89–101, 129; Chicago,
162, 199n; New York, 62–64, 91,
98, 129, 131; slum, 214
Political economy, 48, 118; conflicts,
104; metropolis, 92, 104
Political science, 105
Poole, Ernest, 103–4
Poor, 2, 9, 62–64, 66, 72, 212–18;
moral reform, 103

Union Square (New York), 30, 71,
73
United City Planning Committee,
(UCPC), 113–14
United Labor party (ULP), 12,
29–30, 91, 96, 113, 261n; cam-
paigns, 36, 269n; collapse, 32;
Henry George, 30, 89; Knights of
Labor, 30, 35; nationalization of
property, 39; political program, 35;
radicals, 38; single tax, 37–39; so-
cialists, 30, 33; trade union move-
ment, 29; voting, 90
University of Chicago, 158, 161, 171,
189, 191; sociological studies,
193–97; strikebreakers, 291n
University of Heidelberg, 165
University of Michigan, 164
University Settlement, 98–99, 101
Urban commonwealth, 4, 17, 27
"Urban Community as a Spatial Pat-
tern and a Moral Order, The"
(Park), 204
Urban conflict, 53, 97, 104
Urban development: city planning,
7–8; design, 1, 3, 114–15
Urban discipline, 83, 87–88, 101–2,
104, 108, 273n, 277n
Urban environment: design, 12; rela-
tions, 172
Urbanism, 225–40; social interaction,
239
"Urbanism as a Way of Life" (Wirth),
226, 236–40
Urbanism Committee, National Re-
sources Planning Board, 226
Urbanization, 48; advantages, 19;
natural order, 39
Urban planning, 190; limitations, 217;
origins, 189–224, 190–91, 208–14;
radical alternative, 231; sociologists, 191

Urban politics, 11–12, 88, 90; ma-
chine reform, 11
Urban professionals, 220
Urban reform, 33, 158, 231–35; eco-
nomic planning, 231–32; Pingree,
261n; play movement, 193; single
tax, 39; traditions, 4; urbanism
committee, 229–34
Urban republic, 22, 31, 45; Henry
George, 45; Henry Demarest
Lloyd, 45; municipal government,
45; municipal socialism, 40
Urban society, government, 40
Urban sociology, 157–88, 235
Urban space, 73; scientific manage-
ment, 147
U.S. Steel Corporation, 57, 74
Utilities, 55, 68, 87; manipulation,
64–65; municipal, 33, 39–40, 46,
60, 85, 98; regulation, 233
Utopias, 28, 165

Van Brunt, Henry, 45
Veiller, Lawrence, 61, 67, 77, 101,
139, 142, 150, 227
Vice, 177
Violence, mob, 52–53, 73, 181,
293–94n
Voting, 85, 87, 98; city trenches,
89–91, 96; labor, 16, 95–96, 102,
112

Wages, 35, 52, 55, 58–59, 71–73, 75,
95, 102, 111, 232
Wagner, Robert, 93–94, 129, 131
Wald, Lillian, 128–29
Walking city, 49, 251n
Warner, Sam Bass, Jr., 242
Washington, Booker T., 170–71
Waskof, Arthur, 182, 185, 190
Weber, Adna, 48–49, 54, 58–59, 70,
83, 85, 93

319

Urban Life and Urban Landscape Series

ZANE L. MILLER AND HENRY D. SHAPIRO, GENERAL EDITORS

The series examines the history of urban life and the development of the urban landscape through works that place social, economic, and political issues in the intellectual and cultural context of their times.

Cincinnati, Queen City of the West: 1819–1838

DANIEL AARON

Fragments of Cities: The New American Downtowns and Neighborhoods

LARRY BENNETT

The Lost Dream: Businessmen and City Planning on the Pacific Coast, 1890–1920

MANSEL G. BLACKFORD

Cincinnati Observed: Architecture and History

JOHN CLUBBE

Suburb in the City: Chestnut Hill, Philadelphia, 1850–1990

DAVID R. CONTOSTA

Building Chicago: Suburban Developers and the Creation of a Divided Metropolis

ANN DURKIN KEATING

Silent City on a Hill: Landscapes of Memory and Boston's Mount Auburn Cemetery

BLANCHE LINDEN-WARD

Plague of Strangers: Social Groups and the Origins of City Services in Cincinnati, 1819–1870

ALAN I MARCUS

Polish Immigrants and Industrial Chicago: Workers on the South Side, 1880–1922

   DOMINIC A. PACYGA

The New York Approach: Robert Moses, Urban Liberals, and Redevelopment of the Inner City

   JOEL SCHWARTZ

Hopedale: From Commune to Company Town, 1840–1920

   EDWARD K. SPANN

Washing "The Great Unwashed": Public Baths in Urban America, 1840–1920

   MARILYN THORNTON WILLIAMS